RAISING CHILDREN IN THE MILITARY

Military Life

Military Life is a series of books for service members and their families who must deal with the significant yet often overlooked difficulties unique to life in the military. Each of the titles in the series is a comprehensive presentation of the problems that arise, solutions to these problems, and resources that are of much further help. The authors of these books—who are themselves military members and experienced writers—have personally faced these challenging situations, and understand the many complications that accompany them. This is the first stop for members of the military and their loved ones in search of information on navigating the complex world of military life.

Titles in the Series

The Military Marriage Manual: Tactics for Successful Relationships, by Janelle Hill, Cheryl Lawhorne, and Don Philpott (2010)

Combat-Related Traumatic Brain Injury and PTSD: A Resource and Recovery Guide , by Cheryl Lawhorne and Don Philpott (2010)

Special Needs Families in the Military: A Resource Guide, by Janelle Hill and Don Philpott (2010)

Military Finances: Personal Money Management for Service Members, Veterans, and Their Families, by Cheryl Lawhorne-Scott and Don Philpott (2013)

Sexual Assault in the Military: A Guide for Victims and Families, by Cheryl Lawhorne-Scott, Don Philpott, and Jeff Scott (2014)

Raising Children in the Military , by Cheryl Lawhorne-Scott, Don Philpott, and Jeff Scott (2014)

RAISING CHILDREN IN THE MILITARY

Cheryl Lawhorne-Scott, Don Philpott, and Jeff Scott

ROWMAN & LITTLEFIELD
Lanham • Boulder • New York • Toronto • Plymouth, UK

Published by Rowman & Littlefield
4501 Forbes Boulevard, Suite 200, Lanham, Maryland 20706
www.rowman.com

10 Thornbury Road, Plymouth PL6 7PP, United Kingdom

British Library Cataloguing in Publication Information Available

Library of Congress Cataloging-in-Publication Data

Lawhorne-Scott, Cheryl, 1968–
Raising children in the military / Cheryl Lawhorne-Scott, Don Philpott, and Jeff Scott.
pages cm. — (Military life)
Includes index.
ISBN 978-1-4422-2748-4 (cloth : alk. paper) — ISBN 978-1-4422-2749-1 (electronic)
1. Children of military personnel—United States—Handbooks, manuals, etc. 2. Families of military personnel—United States—Handbooks, manuals, etc. 3. Child rearing—United States—Handbooks, manuals, etc. 4. United States—Armed Forces—Military life—Handbooks, manuals, etc. I. Philpott, Don, 1946– II. Scott, Jeff, 1969– III. Title.
UB403.L39 2014
355.120973—dc23
2013046688

♾™ The paper used in this publication meets the minimum requirements of American National Standard for Information Sciences Permanence of Paper for Printed Library Materials, ANSI/NISO Z39.48-1992.

Printed in the United States of America

CONTENTS

ACKNOWLEDGMENTS

Like all titles in the Military Life Series, this book aims to serve as a one-stop guide covering all the information you need on a specific subject. We are not trying to reinvent the wheel; we are simply gathering information from as many sources as possible so that you don't have to. Almost all the information in this book comes from federal and military websites and is in the public domain. These include the Department of Defense, American Forces Press Service, US Army Medical Department, Department of Veterans Affairs, Department of Health and Human Services, and all branches of the US military. We have tried to extract the essentials. Where more information might be useful, we have provided websites and resources that can help you.

INTRODUCTION

President Barack Obama has made the care and support of military families a top national security policy priority. In a statement issued by the White House in January 2011, he said,

> We recognize that military families come from the active duty Armed Forces, the National Guard, and the Reserves. They support and sustain troops fighting to defend the Nation, they care for our wounded warriors, and they survive our fallen heroes. The well-being of military families is an important indicator of the well-being of the overall force. At a time when America is at war and placing considerable, sustained demands on its troops and their families, it is especially important to address the family, home, and community challenges facing our all-volunteer force. For years to come, military families and Veterans will continue to face unique challenges, and at the same time will also have great potential to continue contributing to our communities and country.

Less than 1 percent of Americans serve in uniform today, but they bear 100 percent of the burden of defending our Nation. Currently, more than 2.2 million service members make up America's all-volunteer force in the active, National Guard, and Reserve components. Since September 11, 2001, more than 2 million troops have been deployed to Iraq and Afghanistan. Fifty-five percent of the force is married, and 40 percent has two children. Only 37 percent of our families live on military installations; the remaining 63 percent live in over four thousand communities nationwide. Multiple deployments, combat injuries, and the challenges of reintegration can have far-reaching effects on not only the troops and their families but also upon America's communities as well. These challenges should be at the forefront of our national discourse, the president said.

Over 1.2 million children have at least one parent serving on active duty; 42.6 percent are five years old or younger. In total, more than 743,000 children have parents in the National Guard or Reserves; of these, 58.5 percent are younger than eleven years.

About 7.8 percent of all military members are single parents: 10.7 percent for the army, 7.6 percent for the navy, 5.8 percent for the air force, and 4.7 percent for the marines. Additionally, of about eighty-four thousand military-married-to-military couples, approximately thirty-six thousand have children.

Living in either military or civilian communities, in urban, suburban, or rural settings, military children experience unique challenges related to military life and culture. These include deployment-related stressors such as parental separation, family reunification, and reintegration. Due to frequent moves, many military children experience disrupted relationships with friends and must adapt to new schools and cultivate new community resources. Some children also experience the trauma of either welcoming home a parent who returns with a combat-related injury or illness or facing a parent's death. Recent research reveals an increase in military child maltreatment and neglect since the start of combat operations and deployments to Afghanistan and Iraq.

Research also indicates that although most military children are healthy and resilient and may even have positive outcomes as a result of certain deployment stressors, some groups are more at risk. Among these are young children; some boys; children with preexisting health and mental health problems; children whose parents serve in the National Guard, are Reserve personnel, or have had multiple deployments; children who do not live close to military communities; children who live in places with limited resources; children in single-parent families with the parent deployed; and children in dual-military-parent families with one or both parents deployed.

Equipped with the right tools, military parents can serve as a buffer against the challenges their children face. Professionals in health care, family, education, recreation, and faith-based services who work with military families can also help reduce the distress that military children experience and can foster individual and family resilience. In part that means becoming familiar with the particular risks that can compromise a military child's health and development. This handbook aims to provide you with the tools you need to successfully navigate the roller-coaster ride that is being a parent in today's military.

SOME STATISTICS

As of January 2013, the United States had 1.429 million people on active duty in the five branches of the armed services, with an additional 850,880 in the seven Reserve components. As of March 2013, more than 50,550 American service members had been wounded in action, and more than 6,650 had lost their lives in Operation Enduring Freedom, Operation Iraqi Freedom, and Operation New Dawn. More than 44,700 children experienced a deployed parent's wounding, injury, illness, or death. Of these children, almost half were elementary-school age; one in four were five years old or younger (US Department of Defense, Personnel and Procurement Statistics, 2012).

With almost 1.5 million active-duty military members, each day around the globe an estimated 540,000 active-duty sponsors care for a family member with special medical or educational needs. Most of those family members are children whom the military refers to as "exceptional family members."

The Exceptional Family Member Program (EFMP) has a personnel function and a family support function. The EFMP personnel function

Covers all active-duty service members; participation is mandatory

Is standard across all armed services

Identifies family members with special medical and/or educational needs and documents the services they require

Considers those needs during the personnel assignment process (especially when approving family members for accompanied travel to overseas locations)

Involves the personnel and medical commands and the Department of Defense educational system overseas

The EFMP family-support function

Is optional

Differs from service to service

Department of Defense policy on family centers allows, but does not require, the military services to offer family-support services to exceptional family members within the military services' family-support systems.

The army and the marines staff their family centers with individuals responsible for providing support to families with exceptional family members. They are called EFMP managers (army) or EFMP coordinators (marines). In the navy, the EFMP staff who support the personnel function may also provide family-support services, but the navy does not staff its family centers with EFMP coordinators.

The air force's Exceptional Family Member Program is designed to provide support to military family members with special needs. Its services include a variety of personnel, medical, and family-support functions. The Exceptional Family Member Program–Family Support (EFMP-FS), which is the community-support function provided by the Airman and Family Readiness Centers (A&FRCs), includes but is not limited to on- and off-base information and referral, parent training, support groups, relocation assistance, financial management, and school information.

The US Coast Guard Special Needs Program is intended to ensure family and coast guard needs are met, to assist service members with appropriate referrals and resources before, during, and after relocation, and to ensure mission readiness. The program works closely with assignment officers, prior to transfer, to ensure appropriate resources are available for family members in proposed areas of relocation. All active-duty members who have family members with professionally diagnosed special needs are required to enroll their dependents in this program.

The Special Needs Identification Assignment Coordination (SNIAC) process provides medical-information-management support for EFMP enrollment functions and coordinates relocations for families who have medical or educational needs. "Both EFMP-FS and SNIAC work together with EFMP-Assignments at the Air Force Personnel Center (AFPC) to provide comprehensive and coordinated medical, education, community support, assignment coordination as well as housing accommodation to families enrolled in the EFMP program."

I

FAMILY LIFE IN THE MILITARY

Most people get married and inherit in-laws. When you marry into the military, you get a very large new family. Be it the army, navy, air force, marines, or coast guard, joining the family can be quite a culture shock. Service members often speak what seems like a different language and use expressions and acronyms that take a lot of getting used to. They tell the time differently. They have rules and standards of conduct that you, as a military spouse, are expected to follow and ways of doing things that may seem very strange at first. There is the chain-of-command structure, and you have to learn to recognize ranks and insignias. Living on base involves heightened levels of security. And all this is on top of getting married, setting up home, and starting a family.

The good news is that while it may all seem very strange and even daunting at first, a lot of help is on hand. Other married couples will be quick to welcome you and help you get organized. Support groups and clubs, social workers and chaplains, and a host of other people are all waiting to help you get acclimatized and familiar with your new, third family.

One huge advantage to being married to someone in the military is the wealth of resources available to you through your new extended family, and this is especially true when you have children. There are family-support services, spouses' clubs, mentoring organizations, child-care facilities, "respite care" for wounded families, volunteer networks, and many other licensed and professional services all aimed at providing you and your family with the support you need, particularly if you have wounded loved ones or children with special needs. All the branches have dedicated, trained, and professional family-support advisors who are available to help you. In the marines, for instance, these advisers, known as family readiness officers, work with Marine Corps Community Services. Your family-support center can put you in touch with the right people. You should never feel alone or helpless. There is always someone to turn to for help.

SINGLE-PARENT FAMILIES

Although the military no longer allows single parents to enlist, members who become single parents (through death of a spouse, separation, divorce, adoption, etc.) and military couples who have children will not be forced to leave the service as long as they meet the family-care requirements of the Department of Defense (DoD) and the various related service regulations. That means they must have a family-care plan. You should develop such a plan whether you expect to be deployed or not; in fact, many units will require you to develop a formal family-care plan. Taking care of these considerations now will help prepare you and your family for any period of separation. When you prepare your plan, be sure to do the following:

- Assign a guardian for your family in a special power of attorney, and make sure that the guardian understands his or her responsibilities.
- Obtain ID and commissary cards, register with the Defense Enrollment Eligibility Reporting System (DEERS), and check to make sure all ID cards have not expired.
- Sign up for Servicemembers' Group Life Insurance (SGLI) or a similar group life insurance and update all beneficiary information.
- Arrange for housing, food, transportation, and emergency needs.
- Inform your spouse or any caretakers about your financial matters.
- Arrange for your guardian to have access to necessary funds.
- Arrange for child care, education, and medical care.
- Prepare a will and designate a guardian in the will.

- Arrange for necessary travel and escort to transfer family members to their guardian.
- Discuss your plans with your older children.

The plan includes three basic elements: short-term care providers, long-term care providers, and care-provision details.

- Short-term care provider: Single-parents and military couples with children must designate a nonmilitary person who will agree, in writing, to accept care of the member's children at any time, twenty-four hours per day, seven days per week, in the event the military member is called to duty or deployed with no notice. Although this person cannot be another military member, he or she can be a military spouse. The short-term care provider must live in the area where the military member is stationed/located and must sign the family-care plan, indicating understanding of the responsibilities being entrusted to him or her.
- Long-term care provider: In addition to the short-term care provider, the military member must also designate a nonmilitary person who will agree, in writing, to provide long-term care for his or her children in the event the military member is deployed for a significant period, selected for an unaccompanied overseas tour, or assigned to a ship at sea. The long-term care provider does not have to live in the local area, but the family-care plan must contain provisions to transfer the child(ren) from the short-term care provider to the long-term care provider (finances, airline tickets, etc.) in the event a no-notice deployment turns into a long-term deployment. The long-term care provider must sign the family-care plan, indicating understanding of the responsibilities being entrusted to him or her.
- Care-provision details: In addition to designating short-term and long-term care providers, the family-care plan must include details regarding the care and support of the children. Family-care plans must include provisions for logistical movement of the family or caregiver. Logistical arrangements include, but are not limited to, arrangements to relocate, if necessary, the caregiver or family, as well as financial, medical, and legal support necessary to ensure continuity of care and support of family members during

the movement. Logistical arrangements must provide for financial support necessary to transport the family or caregiver to a designated location. The military member(s) must also consider a non-military escort for family members requiring assistance, such as infants, children, and elderly and disabled adults.

Family-care plans must also include arrangements for the financial well-being of family members covered by the family-care plan during short- and long-term separations. Arrangements for financial care should include powers of attorney, allotments, or other appropriate means to ensure the self-sufficiency and financial security of family members.

Each service has special provisions in place that allow designated care providers to access military base facilities (commissary, base exchange, post exchange, medical) in order to care for the military dependents when the family-care plan is in effect (i.e., care has been transferred from the military member to the care provider).

COMMANDER REVIEW

The regulations require that the commander or a designated representative review each family-care plan for workability and completeness. The "designated representative" is usually the executive officer or first sergeant. After the initial review, the plans are updated by the member and reviewed at least annually.

TIME PERIODS

When military members first become single parents or military couples have children, they must notify their commander, supervisor, or the commander's designated representative no later than thirty days after the occurrence of change in family circumstances or personal status (sixty days for Guard/Reserve members). After that, military member(s) have sixty days (ninety days for Guard/Reserve members) to submit a completed family-care plan. If mitigating circumstances are involved, the commander or supervisor concerned may grant members an additional thirty days to submit an acceptable family-care plan. Further extensions are not authorized.

The same sixty-day rule applies for active-duty military members who move from one military base to another. They have sixty days to find a short-term care provider who lives in the local area.

Military mothers of newborns receive a four-month deferment from duty away from the home station for the period immediately following the birth of a child. This provision is to assist the member in developing family-care plans and to establish a pattern of child care. Single members or one member of a military couple who adopt receive a four-month deferment from the date the child is placed in the home as part of the formal adoption process. Similarly, Reserve component members receive a four-month deferment from involuntary recall to active duty.

PENALTIES

Failure to produce the required family-care plan within the periods required can result in involuntary separation from the military by reason of parenthood in accordance with DoD Directive 1332.14 (enlisted) or DoD Directive 1332.30 (officers). Failure to produce the required family-care plan in the case of the Reserve member can result in processing for discharge or transfer to an inactive or retired status.

Each branch of the military has its own name for family-support centers and its own programs for new spouses.

Army Community Service Center: Family Team Building
Airman and Family Readiness Center: Heartlink
Marine Corps Community Services Center: LINKS (Lifestyle, Insights, Networking, Knowledge, and Skills)
Navy Fleet and Family-Support Center: COMPASS

SEQUESTRATION

Speaking before five hundred service spouses and educators on July 8, 2013, the army's vice chief of staff didn't pull any punches about the negative impact continued sequestration could have on military programs for children. During a presentation at the Military Child Education Coalition's fifteenth national training seminar in National Harbor, Maryland, Gen. John F. Campbell made clear that fiscal woes facing the country and the army as it transitions out of Afghanistan and into a leaner force structure will also mean leaner funding for programs. "I used to say that everything in Afghanistan was hard, but this is really hard and has to do with sequestration; it has to do with budget; it has to do with downsizing," Campbell said. The general said that what is happening now is not new, however, and pointed out that the conclusion of every major conflict has also involved a downsizing of military forces.

In July 2013, the army announced just such a cut. The number of active brigade combat teams (BCTs) in the army will be reduced from forty-five to thirty-three. Army leaders also said at the time that they expected to name an additional brigade for eliminatation. It's expected that eventually, a total of thirteen BCTs will be eliminated. Many soldiers in those brigades will move into other brigades.

Those moves are in response to force cuts put forth in the Budget Control Act of 2011, which mandated an army reduction in end strength of eighty thousand soldiers. That reduction will reduce the force to 490,000 soldiers by 2017. The reduction does not take into consideration any additional cuts that sequestration will require. Campbell said that if sequestration continues, the army will have to continue downsizing—possibly by an additional one hundred thousand soldiers from the active, Army National Guard, and Army Reserve forces.

"[Secretary of the Army John M. McHugh and Chief of Staff of the Army Gen. Ray Odierno] are committed to making sure that the critical family programs, and the programs that have the most impact on our children will continue to be funded at the levels they are now," Campbell said. He also said the army's chief of staff is determined to keep the school liaison officers program at the same funding levels currently in effect, though the army doesn't yet know if its fiscal year 2014 budget request will be fully funded. Campbell said the army's goal is to make sure programs that "benefit our children most, and that give us the biggest bang for the buck" are able to continue. "But we shouldn't fool ourselves," he said. "It's not going to be the way it was the last 10 years—our nation cannot afford it."

The vice chief also explained that money for many army programs came as part of funding tied to fighting the wars in Iraq and Afghanistan—funding known as the overseas contingency operations (OCO) budget. Now that the army is out of Iraq and moving ahead with pulling out of Afghanistan, OCO funding for those conflicts will diminish. "We had different programs that came on board because we could, and in most cases it was for the right reasons," Campbell said. "What we're doing now is taking a look at all these programs and making sure we're not redundant where we don't have to be."

Campbell said the army would try to do the best it could with the budget it gets. "The bottom line is, the programs that we have we're taking a very hard look at and making sure we pick the right programs that impact the most people—but that will be different at each post, camp or station," he said. "So we're going to power down and depend upon the senior mission and division commanders to provide us that input." Campbell said audience members, on returning to their home stations, could advocate with their commanders for programs that work and could also draw attention to those programs that do not work.

2

HOUSING

Married service members receive a housing allowance while in basic training and follow-on job training—technical school, advanced individual training (AIT), A-School—in order to provide a household for dependents, even though they are also living for free in government quarters (barracks). If you get married before joining the military, this tax-free housing allowance begins on the very first day of your active duty (the first day of basic training).

If you wait until after joining the military to get married, the housing allowance becomes effective on the date of the marriage. However, you need a certified copy of the marriage certificate to change your marital status, and (depending on the state) obtaining this can take a couple of weeks or even a month. Even so, the housing allowance will be backdated to the date of the marriage.

Everyone in the military gets free (or almost free) housing. How the military chooses to provide this to you depends mostly on your marital (dependency) status and your rank. If you are married and living with your spouse and/or minor dependents, you will either live in on-base housing or receive a monetary basic allowance for housing (BAH) to live off base. The BAH amount depends on your rank, location, and whether you have dependents.

If you are in the Guard or Reserves and entitled to a housing allowance, you will receive a special reduced BAH, called BAH Type II, anytime you are on active duty for less than thirty days. If you are on orders to serve on active duty for thirty days or more, you'll receive the full housing allowance rate (the same as active duty).

If you have dependents, you will receive the housing allowance even when staying in the barracks at basic training and/or at technical school, AIT, or A-School. This is because the military makes it mandatory for you to provide adequate housing for your dependents. The allowance will be included as part of your regular paycheck (*Note:* In the military, your monthly pay entitlements are paid twice per month—half on the first of the month and half on the last duty day of the month). For basic training and/or technical school, AIT, or A-School, you will receive the BAH amount for the location where your dependent(s) are residing.

However, if you are single or divorced and are paying child support, you do not receive full-rate BAH while living in the barracks. In this case, special rules apply, and the member receives BAH-DIFF. Unlike basic pay, BAH is an allowance, not pay, and is therefore not taxable.

If you are single, you can expect to spend a few years of your military service residing on base in the dormitory, or barracks. Policies concerning single military members living off base at government expense vary from service to service and even from base to base, depending on the occupancy rate of the barracks or dormitories on the particular base.

Army policy allows single members in the pay grade of E-6 and above to live off base at government expense. However, at some bases, E-5s are allowed to move off base at government expense, depending on the barracks occupancy rates at that base. Air force policy generally allows single E-4s with more than three years of service or more to reside off base at government expense. Navy policy allows single sailors in the pay grades of E-5 and above and E-4s with more than four years of service to reside off base and receive a housing allowance. The Marine Corps allows single E-6s and above to reside off base at government expense. On some bases, depending on the barracks occupancy rate, single E-5s and even some E-4s are authorized to reside off base.

ON-BASE HOUSING

Most places have limited on-base housing, so there is usually a waiting list (sometimes, more than one year!). To qualify for on-base housing, you must be residing with a dependent (in most cases, that means a spouse or minor children). The number of bedrooms you'll be authorized depends on the number and age of the dependents residing with you. Some bases have very, very nice housing; on other bases it barely qualifies for slum status. Utilities (trash, water, gas, electric) are normally free. Cable TV and phone service are not. Furniture is normally not provided (although many bases have "loan closets," which will temporarily loan you furniture). Appliances, such as stoves and refrigerators, are usually provided. Many on-base houses even have dishwashers.

Clothes washers and dryers are usually not provided, but most units—at least in the United States—have hookups. Additionally, many bases have Laundromats located close to the housing area. Overseas, many housing units are condo style, with washers and dryers located in each stairwell.

SPECIAL NEEDS

Five percent of on-base housing has the advantage of being wheelchair accessible, a feature that can be hard to find off base. Life on base has the added advantage that other military families are close by. Becoming part of a supportive community may be easier on base than it is off, where neighbors may not understand or be interested in the military lifestyle. A big factor in the decision about whether to live on base is the wait for housing, which varies from base to base. Some services offer priority housing to eligible families with exceptional family members (EFMs). If an EFM requires special housing or accommodations, such as pocket doors or railings, the base housing office can work with the EFM's medical documentation and physicians to provide certain modifications deemed medically necessary. This is evaluated on a case-by-case basis.

Schools

An important factor in your decision about housing is schools. Investigate both on-base, if available, and off-base schools. Contact them well in advance of the move to begin discussing how your child's unique needs will be met. Meet with administrators of both systems to share your child's individualized education program (IEP) and to see what is available in each system. Your child's IEP should be honored until a new IEP is written, but available services may vary, as might the individual school's approach to special education. Even on a base with a Department of Defense (DoD) school, the child might be transferred off base if the civilian school is determined to be better suited. This more likely if the child faces severe or profound challenges. Schools, both on and off base, develop reputations in the existing military special-needs community. Sometimes contacting a local educational advocate's office is a good idea because advocacy groups are often hired to participate in negotiating IEPs for families. The Military OneSource and the Marine Corps's Special Needs Evaluation Review Team (SNERT) can help you locate advocacy groups in your area. Wrightslaw (http://www.wrightslaw.com) is also a good source for referrals and connectivity in new communities. Those groups will know which schools have a reputation for providing a quality free and appropriate education and which tend to be less enlightened about the implementation of the Individuals with Disabilities Education Act (IDEA). Some schools and/ or their districts use legal due process to "slow-roll" military families out of their area in an attempt to save money and conserve resources, which is not in the child's best interests. Advocates will know which schools or districts have a reputation for this and can prevent placement in undesirable or less appropriate programs.

Schools use a rating system to determine a child's disability level, and part of that rating system involves a mathematical calculation of additional funds a district may provide to a school to implement services for that child. It is important to know what your child's rights and entitlements are, as well as to have a connection with someone who understands how those calculations work, in order to know how to negotiate for services for your child. For instance, your child may be eligible for curbside pickup at a residence or care facility and may require an air-conditioned bus if sensitive to heat sickness or seizures. Your child may need vision therapy, physical therapy, or occupational therapy as deemed educationally appropriate for acquiring a particular set of skills. Perhaps a least restrictive environment needs to be discussed and selected. Schools are required by law to provide a free appropriate public education in the least restrictive environment that is appropriate to the individual student's needs. Perhaps specific, measurable, qualitative, and quantitative goals need to be established to determine progress during the increments of the school year with regard to academic, behavioral, and other categories of instruction. Perhaps your child needs an individual aide or shared access to an aide. Perhaps your child would significantly regress if not placed in a similar services program during the summer break as other children. Special needs are individualized; therefore, so are IEPs. Thus it is incredibly important for parents to be informed, educated, and prepared to advocate for their children because the school's first priority is its budget, not your child; hence, the parent and often an informed companion advocate must represent the best interests of the child. Advocates for hire can be very expensive, but many work with community agencies and grant programs to offset their costs, and others are experienced parents who volunteer to participate and assist.

GOVERNMENT FAMILY HOUSING

The interiors of occupied housing units are not normally inspected as dormitories are (although they may be inspected without notice if the commander receives any kind of safety or sanitary problem report). The housing exterior is an entirely different matter. All of the services are pretty strict in dictating exactly how the outside the house (yard) will be maintained. Most employ personnel to drive by each and every housing unit once per week and write tickets for any discrepancies noted. Receive too many tickets in too short a period, and you will be asked to move off base.

In the United States, most on-base family housing units are duplexes and sometimes fourplexes. For officers and more senior enlisted members, on-base family housing usually consists of either duplexes or single-family dwellings. Sometimes they have fenced-in backyards. If the housing unit has a backyard but no fence, you can usually get permission to install a fence at your own expense (you have to agree to take the fence down when you move out if the next occupant doesn't want it).

The same is true of almost any "improvement" you wish to make to on-base family housing. Usually, you can get permission to do "do-it-yourself" improvements, but you must agree to return the house to its original state if the next person to move in doesn't want to accept your improvements.

Overseas, on-base family housing units generally take the form of high-rise apartment buildings—kind of like condominiums.

Moving out of base housing is a lot harder than moving in. The house interior will be inspected and should be immaculate (many people hire professional cleaners prior to checkout). However, many bases now hire professional cleaners themselves when an occupant moves out, making the process much easier.

More and more military bases are moving to privatized family housing maintained, managed, and sometimes built by private industry. The rent for these privatized units is paid to the housing management agency by military pay allotment and is equal to the member's housing allowance.

OFF-BASE HOUSING

Instead of living in the dormitories or residing in on-base housing, you may be authorized to live off base. In this case, the military will pay you BAH. The amount of this nontaxable allowance depends on your rank, marital (dependency) status, and where you (or your dependents) reside. Once per year, the military hires an independent agency to survey the average housing costs in all of the areas where significant numbers of military personnel live. The Per Diem, Travel and Transportation Allowance Committee uses this data to compute the amount of BAH you will receive each month. It currently covers 100 percent of average housing costs.

One nice feature of the BAH law is that the amount of BAH you receive may never go down while you are living in an area, even if the average cost of housing in that area goes down. Of course, once you move to a different base, your BAH will be recalculated for the current rate in the new location.

An interesting aspect of BAH is the type of housing that the entitlement is based upon. BAH is based on acceptable housing for an individual (or an individual with dependents). For example, a married E-5 is reimbursed based on what DoD considers minimum acceptable housing, a two-bedroom townhouse or duplex. For an O-5 it is a four-bedroom detached home. Although whether one has dependents is a factor, the number of dependents is not.

If you move into off-base housing overseas, your monthly entitlement, the overseas housing allowance (OHA), is recalculated every two weeks. This is because currency rates can fluctuate dramatically overseas, causing housing expenses to go up and down. In addition to OHA, those overseas are entitled to some additional allowances, such as an initial move-in-expense allowance, and reimbursement for costs to improve the security of the off-base residence.

If you are authorized to reside off base, it's very important that you ensure your lease contains a "military clause." A military clause allows you to break your lease in case you are forced to move on official orders.

SPECIAL CONSIDERATIONS

If you are married to a nonmilitary member and/or you have children, the military considers your spouse and children "dependents" and requires you to provide them with adequate support (which includes housing). Because of this, if you are married, you receive a housing allowance at the "with dependent" rate even if you are living in the single dormitories or barracks.

Because living in the barracks or dormitories is mandatory during basic training and job school, and because your dependents are not allowed to travel to basic training or job school (unless the job school is over twenty weeks long at a single location), during these periods you live in the barracks or dormitories and receive BAH for the area where your dependents reside.

When you move to your first permanent duty station, the rules change. Your dependents are allowed to move there at government expense. If they don't move there, that is considered your choice. In such cases, you receive BAH (at the "with dependent" rate) calculated based on your duty station location, regardless of where your dependents actually live.

As long as you are still married, to give up BAH, you would have to reside in on-base family housing. However, unless your dependents move to your duty location, you are not authorized to reside in on-base family housing, because the rules say that to qualify, your dependents must be living with you.

If there is extra space available in the barracks or dormitories, you are allowed to live there and still receive your BAH. However, now that the military is trying to give all single people living in the dormitories their own room, most bases do not have any extra space available. Therefore, as a married person who has voluntarily elected not to be accompanied by dependents, you will likely be required to live off base. You will receive BAH for the area you are assigned to. If you are allowed to live in the dormitory or barracks, you must be prepared to move out, with little or no notice, in case the space is needed (although most commanders/first sergeants will try to give at least two weeks' notice if possible).

The rules change for overseas assignments. If you are assigned overseas and elect not to bring your dependents, you can live in the barracks or dormitories on base and still receive BAH in order to provide them with adequate housing support in the United States.

Note: If you are a wounded warrior, there are lots of ways to get housing grants and assistance for yourself and your family. There are grants for remodeling homes to make them disability friendly. Habitat for Humanity has an extensive building program for combat-disabled veterans and their families. See the "Wounded Warrior" section below for more information.

BUYING YOUR FIRST HOME

Buying a home is always a sound investment, but it can be difficult if you frequently have to relocate. It is also a major decision and one that many young couples have to weigh seriously. With the current (2014) housing market, there has never been a better time to buy, and military couples are eligible for special mortgage rates.

There are many things to consider. Buying a home is not only a big investment but an ongoing one, with upkeep and maintenance expenses, property taxes, and other fees and services to pay for. There is no doubt, however, that if you can afford to buy a house now and perhaps rent it out if you are posted elsewhere, it will steadily appreciate in value and serve as a valuable nest egg in years to come.

Some advantages of buying your own home include savings on your income taxes because your mortgage interest payments are deductible every year. Also, because you own the place, you are not paying rent every month and getting nothing back in return. If you own your home, you can customize it to your liking—something most landlords don't encourage, even if you did want to spend money upgrading another person's property. Another major advantage is that as your house appreciates in value, your equity in the property increases. In a few years, if you need extra cash—to start a family, for instance—you can take out a loan against that equity.

There are downsides as well. Purchasing a home is an expensive initial investment, although buyers can exert a lot of leverage at the moment, such as getting the seller to pay all or some of the closing costs. If anxious to close the deal, the seller might accept these terms. Other costs include legal fees, surveys, deposits, and so on. Then there are the ongoing mortgage, tax, and homeowners insurance payments. You will also be responsible for upkeep and maintenance; if something goes wrong, you have to fix it. You may also have to pay housing association fees.

The decision to buy or not requires much thought. Do you want to be tied down with home ownership and everything that goes with it? Can you afford to buy a property? Do you earn enough to pay the mortgage and other costs every month and not fall into arrears.

If you expect to get a new posting in a couple of years, the house will not likely have appreciated sufficiently for you to recoup your buying costs, and it is probably better to rent. If you think you will be staying put for four or five years, then buying becomes a serious option.

If you buy a house near a base and are relocated, it may be easier to rent your home to another military couple rather than sell it. If you plan on selling each time you move on, you can always rent accommodation on a short lease rather than make a snap decision to buy after looking hurriedly at what is available. Rushed decisions are seldom the right ones.

FREQUENTLY ASKED QUESTIONS

Why Should I Buy Instead of Rent?

A home is an investment. When you rent, you write your monthly check, and that money is gone forever. But when you own your home, you can deduct the cost of your mortgage loan interest from your federal income taxes and usually from your state taxes. This will save you a lot each year, because the interest you pay will make up most of your monthly payment for most of the years of your mortgage. You can also deduct the property taxes you pay as a homeowner. In addition, the value of your home may go up over the years. Finally, you'll enjoy having something that's all yours—a home where your own personal style will tell the world who you are.

What Are "HUD Homes," and Are They a Good Deal?

When someone with a Department of Housing and Urban Development (HUD)–insured mortgage can't meet the payments, the lender forecloses on the home. HUD pays the lender what is owed, takes ownership of the property, and sells it at market value as quickly as possible. These homes can be a very good deal.

Can I Become a Home Buyer Even if I Have Had Bad Credit and Don't Have Much for a Down Payment?

You may be a good candidate for one of the federal mortgage programs. Start by contacting one of the HUD-funded housing counseling agencies that can help you sort through your options. Also contact your local government to see if any local home-buying programs might work for you. Look in the blue pages of your phone directory for your local office of housing and community development or, if you can't find it, contact your mayor's office or your county executive's office.

Should I Use a Real Estate Broker? How Do I Find One?

Using a real estate broker is a very good idea. All the details involved in home buying, particularly the financial ones, can be mind-boggling. A good real estate professional can guide you through the entire process and make the experience much easier. A real estate broker will be well acquainted with all the important things you'll want to know about a neighborhood you may be considering: school quality, number of children in the area, safety, traffic volume, and more. He or she will help you figure the price range you can afford and search the classified ads and multiple listing services for homes you'll want to see. With immediate access to homes as soon as they're put on the market, the broker can save you hours of wasted driving-around time. When it's time to make an offer on a home, the broker can point out ways to structure your deal to save you money. He or she will explain the advantages and disadvantages of different types of mortgages, guide you through the paperwork, and be there to hold your hand and answer last-minute questions when you sign the final papers at closing. And you don't have to pay the broker anything! The home seller—not the buyer—pays the commission.

By the way, if you want to buy a HUD home, you will be required to use a real estate broker to submit your bid. To find a broker who sells HUD homes, check your local yellow pages or the classified ads in your local newspaper.

How Much Money Will I Have to Come Up with to Buy a Home?

That depends on a number of factors, including the cost of the house and the type of mortgage you get. In general, you need to come up with enough money to cover three costs: earnest money, the deposit you make on the home to prove to the seller that your offer is serious; the down payment, a percentage of the cost of the home that you must pay when you go to settlement; and closing costs, the costs associated with processing the paperwork to buy a house.

When you make an offer on a home, your real estate broker will put your earnest money into an escrow account. If the offer is accepted, your earnest money will be applied to the down payment or closing costs. If your offer is not accepted, the money will be returned to you. The amount of your earnest money varies. If you buy a HUD home, for example, your deposit generally will range from $500 to $2,000.

The more money you can put into your down payment, the lower your mortgage payments will be. Some types of loans require 10 to 20 percent of the purchase price. That's why many first-time homebuyers turn to HUD's Federal Housing Administration (FHA) for help. FHA loans require only 3 percent down—and sometimes less.

Closing costs, which you will pay at settlement, average 3 to 4 percent of the price of your home. These costs include various fees your lender charges and other processing expenses. When you apply for your loan, your lender will give you an estimate of the closing costs, so you won't be caught by surprise. If you buy a HUD home, HUD may pay many of your closing costs.

How Do I Know if I Can Get a Loan?

There are many simple mortgage calculators on the Internet that will show how much mortgage you can afford. If that amount is significantly less than the cost of the homes that interest you, then you might want to wait a while longer. Before giving up, contact a real estate broker or a HUD-funded housing counseling agency, which will help you evaluate your loan potential. A broker will know what kinds of mortgages the lenders are offering and can help you choose a program that might be right for you. Another good idea is to get prequalified for a loan—that is, to apply for a mortgage before you actually start looking for a home. Then you'll know exactly how much you can afford to spend, and it will speed the process once you do find the home of your dreams.

How Do I Find a Lender?

You can finance a home with a loan from a bank, a savings and loan, a credit union, a private mortgage company, or various state government lenders. Shopping for a loan is like shopping for any other large purchase: you can save money if you take some time to look around for the best prices. Different lenders can offer quite different interest rates and loan fees, and as you know, a lower interest rate can make a big difference in what you can afford. Talk with several lenders before you decide. Most lenders need three to six weeks for the whole loan approval process. Your real estate broker will be familiar with lenders in the area and what they're offering. Or you can look in your local newspaper's real estate section—most papers list interest rates being offered by local lenders. You can find FHA-approved lenders in the yellow pages of your phone book. HUD does not make loans directly—you must use a HUD-approved lender if you're interested in an FHA loan.

In Addition to the Mortgage Payment, What Other Costs Do I Need to Consider?

Of course you'll have your monthly utilities. If your rent has previously included utilities, this may be new for you. Your real estate broker will be able to help you get information from the seller on what utilities normally cost. In addition, you might have homeowner or condo association dues. You'll definitely have property taxes, and you may also have city or county taxes. Taxes are normally rolled into your mortgage payment. Again, your broker can help you anticipate these costs.

So What Will My Mortgage Cover?

Most loans have four parts: principal, the amount you actually borrowed; interest, money paid to the lender for the money you've borrowed; homeowners insurance, a monthly fee to insure the property against loss from fire, smoke, theft, and other hazards required by most lenders; and property taxes, the annual city/county taxes assessed on your property, divided by the number of mortgage payments you make in a year. Most loans are for thirty years, although fifteen-year loans are available too. During the life of the loan, you'll pay far more in interest than you will in principal—sometimes two or three times more! Because of the way loans are structured, in the first years you'll be paying mostly interest in your monthly payments. In the final years, you'll be paying mostly principal.

What Do I Need to Take with Me When I Apply for a Mortgage?

If you have everything with you when you visit your lender, you'll save a good deal of time. You should have (1) Social Security numbers for both you and your spouse if both of you are applying for the loan; (2) copies of your checking and savings account statements for the past six months; (3) evidence of any other assets, like bonds or stocks; (4) a recent pay stub detailing your earnings; (5) a list of all credit card accounts and the approximate monthly amounts owed on each; (6) a list of account numbers and balances due on outstanding loans, such as car loans; (7) copies of your last two years' income tax statements; and (8) the name and address of someone who can verify your employment. Depending on your lender, you may be asked for other information.

How Do I Know Which Type of Mortgage Is Best for Me?

There are many types of mortgages, and the more you know about them before you start, the better. Most people use a fixed-rate mortgage in which the interest rate stays the same for the term of the loan, which normally is thirty years. The advantage of a fixed-rate mortgage is that you always know exactly how much your mortgage payment will be, and you can plan for it. Another kind of mortgage is an adjustable-rate mortgage (ARM). With this kind of mortgage, your interest rate and monthly payments usually start lower than for a fixed-rate mortgage, but your rate and payment amount can go up or down as often as once or twice a year. The adjustment is tied to a financial index, such as the US Treasury securities index. The advantage of an ARM is that you may be able to afford a more expensive home because your initial interest rate will be lower. There are several government mortgage programs, including Veteran's Administration programs. Most people have heard of FHA mortgages. FHA doesn't actually make loans; instead, it insures them so that if buyers default for some reason, lenders will get their money. This encourages lenders to give mortgages to people who might not otherwise qualify. Talk to your real estate broker about the various kinds of loans before you begin shopping for a mortgage.

When I Find the Home I Want, How Much Should I Offer?

Again, your real estate broker can help you here. But you should consider several things.

1. Is the asking price in line with prices for similar homes in the area?
2. Is the home in good condition, or will you have to spend a substantial amount of money to fix it up? You probably want to get a professional home inspection before you make your offer. Your real estate broker can help you arrange one.
3. How long has the home been on the market? If it's been for sale for a while, the seller may be willing to accept a lower offer.
4. How much mortgage will be required? Make sure you really can afford whatever offer you make.
5. How much do you really want the home? The closer your offer to the asking price, the more likely it is to be accepted. In some cases, you may even want to offer more than the asking price—for instance, if you know you are competing with others for the house.

What If My Offer Is Rejected?

They often are! But don't let that stop you. Now you begin negotiating. Your broker will help you. You may have to offer more money, but you can ask the seller to cover some or all of the closing costs or to make repairs that wouldn't normally be expected. Often negotiations on a price go back and forth several times before a deal is made. Just remember—don't get so caught up in negotiations that you lose sight of what you really want and can afford!

So What Will Happen at Closing?

Basically, you'll sit at a table with your broker, the seller's broker, probably the seller, and a closing agent. The closing agent will have a stack of papers for you and the seller to sign. Although he or she will give you a basic explanation of each paper, you may want to take the time to read each one and/or to consult with your agent to make sure you know exactly what you're signing. After all, you're committing to pay a large amount of money for a lot of years! Before the closing, your lender is required to give you a booklet explaining the closing costs, a "good faith estimate" of how much cash you'll have to supply at closing, and a list of documents you'll need at closing. If you don't get those items, be sure to call your lender before you go to closing. Don't hesitate to ask questions.

MOVING IN

Move-in day is exciting. The new house starts to feel like home, and everyone is relieved to have familiar objects back. Give thought to creating moving-day traditions. They can be a simple as having Chinese takeout the first night in a new home or eating the first meal on boxes even though the table has arrived. Because of the excitement, pay special attention to children, who may wander around the unfamiliar surroundings and find danger. If respite care is needed, contact the family-support center ahead of time to prepare to have help well in advance.

SAFETY IN A NEW HOME

Look over a new home with an eye for hazards such as busy roads or creeks nearby. Hold a family meeting to discuss these hazards with children and establish firm boundaries defining where they are allowed to go. In some cases base housing or certain apartments and condominium associations can post signs, such as "Deaf Child at Play," to alert neighbors and travelers to take extra precautions for hearing- or vision-impaired family members.

If a child is likely to run away from home, talk to the neighbors, local police, local fire department, and/or military police (MPs) about this. Provide them with a current photo and a description of the child. Explain how the child might react if confronted. Be sure to include all contact information on the sheet and give copies to the MPs or local police. Remember to update the photo and contact information as necessary. List any medications and/or diagnoses that can impact first responders' approach to and understanding of volatile situations. You may want to make several copies of this sheet to have on hand in case of emergency and to take with you when you travel.

If you are concerned that despite much vigilance, a child might leave the house unobserved, consider installing extra locks, barriers, or an alarm system. Ask your physician for a letter explaining the medical necessity for these modifications and bring it along with a request to the base housing office or landlord to ask for permission to install extra locks.

Talk to neighbors about your concerns about your child. Give them your phone number and ask them to call if they spot your child moving away from the house alone. If a child is deaf or blind, contact the base or local authorities and ask for a sign alerting drivers to the presence of a deaf or blind child.

If oxygen tanks are in the home, the local fire department needs to know about them. Also, if a child is likely to hide in case of an emergency, tell the fire department. A copy of the child ID sheet made for the police would be appropriate for the fire department as well.

If a child is nonverbal, consider keeping identification and contact information on the child, perhaps on a bracelet or sewn into clothes. It is recommended that you post signs about pets and service animals and identifying disabilities by the front door or a visible window to alert first responders in an emergency.

3

HAVING A BABY

If you are thinking of starting a family, make sure that your health insurance covers prenatal care during pregnancy and delivery and then covers both mother and child thereafter. Consult with your health-benefits advisor.

Women should start taking care of themselves before trying to get pregnant. This is called preconception health. It means knowing how health conditions and risk factors could affect you or your unborn baby if you become pregnant. For example, some foods, habits, and medications can harm your baby—even before he or she is conceived. Some health problems also can affect pregnancy.

Talk to your doctor before pregnancy to learn what you can do to prepare your body. Women should prepare for pregnancy before becoming sexually active. Ideally, women should give themselves at least three months to prepare before getting pregnant.

The following are the five most important things you can do before becoming pregnant:

1. Take 400 μg (0.4 mg) of folic acid every day for at least three months before getting pregnant to lower your risk of some birth defects of the brain and spine. You can get folic acid from some foods, but it's hard to get all you need from foods alone. Taking a vitamin with folic acid is the best and easiest way to be sure you're getting enough. Of course, you should consult with a

health care professional before taking any kind of supplement or medication.

2. Stop smoking and drinking alcohol. Ask your doctor for help.
3. If you have a medical condition, be sure it is under control. Some conditions include asthma, diabetes, depression, high blood pressure, obesity, thyroid disease, and epilepsy. Be sure your vaccinations are up to date.
4. Talk to your doctor about any over-the-counter and prescription medicines you are using. These include dietary and herbal supplements. Some medications are not safe during pregnancy. At the same time, stopping needed medications can also be harmful.
5. Avoid contact with potentially harmful toxic substances or materials at work and at home. Stay away from chemicals and cat or rodent feces.

YOU ARE PREGNANT

You will probably want to tell everyone that you are having a baby, but as a member of a serving military family, you must also tell your command. This is even more important if you are the serving family member and become pregnant so that command can adjust your duties. For a serving father, this is also a good time to put in a request for paternity leave. You may wish to wait until you're out of the first trimester before telling others about the pregnancy.

PRENATAL CARE

Get early and regular prenatal care, which can help keep you and your baby healthy. Babies of mothers who do not get prenatal care are three times more likely to have a low birth weight and five times more likely to die than those born to mothers who do get care, according to the "Prenatal Care Fact Sheet" issued by the Office on Women's Health, US Department of Health and Human Services.

Doctors can spot health problems early when they see mothers regularly. This allows for early treatment, which can cure many problems and prevent others. Doctors also can talk to pregnant women about steps they can take to give their unborn babies a healthy start in life.

Ask your doctor before stopping or starting any medications. Some are unsafe during pregnancy. Keep in mind that even over-the-counter medicines and herbal products may cause side effects or other problems. But not using needed medicines can also be harmful.

Avoid X-rays. If you must have dental work or diagnostic tests, tell your dentist or doctor that you are pregnant so that he or she will take extra care.

Get a flu shot if your baby's due date is between March and July. Pregnant women can get very sick from the flu and may need hospital care.

FOOD DOS AND DON'TS

Eat a variety of healthy foods. Choose fruits, vegetables, whole grains, calcium-rich foods, and foods low in saturated fat. Also make sure to drink plenty of fluids, especially water.

Get all the nutrients you need each day, including iron. Getting enough iron prevents anemia, which is linked to preterm birth and low birth weight. Eating a variety of healthy foods will help you get the nutrients your baby needs. Ask your doctor if you need to take a daily prenatal vitamin or iron supplement to be sure you are getting enough.

Protect yourself and your baby from food-borne illnesses, including toxoplasmosis and *Listeria* infection. Wash fruits and vegetables before eating them. Don't eat under- or uncooked meat or fish. Always handle, clean, cook, eat, and store foods properly.

Avoid fish with lots of mercury, including swordfish, king mackerel, shark, and tilefish.

LIFESTYLE DOS AND DON'TS

Gain a healthy amount of weight. Your doctor can tell you how much weight gain you should aim for during pregnancy. Don't smoke, drink alcohol, or use drugs. These can cause the baby long-term harm and even death. Ask your doctor for help quitting.

Unless your doctor tells you not to, try to get at least 2.5 hours of moderate-intensity aerobic activity a week, but do not start a new exercise routine without consulting your doctor first. It's best to spread your workouts across the week. If you worked out regularly before pregnancy, you can keep up your activity level as long as your health doesn't change and you talk to your doctor about your activity level throughout your pregnancy. Learn more about how to have a fit pregnancy.

Don't take very hot baths or use hot tubs or saunas. Get plenty of sleep and find ways to control stress. Get informed: read books, watch videos, go to a childbirth class, and talk with moms you know. Ask your doctor about childbirth education classes for you and your partner. Classes can help you prepare for the birth.

ENVIRONMENTAL DOS AND DON'TS

Stay away from chemicals like insecticides, solvents (e.g., some cleaners or paint thinners), lead, mercury, and paint (including fumes). Not all products have pregnancy warnings on their labels. If you're unsure if a product is safe, ask your doctor before using it. Talk to your doctor if you are worried that chemicals used in your workplace might be harmful.

If you have a cat, ask your doctor about toxoplasmosis, an infection caused by a parasite sometimes found in cat feces. If not treated, it can cause birth defects. You can lower your risk by avoiding cat litter and wearing gloves when gardening.

Avoid contact with rodents, including pet rodents, and with their urine, droppings, or nesting material. Rodents can carry a virus that can be harmful or even deadly to your unborn baby.

Take steps to avoid illness, such as washing hands frequently. Stay away from secondhand smoke.

Your doctor will give you a schedule of all the appointments you should have while pregnant. Most experts suggest you see your doctor as follows:

- About once a month for weeks four through twenty-eight
- Twice a month for weeks twenty-eight through thirty-six
- Weekly from week thirty-six to birth

If you are older than thirty-five or your pregnancy is high risk, you'll probably see your doctor more often.

FIRST TRIMESTER (WEEKS ONE TO TWELVE)

During the first trimester, your body undergoes many changes. Hormonal changes affect almost every organ system in your body and can trigger symptoms even in the very first weeks of pregnancy. Your period stopping is a clear sign that you are pregnant. Other changes may include the following:

- Extreme tiredness
- Tender, swollen breasts (nipples might also stick out)
- Upset stomach with or without throwing up (morning sickness)
- Cravings or distaste for certain foods
- Mood swings
- Constipation (trouble having bowel movements)
- Need to pass urine more often
- Headache
- Heartburn
- Weight gain or loss

As your body changes, you might need to make changes to your daily routine, such as going to bed earlier or eating frequent, small meals. Fortunately, most of these discomforts will go away as your pregnancy progresses. And some women might not feel any discomfort at all! If you have been pregnant before, you might feel differently this time around. Just as each woman is different, so is each pregnancy.

SECOND TRIMESTER (WEEKS THIRTEEN TO TWENTY-EIGHT)

Most women find the second trimester of pregnancy easier than the first. But it is just as important to stay informed about the pregnancy during these months.

You might notice that symptoms like nausea and fatigue are going away. But other new, more noticeable changes to your body are now happening. Your abdomen will expand as the baby continues to grow. And before this trimester is over, you will feel your baby beginning to move!

As your body changes to make room for your growing baby, you may develop the following:

- Body aches, such as back, abdomen, groin, or thigh pain
- Stretch marks on your abdomen, breasts, thighs, or buttocks
- Darkening of the skin around your nipples
- A line on the skin running from belly button to pubic hairline
- Patches of darker skin, often symmetrical on both sides of the face, usually over the cheeks, forehead, nose, or upper lip (sometimes called the mask of pregnancy)
- Numb or tingling hands (carpal tunnel syndrome)
- Itching on the abdomen, palms, and soles of the feet
- Swelling of the ankles, fingers, and face

Note: Call your doctor if you have nausea, loss of appetite, vomiting, jaundice, or fatigue combined with itching on your abdomen, palms, and soles of your feet. These can be signs of a serious liver problem. Also call your doctor right away if you notice any sudden or extreme swelling, or if you gain a lot of weight really quickly, as this could be a sign of preeclampsia, a medical condition characterized by high blood pressure and high levels of protein in the urine. If left untreated, it can be life threatening.

THIRD TRIMESTER (WEEKS TWENTY-NINE TO FORTY)

You're in the home stretch! Some of the same discomforts you had in your second trimester will continue. Plus, many women find breathing difficult and notice they have to go to the bathroom even more often. This is because the baby is getting bigger and is putting more pressure on your organs. Don't worry, your baby is fine, and these problems will abate once you give birth.

Some new body changes you might notice in the third trimester include the following:

- Shortness of breath
- Heartburn
- Swelling of the ankles, fingers, and face
- Hemorrhoids
- Tender breasts, which may leak a watery premilk called colostrum
- A protruding belly button
- Trouble sleeping
- The baby "dropping," or moving lower in your abdomen
- Contractions, which can be a sign of real or false labor

Note: If you notice any sudden or extreme swelling, or if you gain a lot of weight really quickly, call your doctor right away, as this could be a sign of preeclampsia.

As you near your due date, your cervix thins and softens (called effacing). This normal, natural process helps the birth canal (vagina) open during the birthing process. Your doctor will check your progress with a vaginal exam as you near your due date.

YOUR NEW BABY

Spending time with your baby in those first hours of life is very special. Although you might be tired, your newborn could be quite alert after birth. Cuddle your baby skin to skin. Let him or her get to know your voice and study your face. Your baby can see up to about two feet away. You might notice that your baby throws his or her arms out if someone turns on a light or makes a sudden noise. This is called the startle response. Babies also are born with grasp and sucking reflexes. Put your finger in your baby's palm and watch how he or she knows to squeeze it. Feed your baby when he or she shows signs of hunger.

Right after birth babies need many important tests and procedures to make sure they are healthy. Some of these are even required by law. But as long as the baby is healthy, everything but the Apgar test can wait for at least an hour. Delaying further medical care will preserve the precious first moments of life for you, your partner, and the baby. A baby who has not been poked and prodded may be more willing to nurse and cuddle. So, before delivery, talk to your doctor or midwife about delaying shots, medications, and tests.

GOING HOME

The first few days at home after having your baby are a time for rest and recovery—physically and emotionally. You need to focus your energy on yourself and getting to know your new infant. Even though you may be very excited and have requests for lots of visits from family and friends, try to limit visitors and get as much rest as possible. Ask for help from close family or friends in the first few weeks if you can. They can assist with errands, cooking, and even caring for the baby so that you can shower, sleep, or take a little time for yourself. Don't expect to keep your house perfect. You may find that all you can do is eat, sleep, and care for your baby. And that is perfectly OK. Learn to pace yourself from the first day that you arrive back home. Try to lie down or nap while the baby naps. Don't try to do too much around the house. Allow others to help you, and don't be afraid to ask for help with cleaning, laundry, meals, or caring for the baby.

Your doctor will check your recovery at your postpartum visit, about six weeks after birth. Ask about resuming normal activities, as well as nutrition and fitness plans to help you return to a healthy weight. Also ask your doctor about having sex and birth control. Your period could return in six to eight weeks, or sooner if you do not breastfeed. If you breastfeed, your period might not resume for many months. Still, using reliable birth control is the best way to prevent pregnancy until you want to have another baby.

If you want to diet and are breastfeeding, it is best to wait until your baby is at least two months old. During those first two months, your body needs to recover from childbirth and establish a good milk supply. When you do start to lose weight, try not to lose too much too quickly. This can be harmful to the baby because environmental toxins stored in your body fat can be released into your breast milk. Losing about one pound per week (no more than four pounds per month) has been deemed safe and will not affect your milk supply or the baby's growth.

After childbirth you may feel sad, weepy, and overwhelmed for a few days. Many new mothers have the "baby blues" after giving birth. Changing hormones, anxiety about caring for the baby, and lack of sleep all affect your emotions. Be patient with yourself. These feelings are normal and usually go away quickly. But if sadness lasts more than two weeks, go see your doctor. Don't wait until your postpartum visit. You might have a serious but treatable condition called postpartum depression. Postpartum depression can occur at any time within the first year after birth and can be moderate to severe. Do not be afraid to ask for help if you are feeling like you cannot handle the stresses of newborn care.

Having a support person stay with you for a few days when you first return home after the birth can give you the confidence to go it alone in the weeks ahead. Try to arrange this before delivery.

TIPS FOR NEW DADS

It is important for the father to be involved in every stage of the pregnancy to support and encourage his pregnant partner and learn what his responsibilities are. For first-time parents, pregnancy and the first months of life are a time of both great happiness and apprehension, which is quite normal and understandable. Never forget, however, that help is always on hand. Most bases have a new-parent support program that provides free advice and guidance from the moment you know you are going to have a baby. The support then continues through the early years of your child's life.

A great way to bond with your wife is to sign up for parenting classes with her. Your base might also offer childbirth classes as well.

Fathers serving in the military cannot guarantee that they will be there for the delivery, so together choose someone who will be available to help your wife, drive her to the hospital, and so on. As the big day approaches, make a checklist of what your wife will need to take with her, map the quickest route to the hospital, and get into the habit of making sure that you always have enough gas in your car!

It is also a good idea to discuss the birth itself with your doctor and the hospital. Sometimes called a birth plan, this conversation can specify the preferred method of delivery, the family and friends who can be with you during labor, and any special religious requirements.

Attending birthing classes will enable you to help your wife greatly during labor. Your role is to support and encourage her and also to act as her advocate. And remember to take your camera or video to record the magical moments as your child is born.

In most cases paternity leave, although discretionary, is granted, and it is important to be home for the first few days after your wife and child return from the hospital. They will really need you there. Your wife will be tired and will need loving, and the baby will need near round-the-clock attention for feeding, cleaning, and caring. Work out a roster that works for you both. Many new mothers like to have their own mother around for a few days, but as the new dad, don't let your mother-in-law do all the work. It will take time to get into a routine, and the new baby may not cooperate, but be patient. Remember that child care is also available on most bases.

4

ADOPTION

Adoption is a realistic option for military personnel who want to expand their families, and many military families do adopt either foster children or stepchildren. A number of factors and issues that civilian families do not have to contend with must be taken into account.

Military life does pose special challenges, from frequent moves to new posts to deployments. Some state agencies may consequently be reluctant to work with military families, arguing that these disruptions are not in the best interest of the child or do not provide a stable environment. These arguments should not deter you, and the military will assist you in your adoption quest. For instance, it provides eligibility for extra leave to complete the adoption process, reimbursement for certain expenses, and access to military health care for the adopted child even before the adoption is final.

It is important, therefore, to ensure that deployments do not affect adoption procedures, and there are a number of places to get help with this and to find out more about adopting. Visit your family service center to find out if there's an adoptive-parent support group on or near your installation. AdoptUSKids (http://www.adoptuskids.org) includes information about fostering and adoption resources specifically for military families. AdoptUSKids has also produced a comprehensive guide to adoption for military families titled "Wherever My Family Is: That's Home!" "Adoption for Military Families: How to Get Started," an article on the Military Money website, covers the basics. The "Adoption: Where Do I Start?" factsheet by Child Welfare Information Gateway answers many questions families have when considering adoption. If you live overseas, your installation's school, legal assistance, and medical clinic personnel are often familiar with local resources and services.

The Department of Defense's (DoD) Exceptional Family Member Program (EFMP) helps families with a special-needs member before, during, and after transfer or permanent change of station orders. Note that the military defines "special needs" to mean "physical or mental disabilities or severe illness." This differs from what adoption professionals often refer to as "children with special needs," which include healthy children who are older, in sibling groups, or of color. For information on how "special needs" is defined in adoption, read the Child Welfare Information Gateway's "'Special Needs' Adoption: What Does It Mean?" The Operation Homefront website provides more details about EFMP.

ADOPTION LAWS

State law governs US adoptions. The state statutes search feature on the Information Gateway website provides information on the adoption laws in each state.

Families who want to adopt children from another state need to be aware of the Interstate Compact on the Placement of Children, a legally binding agreement between states that regulates the placement of children across state lines. Your social worker or agency should be familiar with its requirements and can provide you with more information.

Adopting a child born outside the United States requires families to comply with the laws of their state of record, as well as US immigration law and the laws of the country where the child lives. For families interested in intercountry adoption, adopting a child from a country that is a member of the Hague Convention on Intercountry Adoption is different from adopting a child from a non–Hague Convention country. Read Information Gateway's factsheet titled "Intercountry Adoption from Hague Convention and Non–Hague Convention Countries."

For families stationed overseas, the Office of the Judge Advocate General or legal assistance office may be able to point you to applicable laws, policies, and agreements between the United States and countries where military personnel are stationed. You may want to ask how the

Status of Forces Agreement (SOFA), a treaty between a host country and a nation stationing troops in that country, affects the relocation of children from one country to another.

THE HOME STUDY

Generally, a home study—also called a family assessment—follows the same procedure for military and civilian families, although it may differ in the following ways:

- More criminal background checks may be requested because agencies may require background checks for every state in which you have lived.
- For you to adopt a child or infant living in another state, your adoption professional must check that state's requirements before completing the home study.
- Families overseas must have a home study completed and approved by a social worker licensed in the United States to do adoption home studies. Two agencies licensed to place US children with overseas families are Adopt Abroad and Voice for International Development and Adoption. Also, the International Social Service has social workers in 140 of the countries where the United States has military installations.

Information Gateway offers the following resources on home studies:

- "The Adoption Home Study Process," an Information Gateway factsheet, provides information about what a home study includes and topics discussed in this process.
- The National Foster Care and Adoption Directory contains a state-by-state listing of adoption program managers and adoptive-parent support groups.

PERMANENT CHANGE OF STATION OR DEPLOYMENT

In the event of a permanent change of station or deployment, you may be able to have some of your home-study documents transferred to an agency near your new home or installation. Some agencies may require their own forms and protocols for the home study.

In case of deployment, it is very important to keep your command informed about your adoption process to ensure completion and delivery of essential documents. It is important to have appropriate powers of attorney in place for a deployed service member.

Before a child moves to another state for adoption, administrators of the Interstate Compact on the Placement of Children will need to grant approval. When a child has been legally adopted, families are free to move to different states.

ADOPTION PROCESS DURATION

A home study takes at least three months to complete. The time it takes for a child to be placed in your home will vary greatly, depending on the agency or the country. It is not unusual to wait two years or longer for a child to be eligible for an adoptive family. Older children may require more preplacement visits over a longer period to ease their transition into a new family. States' terms for the preplacement plan will vary. Preplacement transition plans are based on agency policy and the needs of the child or children. Out-of-state or overseas families may need to travel to the home state of the child to meet and visit with him or her. Realistic expectations for the waiting period and making use of that time to prepare for the child you would like to parent can help ease the frustration of the wait.

LEAVE

Military service members are not eligible for leave under the Family Medical Leave Act. However, legislative changes make service members eligible for up to twenty-one days of nonchargeable leave (i.e., leave that doesn't count against regular leave time) in conjunction with the adoption of a child. If both parents are in the military, only one can take adoption leave. The following is taken from DoD Instruction 1327.06 (p. 19) from September 30, 2011:

(4) Adoption Leave. A Service member who adopts a child in a qualifying adoption shall receive up to 21 days of non-chargeable leave of absence to be used in connection with the adoption. This absence shall be taken within 12 months following the adoption and may be authorized in conjunction with ordinary leave. In the event that two Service members who are married to each other adopt a child in a qualifying child adoption, only one of the members shall be granted an adoption leave of absence. A qualifying adoption is defined as an adoption where the member is eligible for reimbursement of qualified adoption expenses under section 1052 of Reference (e). (Paragraph 10.6 of Reference (j) provides information on deferment from duty based on adoption.)

COSTS

The costs of adoption can range from $0, if you adopt from the foster care system and use a public agency, to more than $40,000 if you adopt independently (that is, without an agency). This is an area of great fluctuation. Several resources can help defray the costs of adoption:

- Adoption reimbursement: According to DoD Instruction 1341.9, up to $2,000 per child or up to $5,000 per year for qualifying expenses is available to military families whose adoptions were arranged by a qualified adoption agency. Benefits are paid after the adoption is completed.
- Adoption assistance (or adoption subsidies): For some eligible children, this assistance is another possible resource. The subsidies will vary, depending on the child's needs.
- Tax credit: Military families are eligible for an adoption tax credit. For more information, go to the Information Gateway webpage that lists grants, loans, and tax credits for adoption.
- Two Information Gateway factsheets offer more information: "Adoption Assistance for Children Adopted from Foster Care" and "Costs of Adopting."

POSTADOPTION SERVICES

For medical coverage, an adopted child or a child placed for adoption before the adoption is finalized should be enrolled immediately in the Defense Enrollment Eligibility Reporting System (DEERS). Patient-affairs personnel at specific medical treatment facilities may have more information, and details about access and eligibility are available on the TRICARE website (http://www.tricare.mil).

Family service centers located on most major military installations can provide military families with information regarding adoption reimbursement and other familial benefits. Information Gateway has a number of factsheets:

- "Finding and Using Postadoption Services"
- "Parenting Your Adopted Preschooler"
- "Parenting Your Adopted School-Age Child"
- "Parenting Your Adopted Teenager"
- "Selecting and Working with a Therapist Skilled in Adoption"
- "Parenting a Child Who Has Been Sexually Abused: A Guide for Foster and Adoptive Parents"

If you are stationed in the United States, your adoption caseworker or adoption agency can help you find the services available in your state. Information Gateway has a webpage of links to adoption information provided by state child-welfare agencies in all fifty states and the District of Columbia.

Adoptive-parent support groups are a great source of information about the services in your area. Some military installations have active adoptive-parent support groups. Search for support groups by state at http://www.childwelfare.gov/nfcad.

5

DISCOVERING YOUR CHILD HAS A DISABILITY

Learning that your child is developmentally delayed or has a disability can be a stunning blow. Many parents experience an array of feelings, frequently starting with denial and flowing into anger, fear, and guilt. It can be hard to believe that the diagnosis is correct. As parents absorb this new information, they may direct anger at medical personnel or whoever provides information about the child's condition. They may even lash out at other family members as they try to understand what the diagnosis means. Fear stems from not knowing what the future holds, as well as the realization that the complex job of raising a disabled child lies ahead. Many parents also worry that they did something to cause the disability and feel a sense of guilt. Sadness and disappointment are inevitable as you realize you must revise the hopes and dreams you had for your child.

You may be flooded with emotion and feel overwhelmed. However, you can take constructive steps now, and there are many sources of help, support, and reassurance available. No matter what the disability is, tapping into resources available to you will help not only your child but you and your entire family as well.

REACH OUT

First of all, ask any questions you may have of the professional who is seeing your child. If a doctor or professional uses words you don't understand, ask him or her to explain. Don't be embarrassed to say, "Would you please explain that again in a way I can understand?" You are absorbing a large amount of potentially confusing information. If you are unsure about the diagnosis, ask for a second opinion; you are entitled to one.

When a child is diagnosed with a disability, some parents move through the following stages:

- Denial: Often the first reaction people have to any loss is denial. When you have just learned that your child may have a disability, denial might propel you to get a second opinion. That a good idea; doctors are fallible.
- Guilt: It is not unusual for parents to blame themselves for having somehow caused their child's impairment. This can be especially difficult for mothers, who may look back on their pregnancy and wonder if something they did or didn't do caused their child's disability or illness.
- Anger: Anger is a reasonable reaction to the loss of something precious, and you are entitled to feel angry. You might be asking, Why me? Why my child? Many parents eventually use their anger to energize themselves in the struggle to get the best possible services for their child.
- Sorrow: Sadness and disappointment are inevitable as you realize that the future you had envisioned for your child might never materialize. Grief is the natural reaction to loss, and if you discover that your child is especially challenged, you may need to grieve for the healthy child you had dreamed of.
- Anxiety and fear: When you learn that your child is not developing typically, there is good reason to be afraid and anxious. Caring for a child with a disability or chronic illness can be exhausting and confusing. Worries about the future and one's ability to be a good parent are common.
- Acceptance and hope: Finally, the roller-coaster ride starts to slow down and level out. Your child is still disabled or delayed, but you

have a greater understanding of his or her condition and realize that you can take good and loving care of this child. You realize that while your child may not be typical, he or she is loving and lovable.

In 1986, recognizing the importance of getting early help to children with special needs and their families, the US Congress passed an amendment to the Education for All Handicapped Children Act of 1975. It ensured that children with special needs would not have to wait until they were school-age to receive services. Today, the Individuals with Disabilities Education Act (IDEA), Part C, requires all fifty states and jurisdictions to have an early-intervention system in place for all children with disabilities from birth until they turn three. For more information about IDEA, visit Wrightslaw (http://www.wrightslaw.com).

WHAT IS EARLY INTERVENTION?

Every baby and child develops at a unique pace emotionally, intellectually, and physically. When children under age three are discovered to have, or be at risk of developing, a condition or special need that may affect their development, early-intervention services can help their families identify and minimize these delays.

GOALS OF EARLY INTERVENTION

Early intervention provides services with the goal of lessening the effect of any condition that may limit a child's development. It can be remedial or preventive in nature, minimizing or preventing delays. Early intervention is most effective when it focuses on the child and the family together. Services may begin anywhere between birth and age three; however, there are many reasons to begin as early as possible.

WHY START SO YOUNG?

There are many reasons to introduce an exceptional child to early intervention as soon as possible. Most importantly, a child's learning and development are most rapid in the preschool years. If, during these early stages of development, the teachable moments and times of greatest readiness are not taken advantage of, the same skills may take longer to learn when the child is older.

EARLY INTERVENTION STRENGTHENS FAMILIES

Early intervention is also a valuable resource for the parents and siblings of an exceptional child. The families of exceptional children may feel isolated, disappointed, frustrated, or helpless. All of these stresses may affect the whole family's well-being, as well as the child's development. Early intervention helps empower families as they negotiate their way through life with a specially challenged child. It can improve parents' attitudes about themselves and their child as well as give them better information and skills for teaching him or her.

WHO PROVIDES THE SERVICES?

Early-intervention services are required by law and are available throughout the fifty states and territories of the United States. Each state decides which of its agencies will be in charge of early services for infants and toddlers with special needs.

MOST SERVICES ARE FREE

Part C of IDEA requires that evaluations or assessments, development of an individual family service plan (IFSP), and service coordination be provided free of charge to eligible children and their families. Other services may also be provided at no cost to families, although some fees may be assessed on a sliding scale, depending on the income of the child's family. However, the law also states that no family shall be denied services because they cannot afford them. If you have problems with the cost or availability of services, contact your service coordinator or your health-benefits advisor. Early intervention may be paid for under your TRICARE option, your private insurance, or Medicaid. Each child's family has the final say about what services they will accept, and they may reject services they don't want to pay for.

The Department of Defense also has an early-intervention program to meet the needs of children who reside on military bases with DoD schools but who are too young to attend. All DoD early-intervention services are provided at no charge.

REFERRALS AND SERVICE COORDINATORS

Referrals for early-intervention services are usually made by a child's parents or physician, but they can be made by anyone on behalf of a family. Once a child has been referred for early intervention, a service coordinator will be assigned to assist by gathering information from the family, arranging for appropriate assessments and evaluations, and eventually creating an individual family service plan. Your service coordinator will be your contact as evaluations are conducted and meetings are scheduled to discuss the results and will help with assessing and coordinating recommended services.

THE EVALUATION PROCESS

Within forty-five calendar days of the referral, an evaluation must be completed and a service plan put in place if the child is found to be eligible for early intervention. The evaluation will determine whether the child needs early-intervention services. It consists of a general developmental assessment of the child's abilities, including the following:

- A parent interview to discuss concerns about a child's delay(s)
- A review of the child's medical history
- Assessments by specialists in the areas of concern

The evaluation will address the following areas:

- Physical development: The ability to see, hear, and move with purpose or coordination
- Language and speech development: The ability to talk, understand language, and express needs
- Social and emotional development: The ability of a child with typical intelligence to build satisfactory relationships and respond appropriately under normal circumstances
- Adaptive development: The ability to eat, dress, toilet, and perform other self-help skills
- Cognitive development: The ability to think and learn—a measure of intellectual functioning related to the child's ability to think, speak, read, write, or do mathematical calculations

To minimize anxiety during the assessment process, do not allow your child to be separated from you if he or she does not need to be. The anxiety of separation may cause a child to do poorly. Make sure the child is comfortable with the professional doing the assessment. This may take time and require more than one session. The goal is a fair assessment of the child's abilities and weaknesses. However, some assessments might be more difficult to perform with parents present. The professional should discuss this with you and explain why.

DISCUSSING YOUR CHILD'S SPECIAL CHALLENGES

Many parents have mixed feelings about discussing their child's area of weakness. It may feel unloving or disloyal to call attention to the child's delays. However, spelling out concerns and noticing weaknesses are your responsibilities as your child's advocate. Your child will benefit when, because of your shared observations, needed services are made available. Being very honest is a loving choice.

WHO IS ELIGIBLE?

Babies and children may be eligible for services from both the state and the military until they turn three (when school systems usually take over for certain types of disabilities and delays) if they meet the following criteria:

- The child has a diagnosed physical or mental condition that is likely to result in a delay of development.
- The child has a developmental delay in one or more of the following areas: cognitive development (intellect), physical development (including vision and hearing), social or emotional development, self-help, and adaptive skills.
- The child is considered to be at high risk of developing substantial delays if early intervention is not provided.

THE ELIGIBILITY MEETING

After completion of assessments, an eligibility meeting will be held. The evaluations and observations of the child will be compared with the eligibility criteria listed above to determine if he or she qualifies. At this meeting a child will or will not be found eligible for services.

PREPARING FOR THE ELIGIBILITY MEETING

To prepare for this meeting, gather and write down your own information about your child's growth and development and be prepared to share this with the team. You may want to make a small poster about your child to help the team see him or her as unique and much loved. It can be helpful to bring a family member or friend with you. Often you will have been given the results of your child's screening prior to the eligibility meeting. You may be pleasantly surprised or dismayed by the findings.

Don't rush through this meeting. Ask questions of the professionals in the room about your child's ability levels or services you believe might help your child or your family. Remember that formal testing is just one component of your child's assessment. Your observations of and experiences with your child are an important component of the assessment. Don't give up if the assessment team does not place the same importance on an observation that you do. Talk it over with them so that you are able to understand their point of view and they yours.

A PARENT'S PERSPECTIVE

It may feel uncomfortable explaining to a stranger that something is not quite right about your child. It may be tempting to minimize your child's delay because you are so proud of the gains he or she has made and because you love your child so profoundly. Keep mind that in order for your child to qualify for appropriate services, you must present a clear and accurate picture of his or her development.

Individual Family Service Plans

If a child is deemed eligible for early-intervention services, parents and members of their support team will gather again to write an individual family service plan, which will identify the child's current developmental levels, the services that will be provided to advance those levels, and the goals parents would like to see their child reach. Armed with this information, you will be able to specify the direction you would like to see your child move in and to identify milestones along the way. The IFSP will contain valuable information about your child's strengths, needs, likes, and dislikes. This information, combined with results from assessments and medical information from the child's doctor, will provide a thorough description of your child's special needs and goals. Families will revisit this document with their child's service coordinator regularly to assess how goals are being met and to revise or update the steps being taken to assist their child.

The IFSP will include the following components:

- Information about your child's current development
- Information about family resources, priorities, and concerns
- Plan goals
- A detailed description of services needed to help your child reach goals
- A statement about the natural environment where the services will be provided

- The start date for services and their expected duration
- A name of the service coordinator who will help obtain the services identified
- A transition plan for your child

THE IFSP MEETING

The guiding principles of the IFSP are that the family is a child's greatest resource and that a baby's needs are closely tied to the needs of the family. The best way to support children and meet their needs is to support and build on the individual strengths of their families. So the IFSP is a whole-family plan with the parents as the most important part of the IFSP team.

PREPARING FOR YOUR IFSP MEETING

Sitting down with a room full of professionals to discuss challenges and opportunities for your child can be difficult and emotionally draining. However, you are the leading expert on your child, and your input is crucial to the quality of the IFSP. To ensure that you remember to discuss all of your hopes and concerns, it is helpful to write down observations and areas that you are worried about in the days before the meeting. If IFSP meetings are emotionally difficult and no family member is available to attend with you, ask a friend familiar with your child to accompany you. This person can offer moral support as well as another viewpoint. The IFSP will be reviewed at regular intervals to monitor your child's progress and adjust goals accordingly.

TYPES OF SERVICES

The IFSP will define what type of intervention will best benefit your child and your family. The services required to be available to eligible families include the following:

- Assistive technology: Devices or services that allow or improve independence in daily activities (e.g., a curved handle on a spoon for easier self-feeding or a wheelchair)
- Audiology: Therapy for individuals with hearing loss
- Family training: Counseling to help family members understand the special needs of the child and how to best support his or her development
- Medical services: Services from birth to age three for diagnostic or evaluation purposes only
- Nursing services: Services to assess the health status of your child or administer treatments prescribed by a physician
- Nutrition services: Services to address the nutritional needs of your child that may include identification of feeding skills or problems and food habits or preferences
- Occupational therapy: Activities designed to improve fine motor skills (e.g., finger, hand, or arm movements)
- Physical therapy: Activities designed to improve gross motor skills (e.g., leg, back, or whole-body movements)
- Psychological services: Administration and interpretation of psychological tests and information about a child's behavior and possibly counseling, parent-training, and education programs
- Respite care: Care of your child by trained caregivers, giving you a little time off
- Service coordination: Services bringing together the people, information, and resources that your child and family may need
- Specialized instruction: Programs or services specially designed to meet the needs of children with special needs
- Speech and language services: Activities and materials designed to improve your child's ability to express thoughts and communicate information
- Transportation: Provision of the necessary transportation or travel to enable a child and family to receive early-intervention services
- Vision services: Identification and provision of services for children with visual disorders or delays

MAKING THE MOST OF AVAILABLE SERVICES

It is very important for parents to watch how their child is taught and encouraged while receiving services. By modeling this behavior at home, you reinforce the lessons and increase the speed with which your child will master the new skills being addressed. Every session, whether at home or at a center, offers a chance for the service provider and the family to share information about the child. A child's parents know him or her best and can share daily observations. The service provider can offer ideas about how to help the child in the home environment. A cooperative partnership between the family, the service coordinator, the teachers, and the service provider will benefit the child profoundly.

YOUR ROLE AS ADVOCATE

When a parent first realizes that a child may face more challenges than his or her peers, the reaction can be emotional. Over time, the family accepts these different circumstances. The realization that children will need specific services to mitigate delays turns many parents into advocates.

Parents are natural advocates for their children. They are their child's first teachers, they know their child better than anyone else, and they have their child's best interests at heart. Children need their parents to play an active role in planning their education. The law gives parents the power to make educational decisions for their children. How can they best use this power for the benefit the child? For detailed information about how to become an advocate for your child, see "Advocating for Your Child" on the Military OneSource website (http://www.militaryonesource.mil/12038/EFMP/PTK_SCORs/PTK_Mod5_Sept2011.pdf).

YOUR RIGHTS

Under the Individuals with Disabilities Education Act, parents have the right to

- Choose whether to have a child evaluated and to have it done in a timely manner
- Go through the early-intervention process in their own language
- Receive full copies of all evaluation results and notice regarding each aspect of the program
- Refuse any specific service without losing the right to other services
- Bring an advocate or attorney to any meeting or consult with one at any stage of the process
- Keep all information regarding the family confidential
- Examine and correct all records regarding the child and family
- Withhold or withdraw consent at any stage of the process
- Be told in advance of any possible changes in the child's evaluation or services
- Be involved in all stages of early intervention
- Elect not to participate in the early-intervention program

The parents' role is vital, for they are the most important people in their child's life and know their child best. To ensure that early-intervention services are meeting your child's needs, organize and keep track of all paperwork throughout the early-intervention process. Learn about assistive technology so that you will be informed enough to ask for devices that might aid your child. Be aware of your rights and those of your family and be an active participant in all stages of early intervention.

CHALLENGES AND SUPPORT

Sometimes, even though parents may suspect their child has a delay, they hesitate to ask for help, perhaps hoping that the child will catch up to his or her peers without additional help. If you are hesitating, consider that there is nothing to lose by asking to have your child screened. Either necessary help will be offered, or you will receive reassuring answers to your questions.

Challenges

Learning how to find appropriate services for your child can be difficult, and military families must also deal with the complication of relocating and starting the process over again. It is very important to carry documentation about your child's early-intervention program with you to your new home. Once in the new location, seek early-intervention services quickly, as there may be a waiting list or other delays. To find early-intervention providers in your area, call the National Dissemination Center for Children with Disabilities (NICHCY) at (800) 695-0285.

Although all states have early-intervention services, all programs are not equal, and a child may not be eligible for the same services at the new location. You may also need to demonstrate residency before you can apply for services.

Support

Members of the military have many groups and agencies to turn to for help with their exceptional children. Please take advantage of the many resources that have been put in place. Remember that you are not alone and that knowledgeable people are ready and waiting to help. Being the caretaker of a special-needs child can be physically exhausting as well as emotionally draining. By finding people to talk to about your life, your child, and your unique stresses, you will be helping yourself as well as your child. Caretakers need care too. If you think you might benefit from counseling, contact your family service center at http://www.militaryinstallations.dod.milor Military OneSource at http://www.militaryonesource.comor call (800) 342-9647. Help is close by.

WHAT CAN I DO?

Learn about your child's condition. Search your library and the Internet for information on your child's condition. Jot down questions that occur to you as you go through your day, and ask your doctor about them. If you don't understand something, don't be embarrassed to say so.

Contact the Specialized Training of Military Parents (STOMP) project, a valuable online resource. You will find support and advice for military parents regardless of the special challenges your child faces. Join the list serve and correspond with other parents of specially challenged children at http://www.stompproject.orgor call (800) 5-PARENT (800-572-7368; voice and TTY).

Seek out other parents of children with disabilities. Realize that you are not alone. Your Exceptional Family Member Program (EFMP) representative can help you find other military families who have faced similar challenges. To find the closest family service center and EFMP coordinator, go to http://www.militaryinstallations.dod.mil.

Seek out your state parent training center (PTC). Every state has PTCs, which serve families with children with all disabilities and can help you obtain appropriate educational services for you child. PTCs train parents and professionals and can help resolve problems between schools and families. To find a PTC in your state, go to http://www.taalliance.org.

FAMILY CONNECTIONS

Keep talking to your spouse. The more you communicate in challenging times, the stronger you will be as a couple. You will probably not react to this new information about your child the same way, but try to explain how you feel and listen carefully as your spouse shares feelings as well. Sometimes agreement is less important than understanding. If there are other children in the home, be aware of their needs as well. If talking about the disability is too difficult at this time, ask another adult to try to establish a bond with your child so that your child has someone to talk to about his or her feelings without upsetting Mom or Dad.

6

CHILD-CARE AND PRESCHOOL OPTIONS

Access to quality child care remains a focus of leadership and families across the armed forces. Military families face challenges not found in other work environments. Shifting work schedules that are often longer than the typical eight-hour day, as well as the ever-present possibility of deployment anywhere in the world at a moment's notice, require a flexible child-care system that maintains high standards.

Child-care programs are needed to support Reserve component families and geographically dispersed active-duty military families while the service member is deployed. Guard and Reserve families are experiencing significantly increased mobilization rates, and families with previously limited exposure to the military now must deal with the likelihood of multiple or longer deployments.

Programs are also needed to meet the child-care needs of families living in areas in the continental United States where on-installation military child care is unavailable or there is a long waiting list. In addition, programs such as respite child care can provide temporary relief or a short break to the parent or guardian. The Department of Defense (DoD) currently supports deployed families by offering respite child care during and immediately following deployment, providing up to sixteen hours of free child care per month, per child, for children up to age twelve.

Child care during deployment must be provided in community child-care centers and family child-care homes that are state-licensed or regulated with annual oversight inspections that protect the health, safety, and well-being of children in care. Longer-term child-care services should be delivered through state-licensed and -regulated local child-care centers and nationally accredited programs. Another option is to use family child-care providers in the local community who have, at a minimum, Child Development Associate credentials. In all cases, the level of program oversight must meet the existing minimum standard of an annual inspection by the state regulatory body.

The Departments of Defense, Health and Human Services (HHS), Education, and Agriculture have committed to increasing the availability of quality child-care options, thereby reducing the estimated shortfall of thirty-seven thousand child-care spaces based on available demographic data. These efforts support the president's early-childhood platform goal to improve child-care quality using state and local resources and have far-reaching implications for increasing quality child care throughout the nation.

PRESCHOOL OPTIONS

Military spouses often work outside the home, attend classes to continue their education, and play the role of single parent when a spouse is deployed or in special training requiring more time away from home. The demands of military service bring frequent deployments, standing duty, training, and unpredictable work schedules with long hours. There has also been an increase in the number of single-parent and dual-military families serving in the armed forces.

All of these factors taken together mean that quality, affordable child care is a necessity for many active-duty families. DoD and the branches of service are constantly reviewing and initiating programs to provide military families and their children with the best possible child-care options.

DoD currently oversees eight hundred child-development centers (CDCs) located on military installations worldwide. These centers offer a safe child-care environment and meet professional standards for early-childhood education. Child care is typically available through these centers for children ages six weeks to twelve years. The centers are generally open Monday through Friday between the hours of 6:00 a.m. and 6:30 p.m. Commanders may decide to extend hours to meet the work and deployment needs and schedules of their installation populations.

CREDENTIALS

While looking for child care, you may hear that a provider or program is certified, licensed, or accredited. Each of these terms refers to a type of approval that a provider receives for meeting certain standards of quality. The rules behind these standards address a range of concerns from health and safety to child development. Understanding the rules that a provider has agreed to follow can help you decide which child-care setting is right for your child.

State Licensing

The goal of state child-care licensing is to ensure the safety and developmental well-being of children while in out-of-home care. Licensing laws vary from state to state, as does oversight of licensing, but this oversight usually involves periodic inspections of facilities. Be sure to ask about licensing requirements in your state.

Certification

DoD certification of child-care programs is comparable to the state licensing process. Although licensing standards vary from state to state, DoD standards are the same worldwide. You can expect to see the same level of quality when you move from one installation to another. DoD standards address health, safety, parent involvement, staff training requirements, and developmentally appropriate practices.

Whether you're looking at CDCs, family child care (FCC) homes (also known as child-development homes), or school-age care (SAC) programs, you'll find that all child-care facilities on military installations are required to be DoD certified. The requirements for certification are similar in all services. Military child-care programs are all based on the same DoD instructions and certification checklist. Where they differ, the standards must be more stringent than those set by DoD. The rules are specific to the type of care and the age of the children.

Accreditation

All CDCs and SAC programs on military installations are accredited by a national accrediting body. FCC providers are encouraged and supported in their effort to seek accreditation from the National Association for Family Child Care. Whereas 8 to 10 percent of civilian childcare centers are accredited, 97 percent of centers at military installations have earned that status.

Providers first assess their own program in detail, and then the accrediting organization observes, reviews documentation, and talks with people in the program. Most programs then spend time making adjustments before accreditation is awarded. Accreditation must be renewed regularly by the accrediting organization. As a result, providers are continually evaluating and looking for ways to improve their programs. Studies have shown that accredited programs have more child-initiated activities, higher staff morale, better-defined goals, and a more culturally diverse curriculum than nonaccredited care.

If you can't use military child care because you live too far away from an installation or there aren't enough spaces, new programs help military parents find and afford quality child care off of the installation. Child Care Aware of America, formerly NACCRRA, working with the DoD, provides fee assistance to offset the higher cost of community-based care and offers specialized resource and referral services for eligible military parents.

The need for early learning is clear. Studies prove that children with rich early-learning experiences are better prepared to thrive in school. Yet the United States ranks twenty-eighth in early-learning enrollment. For those who do attend, quality varies widely. Less than one-third of four-year-olds living in poverty attend a high-quality preschool program, and this is especially pronounced in low-income communities. Doing better is more than just a moral and educational imperative; it's smart government: every public dollar spent on preschool returns $7 through increased productivity and savings on public assistance and criminal justice.

CHILD CARE FOR SPECIAL-NEEDS CHILDREN

For working parents, finding high-quality care is a high priority. As a military parent of a special-needs child, finding child care that can accommodate shift work, extended hours, and weekend duty and meet the unique needs of an exceptional child can be challenging.

Look for child care that is "inclusive"—that is, where children with and without special needs are in child care together. Inclusive child care allows children to learn together in an educational atmosphere that supports and nurtures the individual strengths of each child, and each child participates in the daily routines and activities of the class regardless of cognitive or physical impairments. Every child deserves the opportunity to interact with other people regardless of his or her ability level.

Most military installations have special resource teams to help parents of special-needs kids find appropriate child care. These teams may comprise child-care specialists, an Exceptional Family Member Program (EFMP) advocate, a public health nurse, and the parents. This team will explore child-care and youth activities for children with certain special needs who are involved in installation child-care or youth programs. The team will identify the care options available to best meet the child's needs as well as consider any increased technical support, special services, or staffing that may be necessary to care for the child appropriately.

For more information about child care, check with the installation's resource and referral office. A resource specialist can guide you through the registration process, accreditation and fees, and the exploration of both on- and off-base options to choose the best care for your child. Installations have different names for the office that manages the child-care programs, so if the name of the office is unknown, the best place to start is to ask at the home installation's child-development center which office provides local child-care resource and referral services. Telephone numbers of all CDCs and school-age programs at can be found at http://www.militaryhomefront.dod.mil/efm.

It is possible for a base child-development center to inform you that it cannot provide care for your extraordinary family member (EFM) under certain circumstances. In this case, the EFMP coordinator and the command should continue to work with the family in order to identify in-home or related appropriate care. It is important, in selecting a duty station, to explore this issue ahead of time because it can happen that a base can accommodate the EFM but not the child-care center, and ultimately the military parent faces a conundrum because care is not guaranteed. Try to work preventatively to ensure this does not happen.

SOME QUESTIONS TO ASK

What are the priorities for placement on the list at this installation?

I have more than one child. What is your policy on placing siblings? Is a discount offered when more than one child is enrolled?

What process do you use for keeping my data up to date? Will you get in touch with me, or will I be responsible for periodically updating you?

How long might I have to wait for a space to open up in my child's age group?

My child is an EFM, and I am on deployment status with a pending departure date. Does this impact priority placement for my child?

I will need child care in the interim. Will you help me find it?

What is your child/provider ratio?

Will the center adapt the physical environment to meet my child's needs with the goal of increasing his or her participation?

Will the providers adapt materials and curriculum to promote independence and capitalize on my child's favorite activities?

Do the providers have experience working with adaptive devices?

What types of training have the providers had?

How will the center implement and monitor my child's individual family service or individualized education plan?

Will the center allow me to work with the care providers to show proper positioning, use of equipment, medication administration, and so forth?

Will therapists have a quiet area to work with my child?

How will the center facilitate diapering? (Sometimes centers will not have changing tables in rooms for three- and four-year-olds, let alone much older children requiring support with activities of daily living.)

Do you have staff members who know American Sign Language or have experience working with augmentative communication devices?

What are your emergency medical procedures? How close are you to a medical facility? Do you have a nurse on staff?

Does the center have a disciplinary policy? (If yes, ask for a copy.)

Does the center have a method for filing complaints? Whom would I speak with?

Do you provide emergency respite care?

What safety measures are in place to keep the children safe from intruders?

What do you require in terms of verifying the identity of someone picking a child up from school?

Do you have someone on staff qualified to administer prescription medications? What are your policies for providing emergency medication, such as at the onset of seizures or allergic reactions?

Is this a peanut- or other-nut-free facility?

If the facility provides food or beverages to the EFM during the day, with whom can we review all ingredient labels to ensure our EFM is not accidentally exposed to a dangerous ingredient?

7

EDUCATION AND DISRUPTIONS IN SCHOOLING

There are 1.9 million children with a parent serving in the military; 220,000 of these children have a parent currently deployed. There are 153,669 single parents serving in the military. The demands of extended conflict add to the challenges military families face. Research suggests that children of deployed parents experience more stress than their peers. Although these kids are often described as a resilient group, the cumulative effects of multiple moves and significant parental absences can erode this resilience. Too many of our military children in public schools feel like their classmates and teachers do not understand what they are going through. Between frequent moves and service member time away from home, many parents worry about whether their children are getting a good education. A recent survey found 34 percent are "less or not confident" that their child's school is responsive to the unique aspects of military family life.

The quality of education available to military children can affect overall recruitment, retention, and morale. Military families frequently say that the quality of their children's education is one of their most important criteria when selecting a place to live. Military children face added stressors due to frequent relocations. The differences between state standards and requirements for academic and athletic participation, when coupled with frequent relocations, can negatively impact achievement and participation for military children. An information-packed resource is the Military Child Education Coalition (MCEC) at www.MilitaryChild.org.

Joining Forces: Taking Action to Serve America's Families is a national initiative that mobilizes all sectors of society to give our service members and their families all of the opportunities and support they have earned.

- The education secretary has pledged that the Department of Education will make supporting military families a supplemental priority for its discretionary grant programs.
- In order to encourage quality reintegration time, the Departments of Education and Defense (DoD) will provide guidance to school districts based on best practices for approving student absences relating to "block leave."
- The Department of Education will continue the Specialized Training of Military Parents (STOMP) project, dedicated to serving military parents of children with special needs.
- The Department of Education has greatly simplified the Free Application for Federal Student Aid (FAFSA).
- The Departments of Defense, Health and Human Services, Education, and Agriculture have committed to increasing the availability of quality child-care options, thereby reducing the estimated shortfall of thirty-seven thousand child-care spaces based on available demographic data.

Key actions include the following:

- Secretary's Priority for Military Families: This priority for discretionary grants can now be applied to favor grant applications to meet the needs of service members, spouses, military-connected children, and veterans. The Department of Education is now seeking means of collecting and reporting data to promote transparency around the performance of military-connected children as part of the Elementary and Secondary Education Act. The department is also working to improve its impact-aid funding of school districts serving military children.
- Specialized Training of Military Parents: The department is committed to the continuation of this project.

- Free Application for Federal Student Aid: The Office of Postsecondary Education sent out a "dear colleague" letter to remind financial aid administrators of their ability to exercise documented professional judgment when determining eligibility of students for federal student aid. It encourages aid administrators to consider the special circumstances that may arise for members of the US armed forces and their families and reminds them about FAFSA reporting and the treatment of combat pay in the calculation of a student's expected family contribution.
- Quality child care: The department has contributed technical assistance and information about education resources at meetings of the Subcommittee on Child Care, which is part of the Interagency Policy Committee for Military Families. The department has also provided the DoD child-care liaison with contact information for the Individuals with Disabilities Education Act (IDEA) 619 state coordinators and IDEA Part C coordinators in their state to expand their awareness of state and local resources and access to existing community networks.

Virtually all school districts are educating at least one child whose parent or guardian is serving in our armed forces, whether stationed in the United States or abroad and whether on active duty or in the National Guard or Reserves. Of the more than 1.2 million school-age children of service men and women, more than 80 percent attend public schools.

Military children encounter challenges related to enrollment, eligibility, placement, and graduation due to frequent relocations in the course of their families' service to our country. The average military child will attend between six and nine schools between kindergarten and twelfth grade. Over one-third of army personnel reported problems related to transferring their child(ren) to a new school.

The Interstate Compact on Educational Opportunities for Military Children provides for uniform treatment of military children transferring between school districts and states. It was developed by the Council of State Governments' National Center for Interstate Compacts, the Department of Defense, national associations, federal and state officials, departments of education, school administrators, and military families. Each state must adopt the compact through its legislative process. Although participation is voluntary, more than forty states have adopted the compact. Each state appoints representation to a governing commission responsible for enacting rules to implement the compact. Each participating state also creates a state council based on the requirements of its state legislation.

Eligibility for coverage by the compact requires that children's parents be

- Active-duty members of the uniformed services, National Guard, or Reserves on active-duty orders
- Members or veterans who have been medically discharged or retired for one year
- Members who have died on active duty

The compact covers issues such as

- Enrollment

  - Educational records
  - Immunizations
  - Kindergarten and first-grade entrance age

- Placement and attendance

  - Course and educational-program placement
  - Special education services
  - Placement flexibility
  - Absence related to deployment activities

- Eligibility

  - Eligibility for student enrollment
  - Eligibility for extracurricular participation

- Graduation

  - Waiving courses required for graduation if similar course work has been completed
  - Flexibility in accepting state exit or end-of-course exams, national achievement tests, or alternative testing in lieu of testing requirements for graduation in the receiving state

- Allowing a student to receive a diploma from the sending school instead of the receiving school

COMPACT ARTICLES

Interstate Compact Article IV.A—Unofficial or "Hand-Carried" Education Records

In the event that official education records cannot be released to the parents for the purpose of transfer, the custodian of the records in the sending state shall prepare and furnish to the parent a complete set of unofficial educational records containing uniform information as determined by the Interstate Commission. Upon receipt of the unofficial education records by a school in the receiving state, the school shall enroll and appropriately place the student based on the information provided in the unofficial records pending validation by the official records, as quickly as possible.

Interstate Compact Article IV.B—Official Education Records/Transcripts

Simultaneously with the enrollment and conditional placement of the student, the school in the receiving state shall request the student's official education record from the school in the sending state. Upon receipt of this request, the school in the sending state will process and furnish the official education records to the school in the receiving state within ten days or within such time as is reasonably determined under the rules promulgated by the Interstate Commission.

Interstate Compact Article IV.C—Immunizations

Compacting states shall allow thirty days from the date of enrollment, or such time as is reasonably determined under the rules promulgated by the Interstate Commission, for students to obtain any immunization(s) required by the receiving state. For a series of immunizations, initial vaccinations must be obtained within thirty days or within such time as is reasonably determined under the rules promulgated by the Interstate Commission.

Interstate Compact Article IV.D—Kindergarten and First-Grade Entrance Age

Students shall be allowed to continue their enrollment at grade level in the receiving state commensurate with their grade level (including kindergarten) from a local education agency in the sending state at the time of transition, regardless of age. A student who has satisfactorily completed the prerequisite grade level in the local education agency in the sending state shall be eligible for enrollment in the next highest grade level in the receiving state, regardless of age. A student transferring after the start of the school year in the receiving state shall enter the school in the receiving state at his or her validated level from an accredited school in the sending state

Interstate Compact Article V.A—Course Placement

When the student transfers before or during the school year, the receiving state school shall initially honor placement of the student in educational courses based on the student's enrollment in the sending state school and/or educational assessments conducted at the school in the sending state if the courses are offered. Course placement includes, but is not limited to, honors, International Baccalaureate, Advanced Placement, vocational, technical, and career-pathways courses. Continuing the student's academic program from the previous school and promoting placement in academically and career-challenging courses should be paramount when considering placement. This does not preclude the school in the receiving state from performing subsequent evaluations to ensure appropriate placement and continued enrollment of the student in the course(s).

Interstate Compact Article V.B—Educational Program Placement

The receiving state school shall initially honor placement of the student in educational programs based on current educational assessments conducted at the school in the sending state or participation/

placement in like programs in the sending state. Such programs include, but are not limited to,

- Gifted and talented programs
- English as a second language programs

This does not preclude the school in the receiving state from performing subsequent evaluations to ensure appropriate placement of the student.

Interstate Compact Article V.C—Special Education Services

In compliance with the federal requirements of the Individuals with Disabilities Education Act, 20 USC, Section 1400 et seq., the receiving state shall initially provide comparable services to a student with disabilities based on his or her current individualized education program (IEP). In compliance with the requirements of Section 504 of the Rehabilitation Act, 29 USC, Section 794, and with Title II of the Americans with Disabilities Act, 42 USC, Sections 12131–65, the receiving state shall make reasonable accommodations and modifications to address the needs of incoming students with disabilities, subject to an existing 504 or Title II plan, to provide the student with equal access to education. This does not preclude the school in the receiving state from performing subsequent evaluations to ensure appropriate placement of the student.

Interstate Compact Article V.E—Absence as Related to Deployment Activities

A student whose parent or legal guardian is an active-duty member of the uniformed services, as defined by the compact, and has been called to duty for, is on leave from, or has immediately returned from deployment to a combat zone or combat-support posting shall be granted additional excused absences at the discretion of the local education agency superintendent to visit with his or her parent or legal guardian relative to such leave or deployment of the parent or guardian.

Interstate Compact Article VI.A—Eligibility for Enrollment

1. Special power of attorney, relative to the guardianship of a child of a military family and executed under applicable law, shall be sufficient for the purposes of enrollment and all other actions requiring parental participation and consent.
2. A local education agency shall be prohibited from charging local tuition to a transitioning military child placed in the care of a noncustodial parent or other person standing in loco parentis who lives in a jurisdiction other than that of the custodial parent. A transitioning military child, placed in the care of a noncustodial parent or other person standing in loco parentis who lives in a jurisdiction other than that of the custodial parent, may continue to attend the school in which he or she was enrolled while residing with the custodial parent.

Interstate Compact Article VI.B—Eligibility for Extracurricular Participation

State and local education agencies shall facilitate the opportunity for transitioning military children's inclusion in extracurricular activities, regardless of application deadlines, to the extent they are otherwise qualified.

Interstate Compact Article VII—Graduation

In order to facilitate the on-time graduation of children of military families, states and local education agencies shall incorporate procedures in Article VII, Sections A through C.

Interstate Compact Article VII.A—Waiver Requirements

Local education agency administrative officials shall waive specific courses required for graduation if similar course work has been satisfactorily completed in another local education agency or shall provide reasonable justification for denial. Should a waiver not be granted to a student who would qualify to graduate from the sending school, the local education agency shall provide an alternative means of acquiring required coursework so that graduation may occur on time.

Interstate Compact Article VII.B—Exit Exams

States shall accept the one of following:

1. Exit or end-of-course exams required for graduation from the sending state
2. National norm-referenced achievement tests
3. Alternative testing, in lieu of testing requirements for graduation in the receiving state

In the event the above alternatives cannot be accommodated by the receiving state for a student transferring in his or her senior year, then the provisions of Article VII, Section C shall apply.

Interstate Compact Article VII.C—Transfers during Senior Year

Should a military student transferring at the beginning of or during his or her senior year be ineligible to graduate from the receiving local education agency after all alternatives have been considered, the sending and receiving local education agencies shall ensure the receipt of a diploma from the sending local education agency, if the student meets the graduation requirements of the sending local education agency. In the event that one of the states in question is not a member of this compact, the member state shall use best efforts to facilitate the on-time graduation of the student in accordance with Sections A and B of this article.

Contact the schools liaison officer at your local installation for more information.

FURTHER EDUCATION

The Veterans Administration (VA) will continue to ease the post–September 11 GI Bill application process, including transferability to spouses or children for service members with over six years of service. This benefit offers transferability to a family member once the service member has been in longer than six years and agrees to serve four additional years. As of December 1, 2010, the VA has issued over $6.6 billion in tuition, housing, and stipends for 413,313 student veterans or eligible family members pursuing higher education. Early in the program's implementation, the VA took unprecedented steps to expedite over $350 million in advance payments and is in the process of automating application processing and payment functions. To further encourage more veterans to use this historic program, in February 2010, the VA launched a nationwide post–September 11 GI Bill advertising campaign through college newspapers, radio announcements, outdoor posters, and information handouts at sixty schools with large veteran student populations. The VA also administers the Marine Gunnery Sergeant John David Fry Scholarship for children of service members killed in the line of duty after September 10, 2001. Eligible children may receive up to the highest public, in-state undergraduate tuition and fees, plus a monthly living stipend and allowance under this program.

The Department of Education has greatly simplified the Free Application for Federal Student Aid. As part of an overall strategy to increase access to postsecondary education and meet President Barack Obama's goal of having "the best educated, most competitive workforce in the world" by 2020, this process has been overhauled, eliminating an administrative barrier to financial aid for military spouses. Applicants (both students and parents) now have the ability to retrieve their tax information online directly from the Internal Revenue Service and to prepopulate that data directly into their applications. This not only makes it easier for families to complete the application but also increases the accuracy of submissions. In an effort to better inform students and families as they make decisions about college, the Department of Education also provides federal Pell Grant award and student loan eligibility estimates to applicants immediately upon completion of the FAFSA rather than requiring them to wait several weeks. In addition, the department provides graduation and retention rates for schools the student is interested in attending; it also commits to sending guidance to all financial aid officers highlighting the need for sensitivity to military personnel and families, including Guard and Reserve personnel, and emphasizing flexibility in cases where a military family may lose financial aid due to temporary spikes in pay due to activation and deployment.

JOB OPPORTUNITIES

The Department of the Interior, one of the largest federal employers of youth ages fifteen to twenty-five in conservation, will partner with DoD to identify military youth for employment opportunities. These opportunities reside in a wide range of educational, recreation and conservation, and cultural programs, including First Lady Michelle Obama's Let's Move Outside Initiative, the National Park Service's Junior Ranger Program and Parks as Classrooms, the US Fish and Wildlife Service's Let's Go Outside and Nature Rocks, and the Bureau of Land Management's Take It Outside Program.

8

SPECIAL NEEDS

Of 1.5 million active-duty military members, each day around the globe an estimated 540,000 active-duty sponsors are caring for family members with special medical or educational needs. Most of those family members are children. Special-needs children have been diagnosed with a physical or mental condition likely to result in a delay of development. This delay can be cognitive (intellect), physical (including vision and hearing), social, or emotional or involve self-help or adaptive skills.

When you are told that your child has a disability or is developmentally delayed it is obviously a shattering blow but it is certainly one that can and must be overcome. Parents often feel guilt that perhaps they did something to contribute to their child's disability. However, once they have been given all the facts and with the help of counseling are able to absorb this information, they realize that this is not the case and there is hope. In these situations it is essential to look forward to what the future holds. Enormous strides have been made in recent years with respect to training, counseling, and therapy. With the loving support of family, friends, and health and education professionals, there is no reason why your child should not lead a rewarding life. Certainly the child will never be short of loving and, in return, they will bring joy to your life.

Take advantage of all the resources available to you—from medical and educational experts to base and online support groups. No matter what your child's disability, other parents have experienced the same emotions and problems that you are facing. The more support you have the easier it will be to adjust to your new circumstances.

The most important thing is to fully understand the nature and extent of your child's disability. You will probably have to be your child's advocate, which means that you must understand the treatments that are being suggested. If you don't understand what the professionals are saying ask them to explain it again. If the doctor or professional refuses to do this, ask for him or her to be replaced by someone who is more caring and sympathetic.

Specialized Training of Military Parents (STOMP) is the only national parent training and information center providing support and advice to military parents without regard of the type of medical or learning condition their child has. STOMP serves families in four main ways:

- By providing information, training, and workshops about laws, regulations, and resources for military families of children with disabilities
- By connecting families to other families
- By assisting parents and professionals in developing their own community parent-education/-support group
- By providing a voice to raise awareness of issues faced by military families of children with disabilities

STOMP is a one-stop shop for information and training regarding special education and other resources for special-needs children. Founded in 1985, STOMP is a project of Washington PAVE, a grassroots parent-directed organization; it is funded through a grant from the US Department of Education. The STOMP staff are parents of children with disabilities and have experience in raising their children in military communities and traveling with their spouses to different locations. The project provides a wealth of personal experience, a network of personal contacts, and a parent-driven approach.

Parents of children with special needs face many challenges:

- Feelings of isolation and anxiety
- Difficulty navigating disjointed services
- Severe financial worries
- Inadequate information

- Tremendous personal and marital stress
- Insurance bureaucracy
- Limited or no personal or private time
- Living in "survival mode"

These challenges are compounded when the family concerned is military. Although all military families face certain challenges, such as frequent permanent change of station (PCS) moves and times when the military member is placed in harm's way—for instance, during wartime deployments—families with special-needs members face additional difficulties, including the following:

- Establishing continuity in provision of individualized education program (IEP) services when moving from state to state or from state to overseas Department of Defense Dependents Schools and Domestic Dependent Elementary and Secondary Schools. In the United States, the Individuals with Disabilities Education Act (IDEA) requires public schools to develop an IEP for every student with a disability who is found to meet the federal and state requirements for special education. The IEP must be designed to provide the child with a free appropriate public education. The IEP refers both to the educational program to be provided to a child with a disability and to the written document that describes that educational program. At the end of twelfth grade, students with disabilities will receive an IEP diploma if they have successfully met the IEP goals. If they have met the requirements for the high school diploma, then the IEP diploma is not awarded.
- Finding a military member to be present to participate during IEP meetings, medical treatments, and procedures.
- Finding specialists/physicians at a new duty station or location who will take TRICARE (the military health entitlement program) and accept new patients.
- Establishing relationships with key medical and educational personnel in a new location.
- Establishing eligibility for community resources to assist the special-needs family member, as well as facing waiting lists for services needed.

- Identifying within each state the array of services available and differences from state to state.
- Navigating differences in implementation of TRICARE services across regions.
- Dealing with a lack of proximate family and community support due to geographical separations and time differences.
- Dealing with additional financial burdens due to certain allotments and aspects of military pay calculations when considering eligibility (i.e., clothing allowance, separate rations, housing).
- Adjusting to challenges with overseas assignments (i.e., denial of command sponsorship for family members with special needs, which is necessary for eligibility for medical and educational systems) and increasing family separations.
- Implementing aspects of IDEA because of host country agreements (i.e., transition services into vocational programming, community access, provision of related services).
- Navigating certain laws, regulations, and services that do not apply in overseas assignments, such as Section 504 of the Rehabilitation Act, Department of Education regulations for the implementation of IDEA, and Medicaid.
- Dealing with lack of local community support due to the self-containment and isolation of military installations and existing relationships between installations and local communities.

The Department of Defense (DoD) has two very useful organizing tools for military families with special needs: the Special Care Organizational Record (SCOR) for Children with Special Health Care Needs and the SCOR for Adults with Special Health Care Needs. The SCORs are tools for caregivers, providing central repositories for recording and tracking information about their family members' ongoing support and health needs. Although the focus of each SCOR differs, they share the same fundamental goal of making it easier to organize, track, and update information for special-needs family members.

In caring for your family members with special health needs, you may get information and paperwork from many sources. This organizational record helps you organize the most important information in a central place. The SCOR makes it easier for you to find and share key information with others who are part of your family's care team. For example, families can use their SCOR to

- Track changes in medicines or treatments
- List telephone numbers for health care providers and community organizations
- Prepare for appointments
- File information about health history
- Share information with primary care doctors, school nurses, day care staff, and other caregivers
- Review the checklist prior to making a PCS move

Each SCOR is tailored to the unique needs of a special-needs family member. For example, the SCOR for children includes sections for copies of a child's individualized family service plan or IEP paperwork. The SCOR for adults has sections for documenting daily routines, vacation preferences, employment and vocational experiences, and more. Exceptional Family Member Program (EFMP) managers, medical and education professionals, and recognized disability expert Dr. Ann Turnbull vetted each tool.

SCOR FOR CHILDREN WITH SPECIAL HEALTH CARE NEEDS

Some Helpful Hints for Using Your Child's SCOR

- Keep the SCOR where it is easy to find. That way it will always be on hand when you need it.
- Be mindful that your SCOR contains very private information and should be kept in a safe place.
- Keep the SCOR as up to date as possible. Add new information to the SCOR whenever there is a change in a child's medical treatment.
- Bring the SCOR with you to appointments and hospital visits so that information you need will be close at hand.

How to Set Up Your Child's SCOR

Follow these steps:

1. Gather any health information that you already have about your child. This may include reports from recent doctor's visits, immunization records, a summary of a recent hospital stay, this year's school plan, test results or informational pamphlets, and so forth. If you have a TRICARE case manager, this individual may be able to help you gather that information.
2. Look through the pages of the SCOR. Select those that you think will be most beneficial for tracking your child's health and care. Once you have determined what you need, print out those selected pages.
3. Decide what information is most important to keep in the SCOR. What information do you find yourself looking for often? What information do your providers need when caring for your child? Additional, less critical information can be stored in a file drawer or box where you can find it if needed.
4. Put the SCOR together. Organize your SCOR in a way that makes the most sense to you and your child. Here are some supplies that may help you put it together:

   - A three-ring binder or large accordion envelope to hold papers securely
   - Tabbed dividers for creating separate sections
   - Pocket dividers for storing reports
   - Plastic pages for storing business cards and photographs

Things to Remember about the SCOR

Although the SCOR does contain a lot of your child's medical history/information, it is not intended to replace official medical records. It contains very private information (e.g., Social Security numbers, insurance information, medical history). It is imperative that you keep it in a safe place.

CHILD DEVELOPMENT SYSTEM

Frequent family separations and the requirement to move, on average, every three years place military families in situations not often experienced in the civilian world. For military families, finding affordable, high-quality child care is paramount if they are to be ready to perform their missions and jobs. It is also important to military personnel that child-care services be consistent and uniform at installations throughout the military.

Both the army and the marines have implemented a process to determine and review the best placement and support for children with special needs in the child-care setting. In the army, the Special Needs Accommodation Process (SNAP) is a subcommittee of the installation EFMP committee. The corps team membership consists of the installation EFMP manager, the children and youth services (CYS) coordinator, the army public health nurse, and parents, augmented, as appropriate, with CYS program staff, a CYS school liaison officer, school personnel, a representative from the Judge Advocate General's Office, a family advocacy program manager, and other medical personnel.

The installation EFMP manager assumes or designates a team chairperson. The team does the following:

1. Explores child-care installation and youth-supervision options for children and youth with a medical diagnosis that reflects life-threatening conditions, functional limitations, or behavioral or psychological conditions.
2. Determines child-care and youth-supervision placement, considering feasibility of program accommodations and availability of services to support child or youth needs.
3. Recommends a placement setting that accommodates, to the extent possible, the child or youth's individual needs.
4. Develops and implements DA Form 7625-3 (SNAP Team Care Plan).
5. Conducts an annual periodic review of the child or youth's individual SNAP care plan and/or as requested by CYS.
6. Establishes an installation SNAP review team consisting of the garrison commander or designee, the staff judge advocate, the installation EFMP manager, and the CYS coordinator. The re-

view team will be available, upon request, to ensure that a SNAP team has explored all options for reasonable accommodation.

In the Marine Corps, the Special Needs Evaluation Review Team (SNERT) comprises qualified personnel that aim to assess the accommodations necessary for a special-needs child to participate in Marine Corps Children, Youth, and Teen Programs (CYTP) and determine the most appropriate placement for the child. Installation SNERT teams report to the installation commander and shall include, but are not limited to, the following members:

- The CYTP administrator
- The EFMP coordinator
- Medical personnel
- The child's parent(s)
- The child or youth, when appropriate
- Other applicable CYTP or community agency personnel

Additional information about the Marine Corps SNERT can be found in Marine Corps Order P1710.30E, "Marine Corps Children, Youth and Teen Programs," dated June 24, 2004.

When a child is between the ages of fourteen and sixteen, his or her IEP will begin to address the transition process to adulthood. During transition planning, students and their families find out about community agencies and programs that provide services to persons with disabilities after high school. Some of these adult services include job training and placement, assistance in getting housing, and programs on health care and independent living. These transition services should start no later than with the first IEP to be in effect when the child turns sixteen, and they should be updated annually thereafter. Also, no later than one year before reaching the age of majority under state law, a child must be informed of his or her rights under IDEA, if any, that will transfer to him or her upon reaching the age of majority. Remember to include an older child in the IEP process.

In some cases, programs may start earlier with counseling to help an EFM transition to puberty and to set expectations for physical and developmental changes that precede adulthood. Parents should investigate eligibility for Social Security, disability, and related services that a child may be ineligible for until he or she turns eighteen.

9

OVERSEAS SCHOOLS AND HOMESCHOOLING

OVERSEAS SCHOOLING

Thousands of children with parents in the military serving overseas attend schools usually located on base. Although there is an adjustment, especially if the family has recently moved from the United States, most children do fit in and benefit not just from the education received but also from the fact that they are getting it in another country. However, if your child is having difficulty academically, behaviorally, or socially in an overseas school, contact your Non-DoD Schools Program (NDSP) liaison officer, who will initiate the collaborative decisions about what services the school recommends and what options are available to you and your child. If your child is referred for a comprehensive diagnostic evaluation due to a suspected disability or disorder, the area NDSP point of contact (POC) will arrange for the assessments and where they will be conducted. Your permission is needed prior to beginning any funded formalized assessments.

The purpose of the assessments is to provide insight into factors influencing your child's academic and/or behavioral problems that are interfering with his or her educational success. If your child's school does not have the needed special education resources, NDSP special education eligibility allows funding for extra services, such as tutoring, counseling, and speech therapy.

Prior to incurring any expense, the NDSP must authorize payment for the cost of any service. Department of Defense (DoD) sponsors assigned to overseas locations are not authorized to obligate the US government, contract with a private institution, or charge educational fees to Department of Defense Education Activity (DoDEA) appropriations (i.e., Foreign Military Sales, Security Assistance Office, or Military Assistance Program case funds) without obtaining prior approval from the DoDEA NDSP.

Prior to any funded educational services, command sponsorship must be verified. The area NDSP POC for special education must authorize payment for the cost of all services prior to the sponsor's incurring any expense. DoD sponsors assigned to overseas locations are not authorized to obligate the US government, contract with a private institution, or charge educational fees to DoDEA appropriations (e.g., Foreign Military Sales, Security Assistance Office, or Military Assistance Program case funds) without obtaining prior approval from the DoDEA NDSP.

After discussing these issues, you may decide that homeschooling is the best option, whether you are stateside or overseas.

HOME-BASED EDUCATIONAL PROGRAMS

The NDSP provides support and funding for the education of eligible dependents of sponsors assigned at locations where the DoD does not operate a school within commuting distance. This could mean homeschooling your child or joining a homeschooling co-op or some other educational facility.

Parents have the right to homeschool even if a local school is available, but in electing to provide home-based educational instruction, they must proceed through the following steps:

1. Select a home-study program.
2. Submit the following documentation to the local NDSP liaison:

   • A copy of the sponsor's orders plus any amendments.
   • A copy of the sponsor's overseas tour extension approval if the date eligible for return from overseas (DEROS) will

have expired prior to the beginning of school. Documentation of a current DEROS is required for continued NDSP enrollment.

- DoDEA Form 610, "Application for Enrollment in a Non-DoD School," for each dependent. A new DoDEA Form 610 is required anytime there is a change in schools.
- A copy of the child's passport or birth certificate, if the child is applying for entry to kindergarten or first grade, to verify age if the permanent change of station orders don't reflect the birth date or the birth date is incorrect on the orders. It is DoDEA policy that a child must be five and six years old for entrance into kindergarten and first grade, respectively. In the Northern Hemisphere, where the school year starts in August, the child must reach age five or six by September 1 of the enrolling year. In the Southern Hemisphere, where the school year starts in January, the child must reach age five or six by February 1 of the enrolling year.
- A completed "Certification of Command-Sponsored DoD Dependents" if the dependent's name is not listed on the sponsor's orders or in a separate approval authorization.

The maximum allowable school-year rate of reimbursed expenses for home-based educational instruction is $5,700 for grades kindergarten through eight and $7,700 for grades nine through twelve. Reasonable materials may only be ordered for the current grade in which the dependent will be enrolled (on a grade-/age-appropriate basis). Materials may not be ordered for two academic years in one school year. Curriculum materials may be ordered for one grade level above or below the grade of enrollment in one curricular area only.

Allowable homeschooling expenses include

1. Traditional curriculum textbooks and other supplemental materials as may be appropriate for math, science, language arts, social studies, and other subjects on a grade-/age-appropriate basis
2. Instructional CDs and software, curriculum guides, and manipulative materials for math and other subjects
3. Fees charged by local public or private schools for access to libraries, computer labs, and participation in athletic, extracurricu-

lar, or music activities that are normally free of charge in US public schools

4. Fees for curriculum-related online Internet services, such as study programs, library services, and distance learning
5. Rental of curriculum-related equipment such as microscopes or very large band instruments (such as a sousaphone) normally provided by US public schools
6. Required testing materials by either the formal home-study course or another authorized program
7. Advisory teaching service affiliated with the selected formally recognized home-study course
8. Tuition, shipping, lesson postage, Internet, and fax charges associated with a formal, recognized home-study course or other authorized program

Nonallowable homeschooling expenses include

1. Equipment such as computers, keyboards, printers, televisions, fax machines, scanners, calculators, microscopes, and furniture
2. Non-course-specific CDs, videos, and DVDs
3. General reading materials and reference materials (dictionaries, encyclopedias, globes)
4. Purchase or rental of items with broader use beyond the course being studied, such as computer hardware, calculators, and band instruments (except as noted above)
5. Expendable supplies (paper, pencils, markers) normally purchased by parents in the United States
6. Parental training in home-study private instruction
7. Any form of compensation to the parent such as child-care or supervisory costs
8. Travel and transportation costs at or away from post
9. Personal telephone, Internet, satellite, cable, or other available communications subscription fees
10. Fees for museums, cultural events, or performances normally paid for by parents in the United States
11. Private lessons
12. Membership in gymnasiums, cultural clubs, spas, and other private clubs

13. Textbooks, Bibles, workbooks, daily devotionals, or any material primarily for religious instruction
14. Insurance associated with shipping charges
15. Fees to an independent agency for posting credits and issuing transcripts

DOCUMENTATION FOR PAYMENT OR REIMBURSEMENT

Sponsors who elect to purchase educational curriculum materials for homeschooling purposes must submit to the local NDSP liaison receipts and an itemized list indicating the appropriate dependent(s) for each purchase. Sponsors are responsible for out-of-pocket expenses until the purchase is approved and reimbursement is processed. Responsibility for documentation rests with the sponsor. Receipts must be legible. Itemized lists of educational texts or materials must clearly indicate relevance to curriculum areas.

10

MOVING AND COPING WITH FREQUENT MOVES

Because of reassignments, known as permanent change of station (PCS) moves, military families relocate significantly more often than civilian families. Unless the first duty assignment is an unaccompanied (remote) overseas tour, the married military member is entitled to move his or her dependents (and personal property) to the first duty station at government expense. Travel entitlements end when one signs in at the new duty station, so whether one can be reimbursed for dependent travel depends on the date of the marriage.

For example, Airman Jones graduates from Air Force Job Training, then goes home on leave en route to his first duty assignment. While on leave, Airman Jones gets married. He then reports to his first duty station. He will be entitled to move his dependents at government expense because the date of the marriage precedes his signing in at the duty station. PFC Jackson, one the other hand, finishes Army Job Training and reports for his first duty assignment. A couple of weeks later, his fiancée flies down, and they get married. PFC Jackson cannot move his wife and her property to the duty assignment at government expense because the marriage occurred after he completed his assignment move.

There is an exception to the above rule for certain overseas assignments. When a single person is assigned to a "long" overseas tour, the assignment length is generally twenty-four months (the unaccompanied tour length). For an accompanied married person, the tour length is usually thirty-six months. If a single person goes overseas on such a tour, then gets married during the tour, he or she can apply to move his dependents overseas if he agrees to extend his tour length to the accompanied tour length.

In order to move dependents at government expense, one's "orders" must include authorization to do so. This means that if one gets married at the last minute before leaving job training or while on leave en route to the first assignment, the orders won't include this authorization and will have to be amended after arrival. As the military rarely does paperwork very fast, this amendment process can take several weeks. This will delay the reimbursement of dependent moving expenses. If the member got married before joining the military, his or her orders will include dependent moving entitlements, avoiding this delay in reimbursement.

If technical school, advanced individual training, or A-School lasts twenty weeks or longer (at a single location), service members are entitled to move dependents to the school location at government expense. They are then (usually thirty days after arrival) allowed to live with their dependents after duty hours. Single members, of course, cannot move their girl- or boyfriends at government expense; nor may they live off base (even at their own expense) at job training locations.

If the military member elects not to move his or her dependents, the Family Separation Allowance stops because the member is not being forced to live separately (the dependents are allowed to move at government expense, so if they don't move, that's the member's choice). Of course, if the dependents do join the member, the Family Separation Allowance still stops as the member is no longer separated from his or her dependents due to military orders.

If the job training lasts less than twenty weeks, a married person can still elect to move dependents at his or her own expense and will (usually) be allowed to live with them, off base (beginning thirty days after arrival), with the school commander's permission. (As long as the student is doing OK in class, such permission is routinely granted.) If the dependents do move to the member's school location, the Family Separation Allowance stops.

MOVING

Being married in the military presents more than its fair share of challenges, including frequent moves. Just as you have got used to one base and made lots of new friends, you receive PCS orders and have to pack up all over again. This is even more difficult if you have children in school and family nearby.

When a family has a special-needs child, these experiences become even more complicated and emotional. As part of the military community, you have access to a lot of help, such as financial aid for the move and, if desired, a sponsor waiting to help at the new duty station. Taking advantage of these resources will benefit the entire family.

The Exceptional Family Member Program

It is mandatory for military service members to enroll a dependent with special needs, whether a spouse or child, in the Exceptional Family Member Program (EFMP). To do so, contact the family-support center at the nearest military installation. This will ensure that your child's medical and educational needs are considered in the selection of a duty station. Service members will be assigned to an area that can meet the educational and medical needs of their exceptional family member (EFM), provided a valid personnel requirement for the service member's grade and specialty is available in such a location.

Service members have the option of accepting assignments where services for EFMs do not exist. Choosing this option usually means that the service member must live apart from the family so that the EFM can continue in a setting that meets his or her needs. Inform the EFMP office at the new duty station that you are coming and what your family's needs are. If respite care or specialized day care is needed, the EFMP coordinator can help suggest available resources.

Family-Support Centers

Once you know you are moving, contact the nearest family-support center and ask to speak with a relocation specialist. The Relocation Assistance Program offers a wealth of information for relocating service members and their families. Be sure to discuss your moving allowances and understand how they are computed. This also a good place to look for resources to help meet the needs of an exceptional child. The family-support center can also connect you to the EFMP and available respite-care programs. To find a family center near you, go to http://www.militaryinstallations.dod.mil.

Planning every detail of the move is the secret to success. Treat the move as an adventure—an exciting new chapter in your marriage. If your partner is deployed and still receives PCS orders, you will need power of attorney to get things done.

- Start making lists of bills to be paid, utilities and services to be cancelled or transferred, people to inform, important telephone numbers to keep, and so on.
- Gather together documents that you will need, such as orders, medical records, birth certificates, marriage certificates, powers of attorney, living wills, and insurance contracts.
- Create a countdown calendar, and enter everything that needs doing three months ahead of time (if you have the luxury of planning time), then everything that needs doing one month out, one week out, and on the day. Keep referring to this calendar, and add to it as you think of tasks.
- Check out your new base and what facilities and services are available. One great thing about the military is that you may well have friends at the new base who can give you useful tips.
- Check out the local chamber of commerce and the Convention and Visitors Bureau if there is one for job opportunities and to familiarize yourself with your new home area.
- Stay in touch with family and friends; they will be a great support group during the move.

Your relocation office should be your first stop when you are considering a move or actually receive orders. This office is staffed by trained professionals who will help manage your move. Their goal is to connect you with the right resources at the right time so that you can execute an efficient and cost-effective move within the military system.

Your installation's relocation office can help you

- Determine your PCS allowances
- Connect with your new installation's relocation office

- Create and customize a moving calendar
- Connect with important installation agencies
- Create a customized booklet of resources
- Access a loan closet
- Understand out-processing requirements
- Obtain a sponsor

PLAN MY MOVE

Plan My Move (http://www.apps.militaryonesource.mil/MOS/f?p= PMM:ENTRY:0) is a comprehensive moving app that includes tools for military families with special needs. It lets you create customized moving tools such as calendars, to-do lists, and arrival checklists, all intended to help you get organized and to make your next move as smooth as possible.

Schools

Ask your child's current teacher to write a letter introducing your child to the new teacher. An overview of what the teacher sees as strengths and weaknesses, as well as a description of what works well with your child, will help the new teacher. Contact the new state's parent training and information center (http://www.taalliance.org) for information on schools in the new area.

Medical Concerns

Before moving, check to see what medical care is available at the new duty station. The provider directory on the TRICARE website (http://www.tricare.mil) can help locate specialty services and lists phone numbers. Contact providers in advance to be sure that they are still network providers and are currently accepting new patients.

If a child has special physical needs, take extra care to ensure that his or her records are kept safe. Before moving, make copies of important documents, and leave copies of papers with grandparents or close friends if possible. Consider checking the medical record out from the existing duty station and delivering it personally to the new duty station.

If this is not allowed, request a full copy of any and all medical records prior to the transfer in the event the record gets lost in transit or arrives incomplete.

Tell the Kids

For some families, news about a move is best presented at a family meeting. If you think the reaction will likely be positive, this probably a good idea. If, however, you think your kids are going to be upset, it may be a good idea to tell each separately before the family meets. This will give each child time to react individually and may avoid a scene where one upset child sets the tone and negatively influences the other children.

Before telling the kids about the move,

- Arm yourself with some of the positive aspects of your new home. Is it closer to friends or family? Is it near beaches or an amusement park?
- Find your new home on a map to show your kids, if they are old enough, and use it to begin the discussion of your journey to your new home.
- Should your child have a special interest, find out if there is a museum on the way to your new home that your child would not be able to visit otherwise.
- Decide the best way to present the move and consider how you will handle various emotional responses.
- Discuss ways your children can keep in touch with friends; perhaps plan a visit before you move away so the good-bye won't feel so final.
- Be positive; if you are upbeat about the move, your kids will be reassured that all is well.
- If your child has concerns or is grieving for his or her old home already, it very important that you let him or her know that you understand this sorrow and that it is natural and normal. You might share some of your own sorrow as well as some aspect of the new home that you are looking forward to.
- Remind your child that the present home was once new, and yet he or she made friends. This will happen again.

- A calendar or time line with pictures of things that will be happening leading up to, during, and after the move may help calm the fears of younger or special-needs children who rely on daily reminders to prepare for what each day will bring.
- Have a family meeting to discuss your children's feelings. Are they are excited, angry, or worried? Reassure your children that all these feelings are normal.
- Find time during normal rituals, such as meal preparation or bedtime, to have one-on-one conversations with your children so that they can share their thoughts and feelings about the move.
- Plan a farewell party. Take lots of photos and collect addresses, e-mail addresses, and phone numbers.
- If your child is old enough, provide a scrapbook for the child to assemble.
- Since many families now have Internet access via computer and cell phone, consider setting up a Web chat service such as Hangouts by Google or Skype so that friends and family can "visit" online. Using social networking applications such as Facebook or MySpace can also connect loved ones and friends over long distances, which is especially important for children during transitions and changes to routines.
- Moving away from the familiar and into the unknown can be scary. Give your children opportunities to express their feelings. Happiness and excitement are much easier to accept and deal with, but negative feelings, like sorrow or anger, are just as valid. If your children feel that they should express only happy thoughts, they will just bury any negative emotions, which may well surface as negative behaviors. This does not mean your child is entitled to set a negative tone for the whole family or that poor behavior is acceptable, but honest talk may diffuse the problem, at least in part.

Packing

Before the movers arrive, set aside the following items in a room with a big sign on the door asking movers to stay out or not to pack:

- Important documents such as school records, dental records, medical records, birth certificates, insurance policies, copies of PCS orders, and a copy of the household inventory form
- Medicine and medical equipment that will travel with you
- Creature comforts, like a pillow, favorite stuffed toys, or some favorite CDs or DVDs
- Valuables such as jewelry, hard drives, laptops, and related personal items that will travel with you

Also consider packing and labeling a few first-night boxes. These boxes might contain sheets, plastic cups, plates and eating utensils, toilet paper, additional medical supplies or equipment, towels, extra toiletries, and other items that will help you settle in while unpacking and establishing your new residence. For young children, adding some special surprises like little books, toys, or games for first-night unpacking can provide a needed distraction.

Overseas Suitability Screening

Before being stationed overseas or at a remote assignment, all families of service members are screened for overseas suitability. The screening is mandatory to determine if members or family member(s) have any special needs requiring special medical or educational attention. The presence of a special need does not mean a family is ineligible to travel overseas; however, it does mean extra care may be necessary to be sure the family is living in an area suitable for all family members.

TRAVELING WITH KIDS

Whether by plane, train, or automobile, traveling with children takes some planning. The following tips will help make the trip go smoothly:

- Be sure to inform the Traffic Management Office that a child has special needs.
- Be proactive in contacting the airlines or other services to ensure there are arrangements for wheelchair or other equipment storage and to find out the locations of accessible bathrooms. If a

wheelchair is needed at the gate, make the calls yourself to be sure one arrives, and double-check at check-in to be sure the airline is fully prepared to support your needs.

- Keep security items within reach.
- Have healthy snacks at hand.
- Bring plastic bags for trash.
- Bring books, cards, and games to help pass the time. A few new items may hold a child's attention longer than an old favorite.
- A child might enjoy being in charge of his or her own travel bag; however, regulate how much is put into this bag so that it doesn't get too heavy!
- Bring an inexpensive umbrella stroller; these can be especially helpful in airports and train stations.
- Tape emergency contact information in children's clothing, or have them wear a medical alert bracelet.
- Take a portable DVD player if possible, along with the child's favorite DVDs and comforting music for bedtime.
- Keep hand wipes ready for frequent hand cleaning after stops and before eating.

Air Travel

The Air Carrier Access Act prohibits airlines from denying service to passengers on the basis of disability and actually requires US air carriers to accommodate the needs of passengers with disabilities. For more information, contact http://www.disabilityinfo.gov. Keep the following things in mind as you prepare for the trip:

- Contact the airline forty-eight hours in advance of the flight if special services are needed, such as a respirator hookup or transportation of an electric wheelchair.
- Ask if the bathrooms are disability accessible on older or small aircraft.
- Remember that assistive devices do not count toward the limit on the number of pieces of carry-on luggage. Wheelchairs (including collapsible battery-powered wheelchairs) and other assistive devices have priority for in-cabin storage space (including in closets), as long as you take advantage of preboarding.

- Ask your physician about the safety of flying if a family member suffers from seizures. Get the physician's recommendation in writing and carry it with you as part of your family's medical records.
- Consider checking a stroller at the gate, as there can be a lot of ground to cover between gates.
- Use a backpack instead of a diaper bag as this will leave your hands free to hold on to kids.
- Bring snacks for the kids as few self-respecting toddlers will eat airplane food, and on many flights only a small bag of pretzels is offered anyway.
- Decide if boarding early would be the best choice for your family. Air-conditioning is generally not turned on until just before take-off, so a squirmy child will have to remain still longer than necessary in an overheated plane. Some families tag team, with one parent boarding early with the bags and the other boarding later with the kids.
- Be sure the car seat you have is compatible with airline seats. Check the airline's website for car seat information.
- If you are traveling with a service animal, notify the airline in advance so that arrangements can be made to seat you and the animal accordingly.
- Ensure that you have appropriate identification and boarding passes within easy reach for security.
- Ensure that any medicines that may qualify as liquids, aerosols, or gels are properly labeled as prescription or required medicines in order to pass through security.
- If hygiene items are required, pack two to three times the needed amount for carry on in order to accommodate unexpected airline delays. The same holds for special foods or medications in the event of an airline delay or cancellation that might last overnight.
- Sometimes the military will pay for first-class accommodations in the event that transporting an EFM requires extra space or leg-room or the ability to recline fully. If your doctor justifies it in writing, there is a process to get special approval for financial coverage of that requirement.

Traveling by Train

If you are traveling by train, Amtrak will assist those using wheelchairs in the case of high or low platforms or bi-level trains. Your child may remain in the wheelchair en route, or the chair may be stowed. Should your child require oxygen, you must make advance reservations and give notice of your need to bring oxygen aboard at least twelve hours before you board. Call (800) USA-RAIL (7245) for more information about bringing oxygen on an Amtrak train, as well as station accessibility.

Train travel means that more interaction with children is possible than in a car, especially if there is only one driver. Be sure to bring activities your child enjoys, such as favorite stories, card games, and healthy snacks. Many Amtrak trains now offer wireless Internet connectivity and electrical outlets at the seats so that DVD players, laptops, and phones can charge during travel. Check to find out if your particular train service offers these features. Amtrak does sell a limited selection of meals, snacks, and beverages on their trains; check ahead of time to be sure that what is available meets any dietary restrictions of the EFM. If not, plan ahead to bring your own food. Trains can also be delayed on the tracks at arrival or departure. Sometimes trains can be delayed en route significantly. It doesn't hurt to pack some extra toilet paper, hygiene items, hand sanitizer, snacks, and items to pass more time than you think you'll spend—just in case.

Traveling by Car

Car travel affords a family greater flexibility than plane or train travel. You can stop to explore or stretch your legs whenever you like. To make the most of the journey, plan a route with places of interest along the way. Give children a map with the route to the new home and stops along the way clearly marked. Car games will help pass the time. Download a map of the United States (http://www.eduplace.com) and have the children color in a state each time they spot a license plate from that state. Have a scavenger hunt with each family member trying to spot items on a list.

In some cases, EFMs traveling by car should plan for periodic stops or select a route that is close to medical facilities. Other times, a single parent cannot drive long distances with an EFM because the EFM may require monitoring, and a medical attendant may be unable to travel with the adult. Many times driving is a full-time requirement, and the EFM's medical needs cannot be attended to simultaneously or the drive depletes the energy of the adult, who is ultimately too tired to care for the EFM. Talk to the EFM's doctor and the command about this situation because, in certain cases, the military will pay (or reimburse you) for the expense of transporting your automobile to the new duty station and provide alternate transportation to ensure the EFM's care remains the priority and to accommodate care and safety requirements. This type of situation is evaluated on a case-by-case basis, though precedents have already been established for reasonable accommodations.

Temporary Lodging

For information about temporary lodging, go to http://www.military. com/Travel/Content1/0,,ML_overview,00.html. Make reservations as far in advance as possible. Mention your family's EFMP status, as some bases have special accommodations. Be sure to ask for wheelchair-accessible rooms or rooms with TTY for the deaf or hearing impaired, if available. Many Morale, Welfare, and Recreation facilities also have special rooms for families traveling with service animals.

PERMANENT CHANGE OF STATION ALLOWANCES

Various allowances are associated with most moves both within and outside the continental United States. Do not assume that you will receive any of these allowances. Allowances change periodically. Check with the finance office on your installation to determine the exact amount of your allowances. For additional information, you can visit the Per Diem, Travel and Transportation Allowance Committee website, the official source for the most up-to-date changes to benefits and allowances.

HOUSING OFFICE

Your installation housing office can help you with the following:

- Determining your housing allowances
- Determining availability of government housing at your new location
- Understanding your housing privatization options at your new location
- Finding local community housing at your new location
- Arranging for temporary lodging

The Department of Defense's (DoD) Automated Housing Referral Network (http://www.ahrn.com) can help you look for housing.

HOUSEHOLD GOODS

Household goods include items associated with the home and all personal effects belonging to members and dependents, on the effective date of the PCS or temporary duty order, that an authorized commercial transporter can legally transport. Household goods also include professional books, papers, and equipment; spare privately owned vehicle (POV) parts and a pickup tailgate when removed; integral or attached vehicle parts that must be removed due to their high vulnerability to pilferage or damage (e.g., seats, tops, winches, spare tires, portable auxiliary gasoline cans, and miscellaneous associated hardware); vehicles other than POVs (such as golf carts, motorcycles, mopeds, jet skis, hang gliders, snowmobiles) and their associated trailers; and boats and single-occupant ultralight vehicles for recreation or sport purposes (weighing less than 155 pounds if uncovered or less than 254 pounds if powered; having a fuel capacity not to exceed five gallons, airspeed not to exceed fifty-five knots, and power-off stall speed not to exceed twenty-four knots).

Household goods do not include the following:

- Personal carry-on baggage on an airplane, bus, or train
- Cars, trucks, vans, and similar motor vehicles
- Airplanes, mobile homes, camper trailers, and farming vehicles

- Live animals, including birds, fish, and reptiles
- Cordwood and building materials
- Items for resale, disposal, or commercial use rather than for use by members and dependents
- Privately owned live ammunition
- Articles that otherwise would qualify as household goods but are acquired after the effective date of PCS orders, except bona fide replacements for articles that have become inadequate, worn-out, broken, or unserviceable on or after the effective date of orders

PERSONALLY OWNED VEHICLE

One personally owned vehicle belonging to you or a family member may be shipped overseas at government expense. It must, however, be for you or your family member's personal use only. If you desire to make your own arrangements and ship an additional POV, consult your transportation office for any restrictions that may apply. You may be required to pay an import duty on a second POV. A motorcycle or moped may be considered a POV if the member does not ship a vehicle with four or more wheels under the same set of military orders. A vehicle under a long-term lease (twelve months or longer) may be shipped with written permission from the leasing company.

The POV should be delivered to the port prior to the departure of the member on whose orders the shipment is to be made. The member must have a minimum of twelve months remaining on overseas tour at the time the vehicle is delivered to the loading port. A military spouse who delivers the vehicle to the loading port must have a special power of attorney.

Personally procured moves (PPM), or do-it-yourself moves, allow you to personally move household goods and collect an incentive payment of up to 95 percent of the government's estimate to move your household goods. You can do a PPM for PCS orders, temporary duty assignment, separation or retirement, or assignment to, from, or between government quarters. You can use certain vehicles to move your household goods instead of having the government ship them. You may use this option to move all or a portion of the authorized Joint Federal

Travel Regulations weight allowance. All of the details can be found at http://www.move.mil.

TRANSPORTATION OFFICE

All moving transactions are to be handled through DoD's worldwide moving website (http://www.move.mil). First log on and create an account. You will then be prompted to research your allowances and to send a message to your transportation office. You will use Move.mil to manage your move; you can work through your allowances, book and track your shipment, and file claims if necessary. You will also be prompted at the end of the move to fill in a customer-satisfaction survey. It is a one-stop, self-help program designed to put you in charge of the shipment and storage of your personal property.

Alternatively, you can make an appointment with your transportation office as soon as you have a copy of your PCS orders. The earlier you call or visit, the greater your chances of moving on your desired date. The counselor will explain your PCS move allowances in detail and walk you through the pros and cons of having the government move you versus managing the move yourself. If you choose a government move, the counselor will book your shipment and let you know the exact dates the movers will come. If you choose to move yourself, the counselor will give you recommendations and tips for making that PPM as smooth as possible. The transportation office can also give you information about household goods allowances and shipping a pet or POV.

UNACCOMPANIED BAGGAGE

If you are moving overseas, your shipment allowance for personal property will probably include a surface shipment and an unaccompanied baggage shipment sent by air. The air shipment is coordinated to be available to you when you arrive at your destination. The unaccompanied baggage shipment should include items that you need upon arrival such as clothes, linens, and baby or medical equipment. You will arrange for the unaccompanied baggage shipment when you organize your move via either Move.mil(DoD's self-counseling and shipment-management system) or your local transportation office. Your installation will also have a loan closet from which to borrow items you need when you arrive. This is especially important if you were not authorized an unaccompanied baggage shipment.

Other resources include the following:

- Army Community Service Center
- Airman and Family Readiness Center (air force)
- Fleet and Family-Support Center (navy)
- Marine Corps Community Services

MOVING WITH CHILDREN

Moving is particularly hard on children, especially if they are in school, have made lots of friends, and have favorite teachers. It is important to talk to them as soon as you know you are moving to address any anxiety or resentment they may feel and get them used to the idea. Spend time with them on the computer exploring your new home area—looking at the schools, attractions, sports facilities, and so on. If possible, try to make a quick visit so that they will have a clearer idea of where they are moving to.

Get them involved in the planning, but try to conduct your family routine normally so that there is as little disruption as possible. This will help reassure children. Sudden changes to their routine will make them anxious.

Younger children are more able to take a move in stride because their lives are constantly changing anyhow, but teenagers will need careful handling. As teens, they are already dealing with all sorts of emotional and developmental issues, and a move is the last thing they want, especially if they have started dating or just won a place on one of the school's sports teams. Get them involved from day one and keep them involved throughout the process. Many bases run relocation briefings, and it is a good idea to encourage your teenager to attend these with you.

If you have a special-needs child, you should talk to your advisor or coordinator so that things—such as the right school, medical specialists, and support groups—are in place on your arrival at your new home.

Setting these services up ahead of time will ease the transition for everyone.

Frequent moves pose significant challenges for all military families, and the impact on children is often not fully appreciated. It can lead to a wide range of issues that may have emotional, psychological, and even physical consequences both at the time and down the road. It is essential when moving to monitor your kids' behavior closely, to talk to them to allay their fears, and to familiarize them with what is happening. If you suspect that your child is having problems with the move, seek help immediately to address and resolve any issues. Consult with your relocation officer, who will be able to put you in touch with counselors and others best able to help and support you.

11

FAMILY SEPARATION AND DEPLOYMENTS

Twenty percent of active-duty military personnel reported concerns about the impact of their deployment on child-care arrangements, whereas less than half of spouses of deployed personnel reported managing child-care arrangements well or very well.

Married members are entitled to a Family Separation Allowance when separated from their dependents due to military orders. There are no restrictions on how this money is spent. The tax-free allowance begins after separation of thirty days. This means married people in basic training and technical school (if the technical school duration is less than twenty weeks) begin to receive this pay thirty days after going on active duty. Single personnel do not receive this allowance.

COMBAT DUTY

Since September 11, 2001, more than 2 million service members have deployed to Iraq or Afghanistan. The duration and the frequency of deployments are unprecedented since the establishment of America's all-volunteer force in 1973. This increased exposure to combat stress has led to a growing number of service members with posttraumatic stress disorder (PTSD) and traumatic brain injury (TBI). According to the September 2010 Medical Surveillance Report, service members have self-reported PTSD symptoms 9 percent of the time and depression symptoms more than 27 percent of the time when asked 90 to 180 days postdeployment. Additionally, more than 19 percent of service members returning from combat reported potentially experiencing TBI during deployment.

Military families are not immune to the stresses of deployment. There is a growing body of research on the impact of prolonged deployment and trauma-related stress on military families, particularly spouses and children. There are approximately seven hundred thousand military spouses and an additional four hundred thousand spouses of Reserve members. More than seven thousand children have experienced one or more parental deployments. Currently, about 220,000 children have a parent deployed. The cumulative impact of multiple deployments is associated with more emotional difficulties among military children and more mental health diagnoses among spouses. A 2010 study reports an 11 percent increase in outpatient visits for behavioral health issues among a group of three- to eight-year-old children of military parents and increases of 18 percent in behavioral disorders and 19 percent in stress disorders during a parent's deployment. Mitigating these negative effects requires a robust psychological health plan, including better data collection, reduced stigma-related barriers, and stronger chain-of-command involvement.

Although many military families are thriving, common stressors can erode their resilience. Many of these stressful situations are preventable. In addition to the compounding effects of deployments, occasional financial stress, especially with regard to housing and home ownership, substance abuse, and incarceration, has caused excessive strain for certain military families. For instance, in surveys conducted by the Department of Defense (DoD), military families have listed personal financial management as number two on their list of biggest sources of stress. Furthermore, homelessness and home foreclosure can be realities in some veteran families, although this is not widespread. In the direst situations, families must cope with incarceration. According the Department of Justice's most recent survey of incarcerated veterans, an estimated 60 percent of the 140,000 veterans in federal and state prisons struggled with substance-use disorders, while approximately 25 percent reported being under the influence of drugs at the time of their offense. Substance abuse, incarceration, and the other stressors aforementioned can be viewed as the result of missed opportunities for preventive actions. Early recognition and treatment seeking signal new strength for our military families.

FAMILY IMPACT

Waiting for a loved one to deploy is hard on children as well as spouses. Children may not understand why a parent must go away and may fear the parent is leaving forever. Because children are not very good at verbalizing their worries, they tend to express them behaviorally. Be sure your children have many chances to express how they are feeling. The following ideas may help your family prepare for and get through a period of separation due to deployment:

- Use your own words to help children find theirs. For example, "I don't want Daddy to leave, and waiting for him to leave makes me feel sort of sad and worried. Do you ever feel that way?"
- Explain that although many things will be different, many things will be the same.
- If the child plays imaginary games with dolls or animals, try to introduce the idea of one member of the doll family leaving. Let the other dolls say how they feel about this.
- Use a map or a globe to show where the deployed parent will be.
- Use a calendar to show children when the deployment will take place, as they may not understand how long three weeks is. Some families cross a day off the calendar; others count with buttons or M&Ms from a jar.

Be sure that the departing parent has time with each child before deploying. Hug often. Take photos of each child with the departing parent. Sometimes a parent will go to Build-A-Bear and get a recording of his or her voice installed in the paw, so the child can squeeze it and hear a short, loving message from the parent. Others video-record stories, loving messages, and songs for their children to listen to while the parent is away. Photos can also be placed on everything from mugs, to T-shirts and blankets, to pillowcases, which can give children something to enjoy as a keepsake during the absence.

The departing parent might schedule a trip to the child's school to meet with the teacher. The point of this trip is to ensure the teacher knows about the change in the family dynamics. Let the child show you around his or her school world and perhaps hear you tell the teacher how proud you are of him or her. You will be able to ask better questions about your child's day if you are familiar with his or her school. Many schools can Skype, iChat, or otherwise virtually assist the deployed parent in participating in individualized education program meetings and school communications; many are willing to do so if asked ahead of time.

Have a family meeting about ways to keep in touch during the deployment. Letters, pictures, tapes, and movies are all good ways to stay connected. Communications and care packages should also come from the child to the parent so that they can remain as engaged and involved as possible.

Remember to send children letters addressed just to them on occasion. Children enjoy few things more than receiving their own mail! A letter to the family pet will also bring a smile to a child's face.

Find the best way for the child to mark the days until the end of the deployment. This may entail making X's on the calendar or ripping links off a paper chain.

Remember that a child's not expressing feelings doesn't mean he or she is not troubled. If a child is acting out, this may be the result of unexpressed emotions. Help the child name these feelings.

It is fine and even healthy for children to see you feel sad too, but if you are really about to fall apart, try to do this away from your kids. Strong emotions in a parent can be scary to a child. Remind children that they are still safe and that a deployed parent is still a member of the family.

Do not minimize the child's grief. To the child it may feel like a parent is lost forever. Grief without understanding is difficult to work through.

Children may punish the parent who is still there for the disappearance of the parent who has left. Often deployed parents are not aware of major behavioral changes that occur after their departure. Parents must be prepared for anger, frustration, sadness, and confusion to lead to acting-out behavior.

Taking time to gather and prepare the proper documents in advance of deployment allows service members to choose people to act on their behalf, to make their wishes known to loved ones, and, if they choose, to give legally binding instructions. Although it may be uncomfortable to talk about certain possibilities, doing so in advance may avoid conflict and allow for quick and decisive action in the event of an emergency. Service members and their families should gather identification documents such as birth certificates, marriage certificates, and any other similar documents that can verify family relationships.

DEPLOYMENT PHASES

The emotional cycle of an extended deployment (six months or longer) falls into five distinct stages: predeployment, deployment, sustainment, redeployment, and postdeployment. Each stage is characterized both by a time frame and specific emotional challenges that each family member must deal with and master. Failure to adequately negotiate these challenges can lead to significant strife—for both family members and the deployed service member. Providing information early about what to expect, especially for families who have not endured a lengthy separation before, can go a long way toward "normalizing" and facilitating positive coping with the deployment experience.

Predeployment Checklist

General

- Have you and your spouse discussed your feelings about the deployment and the deployed spouse's return?
- Have the children been included in discussions about where the deployed parent is going, when he or she is coming home, and why he or she is leaving?
- Have you reached an agreement on the frequency of letter writing and phone calls?
- Do you have current family snapshots?
- Has the deploying spouse recorded the children's favorite bedtime stories or songs on cassettes?

- Do both the deploying and the staying parent or guardian understand what the Airman and Family Readiness Center, Family Services, Air Force Aid Society, American Red Cross, chaplain, and so forth, can do for them and how to contact these organizations and individuals?

Security

- Has the home been given a security check?
- Do all window locks work?
- Do the windows open, or are they painted shut?
- Do all door locks work properly?
- Do you have keys for all doors or combinations for all padlocks?
- Do the smoke alarms function, and do you know how to test them?
- Are all emergency numbers posted where they can be referred to easily?
- Is there an appropriate message on the answering machine? (Having a male voice sometimes discourages prank phone calls)
- Do you need to change your phone number to an unlisted number?

Medical

- Do you know how to access and use the medical facilities?
- Do you know your pediatrician's name and have his or her phone number?
- Do you know your children's dentist or orthodontist and their appointment schedules

Financial

- Have you determined who will pay the bills?
- Do you have a spending plan?
- Do you both understand the spending plan?
- Does your spending plan consider the following?

    - Rent/mortgage
    - Utilities
    - Food
    - Automobile maintenance

- Insurance
- Loan payments
- Emergencies
- Long-distance phone calls
- Postage
- Telegrams
- Travel (leave)
- Entertainment
- Presents
- Savings

- Has an allotment been established?
- Will the allotment be in effect in time?
- Is there a backup plan if the allotment is late?
- Have you established two checking accounts?
- Have you decided on a procedure for filing income taxes?

Legal

- Do you know your spouse's Social Security number?
- Have you signed a power of attorney?
- Do you have current wills?
- Have guardians for the children been named in the wills?
- Does everyone who qualifies have a government ID card?
- Will any ID cards need renewing?
- If ID needs renewing, has Form DD 1172 been completed?
- Is the military member's emergency data on record and current?
- Do you know the process for moving your household goods?

Important Papers

Are the following important papers current and in an accessible safety deposit box?

- Power of attorney
- Wills
- Insurance policies
- Real estate documents (deeds, titles, mortgages, leases)
- Bank account numbers

- Charge or credit account numbers
- Savings bonds
- Birth certificates
- Marriage certificates
- Naturalization papers
- Citizenship papers
- Family Social Security numbers
- Inventory of household goods
- Car title(s)

Important Phone Numbers

Do you have the following important numbers where you can refer to them easily:

- Police
- Fire
- Medical (hospital/doctor)
- Service member's contact number
- Service member's unit in local area
- Spouses in the unit/squadron
- Reliable neighbors
- Relatives
- Children's school
- Spouse's workplace
- Utilities
- Repair shops
- Insurance company
- Airman and Family Readiness Center

Household Maintenance

- Do you know whom to call if something breaks?
- Do you know how to operate the furnace?
- Does the furnace have clean filters?
- Does the furnace need periodic supplies of oil or gas?
- Is the hot-water heater operating properly?
- Are any pipes or faucets leaking?
- Are toilets operating correctly?

- Are all drains operating correctly?
- Are the following appliances operating correctly?

  - Stove
  - Refrigerator
  - Freezer
  - Dishwasher
  - Clothes washer
  - Clothes dryer
  - Television
  - Air conditioner

- Does everyone know where the fuse box is?
- Are the switches in the fuse box labeled?
- Are there extra fuses?
- Is there adequate outside lighting?
- Is there a list of repair people?
- Are there tools in the house?
- Is the lawn mower tuned?
- Is there adequate firewood?

If you or your children are having a particularly difficult time adjusting to the deployment, counseling is readily available through several sources. Call the family service center or contact Military OneSource (http://www.militaryonesource.com). Through TRICARE you are entitled to eight sessions of counseling without a referral from your primary care manager. If more is needed, an authorization can be obtained. Another source of support may be a chaplain. It is important to ask if the chaplain is licensed for marriage or family therapy. The parent at home has a heavy load to carry. When a child is disabled, things can be difficult enough when both parents are available, but with one absent, caregiving may seem overwhelming. Taking care of yourself has never been more important. Do not hesitate to contact your Exceptional Family Member Program coordinator to ask for respite care. The entire family will benefit if the parent at home has the chance to recharge his or her batteries.

Deployment

This stage encompasses the period from departure from home through the first month of the deployment. A roller-coaster ride of mixed emotions is common during the deployment stage. Some military spouses report feeling disoriented and overwhelmed. Others may feel relieved that they no longer have to appear brave and strong. There may be residual anger at tasks left undone. The departure creates a "hole," which can lead to feelings of numbness, sadness, aloneness, or abandonment. It is common to have difficulty sleeping and to feel anxiety about coping. Worries about security issues may ensue. The spouse staying behind may wonder, What if there is a pay problem? Is the house safe? How will I manage if my child gets sick? What if the car breaks down? For many, the deployment stage is an unpleasant, disorganized experience.

On the positive side, the ability to communicate with home from anywhere in the world is a great morale boost. The Defense Satellite Network provides service personnel the ability to call home at no cost, although usually for a fifteen-minute limit. Military families have come to expect phone (and now even video) contact, and most report that the ability to stay in close touch—especially during key events (e.g., birthdays, anniversaries)—greatly helps them to cope with the separation.

Sustainment

The sustainment stage lasts from the first month through the fifth (penultimate) month of deployment. It is a time of establishing new sources of support and new routines. Many families rely on the Family Readiness Group, which serves as a close network that meets on a regular basis to handle problems and disseminate the latest information. Others are more comfortable with family, friends, church, or another religious institution as their main means of emotional support. As challenges come up, most spouses learn that they are able to cope and make important decisions on their own. They report feeling more confident and in control.

Redeployment

The redeployment stage is essentially defined as the month before the deployed family member returns home. This time is generally one of intense anticipation. As during the deployment stage, there can be a surge of conflicting emotions. On the one hand, there is excitement about the homecoming. On the other, there is some apprehension. Some concerns include, Will he or she agree with the changes that I have made? Will I have to give up my independence? Will we get along? Many spouses also experience a burst of energy during this stage. There is often a rush to complete to-do lists before the redeployed mate returns—especially around the home. It is almost inevitable that expectations will be high.

Postdeployment

The postdeployment stage begins with the deployed family member's arrival at home station. As with the predeployment stage, the time frame for this stage is variable, depending on the particular family. Typically, this stage lasts from three to six months. It starts with the homecoming, which can be a wonderfully joyous occasion, with children rushing to the returning parent followed by the warm embrace and kiss of the reunited couple. The unit then comes to attention for one last time, followed by words of praise from the senior commander present. Finally, weapons are turned in, duffle bags are retrieved, and the family goes home.

Homecoming can also be an extremely frustrating and upsetting experience. The date of return may change repeatedly, or units may travel home piecemeal over several days. Despite his or her best intentions, the spouse at home may not be able to meet the returning warrior due to short notice, sick children, inability to find a sitter in the middle of the night or to get off work, and so forth. Returning service personnel may expect to be received as heroes or heroines only to find that they have to make their own way home.

Typically, a honeymoon period follows in which couples reunite physically but not necessarily emotionally. Some spouses express a sense of awkwardness in addition to excitement, wondering, Who is this stranger in my bed? For others, however, the sexual intimacy may require time to reconnect emotionally first.

Eventually, the returning warrior will want to reassert his or her role as a member of the family, which can lead to tension. This essential transition requires considerable patience to accomplish successfully. Warriors may feel pressure to make up for lost time and missed milestones and may want to take back all the responsibilities they had before. However, some things will have changed in their absence: spouses are more autonomous, children have grown, and individual personal priorities in life may be different. It is not realistic to return home and expect everything to be the same as before the deployment. During this period, the spouse who stayed at home may report a sense of lost independence or resentment at having been "abandoned" for six months or more. Reunion with children can also present a challenge.

IMPACT ON CHILDREN

Children's response to a parent's extended deployment is very individualized and also depends on their developmental age—whether they are infants, toddlers, preschoolers, elementary school students, or teenagers. It is reasonable to assume that a sudden negative change in a child's behavior or mood is a predictable response to the stress of having a deployed parent.

Infants (less than one year old) must be held and actively nurtured in order thrive. If a primary caregiver becomes significantly depressed, then the infant will be at risk of developing apathy, refusal to eat, and even weight loss. Early intervention becomes critical to prevent undue harm or neglect. Pediatricians can perform serial exams to ensure growth continues as expected on height/weight charts. Army Community Service and Social Work can assist with parenting skills and eliciting family or community support. Finally, the primary caregiver may also benefit from individual counseling. Babies less than one year old may not recognize the returning warrior and may cry at first when held.

Toddlers (one to three years) will generally take their cue from the primary caregiver. One issue is whether the mother or father is leaving—especially when children are very young. If the nondeploying parent is coping well, toddlers will tend to do well. The converse is also true. If the primary caregiver is not coping well, then toddlers may become sullen and tearful, throw tantrums, or develop sleep disturbance. They will usually respond to increased attention, hugs, and hand-holding. The nondeploying parent may also benefit from sharing day-to-day experiences with other parents facing similar challenges. In particular, it is important for primary caregivers to balance the demands of caring for children alone with their own need for time for themselves. It may take time for toddlers to warm up again to the returning warrior.

Preschoolers (three to six years) may regress in their skills (manifesting difficulty with potty training and reverting to baby talk, thumb sucking, or refusal to sleep alone) and seem clingier. They may be irritable, depressed, aggressive, prone to somatic complaints, and fearful of parents or others leaving. Caregivers will need to reassure them with extra attention and physical closeness (hugs, hand-holding). In addition, it is important to avoid changing family routines, such as having them sleep in their own beds, unless they are very scared. Answers to questions about the deployment should be brief, matter-of-fact, and to the point. This will help to contain the free-floating anxiety caused by an overactive imagination. Preschoolers may feel guilty and scared about the separation.

School-age children (six to twelve years) may whine, complain, become aggressive, or otherwise act out their feelings. They may focus on the deployed parent's missing a key event, asking questions like, "Will he/she/you (the soldier) be here for my birthday." Depressive symptoms may include sleep disturbance and loss of interest in school, eating, or even playing with friends. These children will need to talk about their feelings and will need more physical attention than usual. Expectations regarding school performance may need to be a little lower, but keeping routines as close to normal is best for them. On the warrior's return, they are likely to want a lot of attention.

Teenagers (thirteen to eighteen years) may be irritable and rebellious, pick fights, or participate in other attention-seeking behavior. They may show a lack of interest in school, peers, and school activities. In addition, they are at greater risk for promiscuity, alcohol, and drug use. Although they may deny problems and worries, it is extremely important for caregivers to stay engaged and to be available to talk out their concerns. At first, lowering academic expectations may be helpful;

however, return to their usual school performance should be supported. Sports and social activities should be encouraged to give normal structure to their lives. Likewise, additional responsibility in the family, commensurate with their emotional maturity, will make them feel important and needed. On the warrior's return, it is not uncommon for the teenager to be moody, to appear not to care, and to seem more loyal to the spouse who remained behind.

Unfortunately, some children may have great difficulty adapting to the stress of a parent's deployment. If your child is unable to return to at least some part of his or her normal routine or displays serious problems over several weeks, a visit to the family doctor or mental health counselor is indicated. Children of deployed parents are also more likely to need psychiatric hospitalization—especially in single-parent and blended families. Despite all these obstacles, the vast majority of spouses and family members successfully negotiate the sustainment stage and begin to look forward to their loved ones' return home.

WHAT TO EXPECT FROM YOUR CHILDREN DURING POSTDEPLOYMENT

Children may experience the same confusing feelings as you and your spouse: worry, fear, stress, happiness, and excitement. Depending on their age, they may not understand how the deployed parent could have left if he or she really loved them. During postdeployment, they may be unsure what to expect from the returned parent and may feel uncomfortable or think of him or her as a stranger. It's hard for children to control their excitement. Let them give and get the attention they need from the returned parent before you try to have quiet time alone with your spouse.

Children's reactions to the returning parent will differ according to their age. Some normal reactions you can expect are as follows:

- Infants may cry, fuss, pull away from the returning parent, cling to you or the caregiver.
- Toddlers may be shy, clingy, not recognize the returning parent, cry, have temper tantrums, return to behaviors they had outgrown (e.g., forget toilet training).

- Preschoolers may feel guilty for having made the parent go away, need time to warm up to the returning parent, feel intense anger, act out to get attention, and be demanding.
- School-age children may show excitement and joy, talk constantly to bring the returning parent up to date, boast about the returning parent, and feel guilt about not doing enough or being good enough.
- Teenagers may feel excitement, guilt about not living up to standards, concern about rules and responsibilities; they may also feel too old or unwilling to change plans to meet or spend extended time with the returning parent.

The following are some tips for managing the redeployment and post-deployment phases:

- Prepare children for homecoming with activities, photographs, participation in preparations, and talk about Dad or Mom.
- Children are excited and tend to act out. Accept and discuss these physical, attitudinal, mental, and emotional changes.
- Plan time as a couple and as a family with the children.
- Stay involved with your children's school and social activities.
- Take time for yourself.
- Look into ways to manage stress (e.g., diet, exercise, recreation).
- Make time to rest.
- Negotiate the number of social events you and your family attend.
- Limit your use of alcohol. Remember, consumption of alcohol was restricted during your spouse's deployment, and tolerance is lower.
- Go slowly in getting back into the swing of things.
- Depend on family, your spouse's unit, and friends for support.

Remember . . .

- Go slowly—don't try to make up for lost time.
- Accept that your partner may have changed.
- Take time to get reacquainted.
- Seek help for family members if needed.
- If you feel like you are having trouble coping with the adjustment, it is healthy to ask for help.

Many normal, healthy people occasionally need help handling tough challenges in their lives. Contact a counseling agency, a minister or military chaplain, a military family center, the Veterans Administration, or a community support group in your area.

FOR THE RETURNING MILITARY

Even if you've been through a mobilization or deployment before, this one has been different because of the increased stressors of the time. Regardless of your experience and assignment, you will have a natural period of adjustment. Ease yourself back into the family gradually. If you come on like a Sherman tank and try to bulldoze your way back into your family's life, feelings of resentment will surface. See yourself as a special guest for a while.

Take some time to observe how the family has been running in your absence. You might be tempted to jump right in with "Now that I am home, there are going to be a few changes around here." You will see that some things will change naturally as a result of your presence. If you disagree with how other things have been handled, wait a few days and discuss this openly with your spouse.

Do not try to take over the finances immediately. A complete interrogation regarding the state of the checkbook as soon as you walk through the door is bound to create hostility. Set aside some time when things have calmed down to review the financial situation with your spouse.

Take it easy with the children in terms of discipline. For a while, stick with the rules your spouse has established during your absence. Immediately playing the heavy will not open up opportunities for you and the children to get to know one another again. It is not difficult to understand why some children are afraid of the returning parent if all they have to look forward to is a changing of the guard.

On the other hand, sometimes it is easy to spoil your children. If you have not seen them for a long time or are home for only short periods, you may find yourself not wanting to discipline them. You are probably eager to make up for the time you were unable to spend with them. This is certainly understandable. But do not put your spouse in the position of constantly playing the heavy while you have all the fun with the children.

POSTDEPLOYMENT: SUPPORT RESOURCES FOR HOMECOMINGS

The joy of homecoming is followed by a transition period as the entire family readjusts to being together. Family dynamics often change during the service member's absence, with partners assuming new roles and responsibilities, children growing and maturing, and new family routines and schedules being established. Both the service member and his or her family may have multiple challenges to overcome as they adjust to these changes, reestablish bonds, and confront the many details of managing a household. If the service member experiences any of the long-term health problems sometimes prevalent after deployment, such as depression, PTSD, or TBI, the entire family has an additional challenge to manage. The American Red Cross offers multiple skill-building opportunities for military families to identify and cope effectively with the unique challenges that arise after a deployment.

Coming Home from Deployment: The New "Normal"

Many men and women return from a deployment and successfully adjust to their lives, but most experience at least some difficulty in readjusting or transitioning to family life, their jobs, and living in their communities after a long separation. The Red Cross has developed *Coming Home from Deployment: The New "Normal,"* a booklet to assist all military families with what can be a difficult and complicated transition home.

Workshop Series

Reconnection Workshops, Presented by Walmart

The American Red Cross is pleased to offer the Reconnection Workshops, Presented by Walmart, dedicated to our country's service men and women and their families and loved ones. The goal is to support and ease the transition home.

The Reconnection Workshops, Presented by Walmart focus on individual/small group discussion that enhances the likelihood of positive reconnections among family members and the successful reengagement of the service member in civilian life. Each workshop focuses on a topic area that service members and their families have found relevant to their experience as they transition back home. Current topic areas include managing anger, supporting children, building communication, reconnecting with others, recognizing PTSS and TBI, and other topics critical to reunion adjustment. The workshops are available to all those impacted by a military deployment from all branches of the armed forces. Members of the Reserves and National Guard, active-duty service members, and veterans and their families, including spouses, parents, siblings, and significant others, are invited to participate.

Participants choose the topic they are most interested in from the available options; sessions and materials focus on learning useful tools, effective coping mechanisms, and where to find resources. Available workshops include

- "Communicating Clearly"
- "Exploring Stress and Trauma"
- "Identifying Depression"
- "Relating to Children"
- "Working through Anger"

To register for one or all of these valuable workshops, please e-mail your name, city and state, and the workshop(s) you are interested in attending to reconnection@redcross.org.

COPING WITH STRESS

All marriages undergo stress from time to time. This can be a result of emotional strains, work or financial problems, children, and so on. For military families, many other situations can be very stressful, with deployment and separation and frequent moves topping the list.

When stressed, people react differently. It is difficult for them to eat and sleep. They become irritable and short-tempered. They may say things in the heat of the moment that they would not say otherwise. As couples tend to react differently under stress, one partner may be affected far more than the other, and so the relationship gets out of kilter. The solution is to identify the source of the stress and see what can be done about it. First, you must accept that you are under stress and that this is causing problems in the relationship. Then sit down together and talk about the issues. That alone is often enough to relieve some of the strain. Whatever its cause, the situation is not likely to be resolved easily or quickly, but just recognizing it and having some sort of plan to tackle it is reassuring. Much more importantly, by sitting down with your partner and talking about it, you can work together to resolve it. There is a lot of truth in the saying "A problem shared is a problem halved."

Talking about the problem is half the battle; showing that you care is the other half. Be supportive and loving. Buy your partner something special—it doesn't have to be expensive—but it does show that you are thinking of and there for him or her.

COMMUNICATIONS

The secret to a successful marriage is good communication—being able to talk freely about any subject, to share secrets, fears, and fantasies, to offer advice if asked, and to discuss problems when they arise.

It takes effort to be a good listener. It means not hiding behind your newspaper at breakfast as your partner speaks and mumbling, "Yes, dear." A good listener will put down the paper, look his or her spouse in the eye, and focus on what he or she is saying. What sort of message does it send if your partner is talking and you walk away and turn on the television?

With busy lives to lead, it is important that couples make time to talk to each other. If you are together, you can do this whenever you want. If your partner is deployed, the time you have to communicate is even more precious. Keeping this communication going during deployment may be difficult, but you can stay in touch through precious phone calls, e-mail and the Internet, letters, videos, and so on.

Good communication is also part of the intimacy of marriage and a loving relationship. Saying "I love you" to your partner every day is part of that. It is such an easy thing to say and takes only a moment, but so often, it doesn't get said. It doesn't matter how long you have been married; you can still do little things to communicate to your partner how much you still love him or her and how important he or she is to you. You can send e-mail messages (where appropriate), leave love notes for your partner to find, send flowers with a loving message, and just be encouraging and supportive.

Good communication keeps a marriage alive. When we stop communicating with each other, we tend to drift apart. If couples are not speaking to each other, other emotions can fill that void: anger, resentment, indifference—all negatives that can lead to marital breakup.

It is as important to be a good communicator as it is to be a good listener. The good communicator will choose words carefully so as not to hurt or offend his or her partner. If there is an issue, it is better to ask, "What can we do?" rather than "Why did you let this happen?" When you start a sentence with "you," it can sound as if you are attacking the other person. Pointing fingers is never a good way to start a conversation. You need to spell out the problem and concentrate on ways to resolve it.

Start instead with "I think . . . " or "I am concerned about . . ." This immediately tells your partner that these are your feelings and opens the door for a response about how he or she feels. Once you both know how the other feels, you are better able to work out a solution that suits both. Remember that you are both entitled to your opinion and must respect each other's point of view. Sometimes it is better to agree to disagree—but always do it with love and a hug.

The good communicator will be clear and to the point so there is little chance for misunderstanding. Arguments often result from misunderstandings—you said something and your partner totally misunderstood it.

Gestures and expressions are also important. If you are discussing something intimate or difficult, take hold of your partner's hand to show that you are in this together and that you care for him or her. Even if the subject is very serious, it doesn't hurt to smile at your partner every now and then. This reassuring gesture says, "I love you. We are in this together, and we will work it out together."

The good listener will focus on what is being said and then think before replying. As you are listening, do not think about what time the game starts or what you are doing tomorrow. Your partner deserves your full attention—and should get it.

Body language is every bit as important as the words you say. The wrong body language can send strong, antipathetic signals. If your arms are folded or you are leaning away from your partner, you are putting a barrier between the two of you and distancing yourself. Leaning toward your partner demonstrates genuine interest in what he or she is saying and a desire to be close. Eye contact is critical because it creates a bond. If your eyes start to wander, this shows you are not concentrating. Even eye movements can convey subtle messages. You should always break eye contact by looking down. Turning your eyes upward might convey impatience (i.e., "that was a stupid thing to say"), whereas looking downward can signal thoughtfulness and nonaggression. If your eyes flicker to the left or right it indicates you are uncomfortable (i.e., looking for an escape).

Set aside a time during the day to talk to each other face-to-face. It can be over breakfast or dinner or just before you go to sleep. Several studies show that the more a couple speaks, the stronger their marriage is likely to be; conversely, couples who hardly speak at all are likely to break up.

If you have a particularly difficult subject to discuss, set aside a time especially for it. Don't try to have the conversation while you are cooking dinner or putting the children to bed. Find a time when you can sit down quietly and devote all your attention to the matter at hand and to each other.

There may be times when your partner may not want to communicate. He or she may have returned from a particularly harrowing deployment or be having an issue at work. If you have a strong relationship, don't assume that the lack of communication reflects your having done something wrong. After hearing soothing and sympathetic words, such as "I'm always here for you if you want to talk" or "Is there anything I can do to help," your partner should eventually open up to you, and your relationship should be right back on track.

If, despite your best efforts to communicate, your partner is unwilling to do so, suggest that counseling may help. Your family-support center can offer advice and recommend counselors.

12

FINANCES, TAXES, AND FINANCIAL DIFFICULTIES

Frequent moves and family separations pose financial difficulties for many military families. Not all moving expenses are reimbursable, and it is not uncommon for military personnel to take out a loan in order to finance a permanent change of station (PCS) move. Due to disruptions in employment, PCS moves also negatively impact the earning power of military spouses. For these reasons, it is not surprising that over half of families of enlisted personnel report occasional and even frequent difficulty paying bills.

Discuss finances with your spouse. It is important for you to be able to manage the family finances if he or she is deployed. You can get a lot of information about pay and compensation from http://militarypay. defense.gov. Most bases have an income tax assistance program that you can turn to for advice. It is also important to familiarize yourself with your spouse's leave and earnings statement, which provides details about pay, allowances, and vacation time accrued.

Federal taxes must be paid on all income, including wages, interest earned on bank accounts, and so on. However, some tax benefits may arise from service in a combat zone, and certain expenses incurred by the service member may generate other benefits, such as exclusions, deductions, and credits. The Combat Zone Tax Exclusion, for instance, renders certain pay tax-free, and you do not have to report it on tax returns.

The deadline for filing returns and paying any tax due is automatically extended for those serving in the armed forces in a combat zone, in a qualified hazardous duty area, or on deployment outside the United States while participating in a contingency operation. Combat zones are designated by a presidential executive order as areas in which the US armed forces are engaging or have engaged in combat. There are currently three such combat zones (including the airspace above each):

- Arabian peninsula areas, beginning January 17, 1991: the Persian Gulf, the Red Sea, the Gulf of Oman, the part of the Arabian Sea north of latitude 10° north and west of longitude 68° east, the Gulf of Aden, and the countries of Bahrain, Iraq, Kuwait, Oman, Qatar, Saudi Arabia, and the United Arab Emirates
- Kosovo area, beginning March 24, 1999—Federal Republic of Yugoslavia (Serbia and Montenegro), Albania, the Adriatic Sea, and the Ionian Sea north of the 39th parallel
- Afghanistan, beginning September 19, 2001

In general, the deadlines for performing certain actions applicable to taxes are extended for the period of the service member's service in the combat zone, plus 180 days after the last day in the combat zone. This extension applies to the filing and payment of income taxes that would have been due on April 15.

Members of the US armed forces who perform military service in an area outside a combat zone qualify for suspension-of-time provisions if their service is in direct support of military operations in the combat zone and they receive special pay for duty subject to hostile fire or imminent danger as certified by the Department of Defense (DoD).

The deadline-extension provisions apply not only to members serving in the US armed forces (or individuals serving in support thereof) in a combat zone but to their spouses as well, with two exceptions: (1) if you are hospitalized in the United States as a result of injuries received while serving in a combat zone, the deadline-extension provisions will not apply to your spouse, and (2) the deadline-extension provisions for a spouse do not apply for any tax year beginning more than two years after the date of the termination of the combat zone designation.

Filing individual income tax returns for your dependent children is not required while your husband is in the combat zone. Instead, these returns will be timely if filed on or before the deadline for filing your joint income tax return under the applicable deadline extensions. When filing your children's individual income tax returns, put "COMBAT ZONE" in red at the top of those returns.

TAX EXCLUSIONS

The Combat Zone Tax Exclusion

If you serve in a combat zone as an enlisted person or as a warrant officer (including as a commissioned warrant officer) for any part of a month, all your military pay received for military service that month is excluded from your gross income. For commissioned officers, the monthly exclusion is capped at the highest enlisted pay, plus any hostile-fire or imminent-danger pay received.

Military pay received by enlisted personnel who are hospitalized as a result of injuries sustained while serving in a combat zone is excluded from gross income for the period of hospitalization. Commissioned officers have a similar exclusion, limited to the maximum enlisted-pay amount per month. These exclusions from gross income for hospitalized enlisted personnel and commissioned officers end two years after the date of termination of their service in the combat zone.

Annual leave payments to enlisted members of the US armed forces upon discharge from service are excluded from gross income to the extent the annual leave was accrued during any month in any part of which the member served in a combat zone. If you are a commissioned officer, a portion of the annual leave payment you receive for leave accrued during any month in any part of which you served in a combat zone may be excluded. The annual leave payment is not excludable to the extent it exceeds the maximum enlisted-pay amount for the month of service to which it relates, less the amount of military pay already excluded for that month. Although received in a month that you were outside the combat zone, a reenlistment bonus is excluded from gross income because you completed the necessary action for entitlement to the reenlistment bonus in a month during which you served in the combat zone.

A recent law change makes it possible for members of the military to count tax-free combat pay when figuring how much they can contribute to a Roth or traditional individual retirement account (IRA). Before this change, members of the military whose earnings came from tax-free combat pay were often barred from putting money into an IRA because taxpayers usually must have taxable earned income. Taxpayers choosing to put money into a Roth IRA don't need to report these contributions on their individual tax returns. Roth contributions are not deductible, but distributions, usually after retirement, are normally tax-free. Income limits and other special rules apply.

CHANGING TAX WITHHOLDINGS

You may want to change your income tax withholdings. You can do this using myPay (https://mypay.dfas.mil) or by contacting your human resources or pay office and stating how much you want withheld.

THRIFT SAVINGS PLAN

The Thrift Savings Plan (TSP) is a retirement savings plan with special tax advantages for federal government employees and service members. Participation is optional, and service members must join TSP while they are still serving in the military. TSP is similar to traditional 401(k) plans often sponsored by private employers; contributions to TSP accounts are not taxed at the time they are made, but distributions from the accounts are generally subject to income tax at the time of withdrawal. Veterans who do not sign up for TSP while in service cannot join the plan after leaving the military. TSP contributions are subject to certain limitations. Detailed information about TSP is available at http://www. tsp.gov.

FINANCIAL COUNSELING

Money issues probably cause more arguments between married couples than anything else; this is true even for nonmilitary families. The issues can be so serious and cause such friction that they lead to separation and divorce. Often the difficulties have to do not with how much money the couple has but with how it should be spent.

It used to be that a married couple could get by with one partner working and the other staying at home. Unfortunately, times and the economic climate have changed, and now both partners have to work in order to earn enough to pay all the bills. One partner's becoming unemployed can cause a serious financial crunch. Many other situations can also get out of hand. One partner may run up a massive credit card debt. One may want to save every penny, whereas the other wants to spend. One may insist on having a separate bank account and refuse to disclose how much is in it. As a couple you may enjoy eating out and not realize just how much it is costing you every month. All of these scenarios can quickly become a recipe for disaster.

Two things are essential for sound financial management as a couple: communication and budgeting. You must talk honestly about your financial situation and shared expectations, agree on an appropriate budget, and stick to it. If you find you can't do this, you probably need to seek financial counseling.

Married couples shouldn't have secrets, especially over money. Sit down and work out a financial road map for your future. Where do you want to be in ten, twenty, or thirty years' time? Do you want to own a home? Do you want to have money set aside for the children's college fund or as a retirement nest egg? If your answer to any of these questions is yes, try to work out a time frame to achieve these goals. That will determine how much you need to save. Then list all your household expenses. Compare the total with how much is coming in. Do you have any money left over to save? If not, where can you make cuts? What lifestyle changes can you make to reduce spending in order to achieve your long-term goals?

That is where budgeting comes in. Budgeting entails not just managing your money but introducing ways to make it go further. Coupons can add up to hundreds of dollars in grocery savings over a year. Commissaries overseas will even accept them up to six months after their expiry date. You can join a discount warehouse and buy in bulk. If you don't want to buy twenty-four toilet paper rolls at a time, split your shopping with friends so that you all save. Also, pay your bills early rather than waiting until the last minute and accidentally incurring late penalties.

Another great way to budget is to plan your week's meals and to buy only those items when you do your weekly shopping. This prevents impulse purchases and the temptation to eat out. Packed lunches are cheaper than restaurant meals. Remember that all the small savings add up to big savings.

Another important element of budgeting is to ensure that you both have your own money to do with as you wish. It does not have to be a huge amount, but you should agree on how much each of you should get to spend however you like.

Sound financial management is an ongoing process. Revisit your financial strategy every year or so. Are you still on track? Have your circumstances changed? If so, how has this impacted your budget planning, and what changes do you need to make to get back on track?

Although both of you must know what bills need paying, it makes sense for one person to manage household expenses, write checks, and so on. If one partner is deployed, it is even more important for the other partner to do this. Keep all the bills and other financial documents together in a secure place. Keeping a separate file for all items you will need for your annual tax filing will save you a lot of trouble later on.

Discuss upcoming expenditures and jointly agree that they are justified. If you need to consult a financial advisor or tax preparer, go as a couple so that you can both ask questions and express opinions. If you still have issues over finances, you should seek help. In the first instance, you can speak to an on-base financial adviser, your bank manager, or a tax preparer. Alternatively, you can go to http://www.consumer. gov, which provides advice on a wide range of financial issues. If you still need help, you can turn to many resources, from financial and marriage councilors to nonprofit financial and credit-counseling organizations.

FINANCIAL PLANNING

All families must make plans for the future (short and long range). Most families have at one time or another faced challenges. Some of these challenges may be associated with meeting the needs of a special-needs family member. Families must plan for the time their special needs children are no longer eligible for some services because of their age. Exit from the public school system is a major transition point for families.

Financial planning involves many complex, emotional issues, especially for families with a member with disabilities. Challenging as it may be, planning can generate some realistic goals for the support of the special-needs family member when the parent or caregiver is no longer able to provide care.

Although financial-planning services can be very expensive in the civilian world, the services offered through Personal Financial Management (PFM) Program offices, Military OneSource, and the Military and Family Life Counseling (MFLC) Program are free of charge. Service members, DoD civilians, and their family members seeking financial counseling through Military OneSource or the MFLC program may receive up to twelve sessions. For those unable to attend face-to-face meetings, Military OneSource arranges telephone and online consultations.

Per DoD policy, the service branches are required to make personal financial-management programs, as well as financial-planning and financial-counseling services, available to service members and their families.

BRANCH SUPPORT SERVICES

Army

- Army Emergency Relief (AER): AER (www.aerhq.org) is a nonprofit organization that assists soldiers and their family members by providing emergency financial assistance, when there is a valid need, in the form of interest-free loans, grants, or a combination of the two.
- Army National Guard Consumer Affairs and Financial Assistance: The Army National Guard program provides financial education for soldiers, civilians, and their families through classes, training, and information. More information on available classes can be found through the National Guard Family Assistance Centers (https://www. jointservicessupport.org/fp/Default.aspx).

- Army OneSource Financial Readiness: Army OneSource (http:// www.myarmyonesource.com) is the website of Army Community Service (ACS), the organization that provides family programs and services to members of the army. This website assists soldiers, civilians, and their families by providing budgeting and planning calculators, links to information on retirement planning, and online financial training, as well as a link to an Internet application that creates a graphic display of a visitor's financial profile.
- Army Reserve Family Programs: Army Reserve Family Programs' Financial Readiness Program (https://www.arfp.org/index.php/ programs/financial-readiness) assists and educates soldiers and their families by providing information on financial planning, financial-readiness training, the TSP, and taxes.

Marine Corps

- Marine Corps Personal Financial Management: The PFM Program (http://www.mccs-sc.com/support/pfmp.asp) provides eligible personnel with education, training, counseling, information, and referrals for personal financial issues.
- Marine Corps Financial Fitness Online Resource Center: This website (http://www.humtech.com/htoffice/website/sites/financial) provides interactive financial tools and information to assist marines and their families in controlling their finances. Topics include financial planning, saving and investing, banking, credit decisions, using credit cards wisely, applying for credit, managing debt, and a "financial fitness checkup" application.
- Navy-Marine Corps Relief Society (NMCRS): NMCRS (http://www. nmcrs.org) is a private, nonprofit organization that provides financial, educational, and other assistance to members of the navy and marines, eligible family members, and survivors, when a valid need exists. NMCRS provides interest-free loans and grants to sailors, marines, and their families to meet emergency financial needs. NMCRS also provides financial education services such as budget counseling.

Navy

- Fleet and Family Support Center (FFSC) Personal Financial Management: The FFSC PFM program (http://www.navylifepnw.com/site/252/Financial-Management.aspx) assists members of the navy family by providing information, classes, training, and counseling to combat financial mismanagement, as well as proactive training to prepare sailors and their families for future financial challenges.
- Navy–Marine Corps Relief Society (NMCRS): NMCRS (http://www.nmcrs.org) is a private, nonprofit organization that provides financial, educational, and other assistance to members of the navy and marines, eligible family members, and survivors, when a valid need exists. NMCRS provides interest-free loans and grants to sailors, marines, and their families to meet emergency financial needs. NMCRS also provides financial education services such as budget counseling.

Air Force

- Air Force Community: The Air Force Community website (http://www.military.com/Community/Home/1,14700,AIRFRC,00.html) provides information and links on a number of financial-readiness topics, including credit and money management, home and car buying, personal finance and investing, tax information, and emergency financial assistance.
- Air Force Aid Society (AFAS): AFAS (http://www.afas.org) is a private, nonprofit organization that provides emergency financial assistance to airmen and their family members. AFAS provides grants and interest-free loans to airmen and their families who demonstrate an emergency financial need for essential costs, such as basic living expenses, medical care, funeral expenses, respite care, vehicle repairs, assistance with other emergencies, pay or allotment problems, and assistance to surviving dependents.
- "Air Force Compensation Fact Sheet": This fact sheet (http://www.af.mil/Portals/1/documents/aboutus/2013%20Benefits%20Fact%20Sheet.pdf) provides information on the benefits, entitlements, and opportunities available through an air force career. The fact sheet also contains Internet links associated with each topic, providing additional valuable information.

Coast Guard

- Coast Guard Mutual Assistance (CGMA): CGMA (http://www. cgmahq.org) is a private, nonprofit organization that provides financial assistance to members of the coast guard community during times of need. CGMA provides persons associated with the coast guard, who demonstrate a financial need, with interest-free loans, personal grants, and confidential financial-counseling and referral services.

FEDERAL AND STATE PROGRAMS WITH BENEFITS FOR SPECIAL-NEEDS FAMILIES

The federal, state, and local governments offer programs designed to aid disabled children and to ensure they receive the medical and educational assistance they need. Military families may use these benefits to augment TRICARE benefits, and several are listed here.

Supplemental Security Income

Supplemental Security Income (SSI) is a monthly payment to low-income individuals with few resources who are disabled, blind, or sixty-five or older. Children may qualify. If you think you or your child might qualify, visit your nearest Social Security office or call the Social Security Administration at (800) 772-1213.

Medicaid

Medicaid is a program that pays for health care for some low-income individuals and families with few resources. Military families struggling with the cost of care for a disabled family member should apply for Medicaid. Benefits may exceed those offered by TRICARE. To apply, go to http://www.cms.hhs.gov.

Medicare

Medicare is a basic health insurance program for Americans over the age of sixty-five and those with disabilities. Qualification for Medicare is based on the Medicare tax paid through work; however, a worker's spouse, minor children, and disabled adult children may also qualify. To learn more, contact http://www.medicare.gov.

Food Stamps and Women, Infants, and Children

Food stamps and Women, Infants, and Children (WIC) are programs designed to provide low-income families with a nutritious diet. Eligibility is based on income and resources. TRICARE manages a WIC program for active-duty family members who are overseas. For information about these nutrition programs, contact http://www.fns.usda.gov.

13

EMPLOYMENT

UNDEREMPLOYMENT OF MILITARY SPOUSES

Frequent relocation, extended deployments, and other unique aspects associated with the military lifestyle can create significant career and employment challenges for military spouses. Wives of military personnel are less likely to be employed than civilian wives, and those who are employed earn significantly less than their civilian counterparts. Spouses of Reservists have also reported difficulty maintaining full-time employment during a spouse's deployment due to child-care issues.

The average age of active-duty military spouses is 31.9. Of the 711,375 active-duty spouses, 66 percent are already in the workforce. According to a September 2008 Department of Defense (DoD) survey, 84 percent of all military spouses have at least some college education, 25 percent hold a bachelor's degree, and 10 percent hold advanced degrees. The majority of military spouses work outside the home to supplement their family income and wish to stay in their current career of choice regardless of relocation. Of military spouses surveyed, 77 percent report wanting or needing to work. Furthermore, 93 percent of the military spouse population is female, and recent studies reveal the extent of the disparity in pay: the overall wage gap between civilian and military wives is 42 percent. This gap represents both lower workforce participation by military wives and lower earnings for employment. In households that moved the year prior to the survey, a common situation in the military, the wage gap rises to over 47 percent.

The challenge is to reduce the barriers that currently prevent military spouses from maintaining a career or employment on a normal progression path regardless of relocation. The lack of broad-based reciprocity among the states in recognizing professional licenses or certificates held by military spouses creates a significant barrier to employment. Additionally, frequent moves result in military spouses incurring high costs for recertification and increased delays before they are able to work due to state licensing requirements in fields such as teaching and medical services. Finally, employers may need more exposure to the benefits of hiring military spouses.

DoD assists with spousal education counseling for all ranks and provides stipends for those pursuing portable career opportunities for entry-level ranks, usually with six years of service or less. Specifically, the Military Spouse Career Advancement Accounts program is focused on E-1 to E-5, W-1 to W-2, and O-1 to O-2 ranks for financial assistance to encourage spouses working on two-year degrees, licenses, and certifications. The Departments of Education and Veterans Affairs works with DoD to assist Military Spouse Career Advancement Account education counselors to help military spouses maximize federal financial aid options, including assistance with GI Bill and Pell grants.

FINDING A JOB AS A MILITARY SPOUSE

Finding a job is difficult enough with the current state of the economy, and it only gets harder if you keep relocating because of permanent changes of station (PCSs). If you work for a national or multinational company with lots of offices, you may be able continue working with your current employer at your new location. Although some jobs are almost recession-proof—teaching, nursing, and so on—getting hired for other jobs can be a challenge. One obstacle is deployment. Many employers might be reluctant to hire you if they think your partner is likely to be deployed, leaving you to look after the home and family and unable to continue with your job responsibilities. The fact that your partner may suddenly be posted to another base is also a handicap because some employers feel it is a waste of time training you for a job if you are not likely to be with them very long.

If you want to find work, however, as a military spouse you have a lot of resources at your disposal. There are opportunities to work on base, which is more convenient. There are also off-base jobs, but many bases are in remote areas, and transport could be a problem. Also, the more remote the area, the fewer the jobs available in any case.

For jobs on base, contact the family-support center to ask how to get in touch with the employment-assistance office, which will have information about job opportunities on and off base, as well as how to apply for federal positions. Let everyone know you are looking for a job. Your friends may hear about an opportunity and pass it on. For off-base jobs, contact the local labor office, scan the local newspapers—their websites often post jobs before they appear in print—and send your résumé around to prospective employers. One way to test the water is to register with a temp agency. Lots of temp jobs lead to permanent employment; plus, they give you an opportunity to decide whether you like working for the company as much as they give the company a chance to test your competencies.

Depending on your skills, there are lots home-based jobs, provided you have a computer and an Internet connection. Opportunities in this area include translation and transcription services, bookkeeping, data entry, call-center services, and so on. Be careful, though, as lots of scams involve working from home, so check your prospective employer out carefully.

Consider going back to school or taking training courses to qualify for more jobs. The DoD offers tuition assistance for military spouses, and there are many on- and offline training and continuing education opportunities.

THE RÉSUMÉ

To apply for almost any job, you will need a résumé, and it is good idea to write one as early as possible. Doing so will allow you to think about your strengths, skills, experience, and qualifications, and the exercise should help you crystalize what jobs you think you are best suited for.

In the current job market, managers receive dozens of resumes. They do not have time to read lengthy listings of skills and complete life histories. For them, less is more. Here are some tips on creating the most effective resumes:

- Know the goal. You want your résumé to motivate employers to call you in for an interview. Then, during your interview, you can discuss your background in as much detail as the employer desires.
- Focus on skills. Employers are more interested in what you can do than in what you want to do. Today's resumes emphasize skills, allowing the employer to compare your skills with those required for the job. (Remember, volunteering is considered real work experience, so don't forget to include appropriate volunteer work when preparing your résumé.) Writing a skills-oriented résumé is easier after you have completed a skills assessment.
- Don't fuss over format. Don't get hung up on which type of résumé to use—functional, chronological, or whatever. Most employers appreciate a job history that tells them what you did and when. You should also state your accomplishments. Again, performing a skills assessment will help you do this.
- Create a scannable résumé. More and more, companies are scanning—rather than reading—resumes, especially if they get a large number of them. Search online to learn how to make your résumé scannable. Research the company. Use its language where you can.

There is no perfect résumé, but you have to feel comfortable with the format you choose and be familiar with what you have written. The employer will use your résumé as the basis for asking detailed questions during your interview.

Tip: Create a one-minute verbal résumé that quickly highlights your experience and skills. Then practice delivering your one-minute résumé aloud until you're comfortable. This will give you the confidence to answer the "Tell me something about yourself" interview question.

FINDING A JOB

Once you decide on your areas of interest, you then have to find out what jobs are available in those areas. There are scores of online job-search sites, such as America's Job Bank, Monster, Career Builder, and so on. Get your résumé out to as many prospective employers as possible.

Your local public and military libraries can be excellent sources of job-search information. Most information of interest to job seekers is located in the reference section. Most public and military libraries offer access to the Internet. Helpful library resources include the following:

- O°NET Online (http://online.onetcenter.org) provides detailed descriptions of most occupations.
- The Encyclopedia of Associations (http://library.dialog.com/bluesheets/html/bl0114.html) addresses of professional and industry associations.
- Dun and Bradstreet and Standard and Poor's Register of Corporations both offer information on individual companies and organizations. As no websites are available for these resources, check the reference section of your local library.
- The *Occupational Outlook Handbook* (http://www.bls.gov/oco/home.htm) addresses the projected needs for various occupations. It may help you choose a career or open the door to a new one.

Libraries also offer newspapers, trade journals, magazines, audio and video cassettes, and computer software packages that aid in career identification and planning. You may also find information on state training, employment, and apprenticeship programs, as well as statistics regarding employment availability, economic climate, and cost of living. Your librarian can show you where to find these resources and how to use them.

Fraternal military associations and veterans' services organizations are good sources of employment information, assistance, and services. Many provide their own job referral and registration services; others sponsor events such as job fairs to expose you to prospective employers. All provide networking opportunities to learn about job requirements and opportunities.

You can sign up with local employment agencies, visit job fairs, and search the local paper's jobs section. Talk to family, friends, and church members to see if they know of any job opportunities. If you are super qualified, hire a headhunter to find a job for you.

Consider temp work as an option. Temping allows you to work on your terms, earn some money, and still have time to look around and attend interviews. Employers are quick to recognize the talents of a good temp, and a lot move into full-time employment this way.

For part-time work, check out the help-wanted ads or look for signs in the windows of retail stores and offices. If you see an ad saying help wanted, check it out, submit an application, and keep your fingers crossed that you get a call.

If you are new to an area where your military spouse has been posted, consider an entry-level job even if you are overqualified for it. It will help you get a foot in the door. Once your experience shines through, you can start to work your way up the corporate ladder.

Another way to get a foot in the door is to volunteer. Many companies offer unpaid internships, and several agencies have volunteer opportunities that could lead to full-time positions.

If it has been some time since you held a job, think about going back to school either full- or part-time to brush up on your skills or acquire new qualifications. Even if you do find work, consider further education. Many employers will allow you time off to study, and some will even pay for your courses if the end results will benefit the company.

If you have an entrepreneurial spirit, consider starting your own business. You could teach art classes or give music lessons, provide child care or babysitting, or do medical transcriptions at home. Bear in mind, however, that people take the plunge into entrepreneurship for many reasons, but not all reasons are the right reasons for opening a business. The following are the most common reasons people consider business ownership as a career:

- They want to be their own boss. Although this is the number one reason given by new entrepreneurs when making the change from employee to self-employed, there are a few important things to consider. Without a boss watching over you, do you have the self-discipline to get things done, to do them right, and to finish them on time? Without a boss to blame, are you willing to take responsibility for mistakes and fix problems yourself? If you eliminate the demands of your boss, will you be able to handle demands from customers and clients, suppliers and vendors, partners, and even yourself?

- They are tired of working nine to five. As an entrepreneur, you can usually set your own schedule, but that does not necessarily mean shorter hours. Many entrepreneurs put in twelve to eighteen hours per day, six or seven days a week. Are you ready to work that hard? Is your drive for entrepreneurial success strong enough to get you through the long hours? You may be able to sleep in and work in the comfort of your home in your fuzzy slippers on occasion, but probably not initially and probably not all the time.
- They are looking for an exciting challenge. Entrepreneurship is full of decisions that can affect your company's success. Every day is a new adventure, and you can learn from your mistakes as well as from your successes. Many successful entrepreneurs claim they are adrenaline junkies, motivated by the excitement of business ownership. That excitement requires taking risks, however, and you must know your own tolerance for risk. Entrepreneurship, as exciting as it may be, means putting everything on the line for your business. Sound too risky to you? Or does it sound like just the adventure you are craving.
- They want to make more money. Entrepreneurship can be an escape from structured pay charts and minimal growth opportunities, and as a small business owner, you benefit directly from your hard work. Despite the potential for big payoffs, however, entrepreneurs sometimes have to for work months—even years— before they begin to see those profits. Oftentimes, they take a pay cut when they start out on their own. Are you willing to sacrifice your current level of pay until your business becomes a success?
- They really want to become an entrepreneur. This is perhaps the most important reason people should undertake entrepreneurship. Entrepreneurship takes time, energy, and money, but it also takes heart. It must be something you want to do in order to succeed because it requires drive and motivation, even in the face of setbacks. If you are considering entrepreneurship just because you haven't found anything else that suits you, make sure you are

honest with yourself about whether you are ready to be an entrepreneur.

ASSESS YOUR SKILLS

Do your skills apply to entrepreneurial success? Many of the skills
needed in entrepreneurship are associated with the military, including
the following:

- Leadership
- Ability to work and get along with all types of people
- Ability to work under pressure and meet deadlines
- Ability to give directions and delegate
- Good planning and organizational skills
- Problem-solving ability
- Familiarity with personnel administration and record keeping
- Flexibility and adaptability
- Capacity for self-direction
- Initiative
- Strong work habits
- Standards of quality and a commitment to excellence

Think about your other skills that might help you become a successful
entrepreneur. Are you good with money with a strong credit history?
Do you have a high energy level? Do you see problems as challenges
and enjoy trying new methods? Listing your skills will not only help you
assess yourself as an entrepreneur but might also tell you what kind of
business you should start.

DEFINE YOUR PERSONALITY

Your personality often helps determine what type of work best suits
you. People preferring structure might find the corporate environment
most suitable, whereas creative types might enjoy flexible jobs with
relaxed policies. As with any job, certain personalities thrive in entrepreneurship. Entrepreneurs tend to be

- Goal-oriented
- Independent
- Self-confident
- Innovative and creative
- Strongly committed
- Highly reliable
- Competitive
- Hardworking
- Organized
- Honest
- Tolerant of failure but driven to achieve
- Idea-oriented
- Motivated by challenge
- Courageous
- Persistent
- Adaptable
- Positive

They also tend to be

- Calculated risk-takers
- Problem solvers
- Good managers

Even if you do not have all of these characteristics, you can still be a successful entrepreneur. Every entrepreneur has a blend of skills and strengths. Think about the skills or traits you don't have and learn to overcome any limitations that present obstacles on the road to entrepreneurship.

FINANCING YOUR SMALL BUSINESS

One of the most common mistakes entrepreneurs make is underestimating their business costs and creating a financial plan based on low cost projections. Every entrepreneurial enterprise has different associated costs. For example, establishing a home-based business will entail little to no cost for acquiring office space; renting office space, on the other hand, will entail low to moderate cost, and building an office will involve high cost. Regardless of your specific needs, every entrepreneur must take two cost types into account: start-up costs and recurring costs. Start-up costs are all of the one-time costs required to start your business, such as a security deposit on office space, furniture and equipment purchases, signage, and so forth. Recurring costs are all of the costs you encounter monthly, such as salary and benefit expenses, insurance fees, monthly rent, and so forth.

Once you have figured your costs, determine whether you will need to borrow money to start your business. If you will, there are several different funding options to consider. Each funding source brings with it a series of pros and cons that you should weigh to find a lender to meet your start-up needs.

Option 1: Banks

Banks are usually the first place people look when they want to borrow money. Banks offer a variety of loans and can often advise you as to which type of loan is best for your needs. Some loans, for example, require you to make set payments of both the principal and interest, whereas others require you to pay back only the interest with a lump payment of the entire principal at the end. The obvious advantage of approaching banks for loans is that they are designed for just that purpose. The downside is that if you have a bad credit history or have accumulated debt, it can be difficult to get approval for a loan at most banks. The best way to determine whether bank loans are appropriate for your needs is to do your research: locate the banks in your region, find out what types of loans they offer, and learn what requirements they have for approving loans.

Option 2: Venture Capital Firms

Venture capital firms invest in small companies in return for equity. They look for companies with potential for high growth and high profitability. Although some venture capitalists will invest in companies that are just beginning, they generally seek to fund companies that have been in business for some time so that they can assess progress, growth, and earned revenues. For that reason, acquiring start-up funding from venture capitalists can be very difficult; also, the earlier the stage of investment, the more equity venture capital firms require. If you are serious about acquiring venture capital funds for your business start-up, look for firms that specifically cater to business in the start-up phase. If you have a thorough, viable business plan and your management team has extensive experience fostering rapid growth in small businesses and creating substantial profits, you will have a much greater chance of receiving venture capital funding.

Option 3: Angel Investors

Angel investors are individuals who invest their own money in entrepreneurial ventures in return for equity. Angel investors can be people you do or do not know; they can also work as individuals or as part of an angel group. Angel investors generally invest smaller amounts of money in companies than do venture capitalists, making them an ideal source for funding when you have exhausted funding from your friends, family, and self but are not yet ready to approach a venture capital firm.

Option 4: Partners

In some cases, you can secure funding from current or potential partners seeking a share of the business. The advantages to partner financing are that partners considering investment are already knowledgeable about the business idea and have confidence in its future, and the approval process may be easier than with a bank or lending firm. The decision you as an entrepreneur must make is whether you are willing to give up a portion of your company in order to obtain this funding or you would rather go to banks or other lenders and maintain your control.

Option 5: Friends and Family

Many people warn against the risks of borrowing money from friends and family, but there are also benefits to acquiring loans this way, and it is an extremely popular source of funding for small businesses. Friends and family already know you, your character, and your credit, debt, and financial-management history. Nevertheless, even friends and family considering making a loan should ask to see a business plan to make sure it is well thought-out. Friends and family will likely give you more relaxed terms on which you must pay back loans, and they may not demand interest. The obvious downside to borrowing from friends and family is the potential inability to repay the loan, damaging not only your finances but theirs, as well as your relationship with those individuals.

Option 6: Self-Financing

Self-financing is the most popular form of financing for small business owners, and it can be extremely advantageous when you approach other lenders. Investing your own money and assets into your business demonstrates your faith that your business will succeed. Different forms of self-financing include borrowing against your retirement fund, taking out personal lines of credit, and utilizing a home equity loan. The disadvantage to financing your business this way is that if your business flounders and you are unable to repay the money, you can lose a lot more than your business. Before putting your home on the line for your business or risking your personal credit history, carefully consider whether self-financing is the right option for you.

FRANCHISE OWNERSHIP

If you are considering business ownership but are hesitant to venture out on your own, you may want to consider becoming a franchisee, or franchise owner. Becoming a business owner can be an intimidating process, but when you purchase a franchise, you get a team of support, which includes marketing assistance, human resources tools, and training. Having others committed to your success as a business owner and willing and able to help when you run into problems is just one of the many advantages of franchise ownership.

Advantages of Franchises

- Higher rate of business success: Perhaps the number-one reason people become franchise owners is because franchises have a higher likelihood of succeeding than do traditional start-up businesses. In fact, according to the US Department of Commerce, 95 percent of franchises are still in business after five years. Franchisors (the companies who sell or grant franchises to individuals) evaluate each prospective franchisee and invest in those they think will thrive as franchise owners for their company. They look for specific skills, experience, motivation, financial capacity, and more to choose people who will be able to afford the franchise, follow the business operational model, and become successful.

- Established brand identity: One key advantage of operating a franchise is the ability to give consumers a brand they know, quality they trust, and the consistency they have come to expect. Purchasing a franchise means purchasing the reputation of the brand, an established customer base, and a set of products or services that have been successfully tested in communities. Whereas new business start-ups must work at building a reputation and generating awareness of the product or service they offer, franchises are often preceded by their reputations and can make an immediate impact.

- No dirty work: Perhaps the most difficult challenge new entrepreneurs face when opening a business of their own is the burden of starting from scratch. The tasks involved can be lengthy and expensive. In a franchise system, however, the work has already been done to develop a product or service, identify and reach a target market, build a reputation, and create a replicable business model. Whereas many new business owners spend the first year (or longer!) testing products, sales tactics, and marketing avenues, franchise owners already know exactly what works and how to reach their target audience effectively.

- Business support: Business owners who start their own business take on a great deal of responsibility: they must market to new customers, provide products and services to existing customers, hire employees, and train those employees to do their jobs properly. In other words, new business owners must be sales representatives, accountants, human resource managers, marketing experts, and more. That is a lot of responsibility. Whereas some individuals may thrive in the multiple roles business owners must take on, others need support in some or all of the aspects of business ownership. Franchisees get the support they need in the form of training and even on-site assistance. In addition, most franchisors provide human resources tools, specialized software, marketing materials, and other valuable resources that independent business owners must find or develop for themselves.

- Easier to finance: If you are looking to start a business with less than perfect credit and need to apply for a business loan, a franchise's established history may help you get your financing. Because new business start-ups are extremely risky, banks are often hesitant to hand out loans without a history of business and credit management in a borrower's past. Prospective franchisees applying for a business loan have the advantage of a tested product or service, a successful business model, and a core of support from the franchisor. Banks know that franchises have a higher likelihood of success than other new businesses; as a result, it is often easier to secure a business loan for a franchise than for a business start-up.

Disadvantages of Franchises

Does franchise ownership seem too good to be true? Although there are many advantages to owning a franchise, there are downsides as well. Although these disadvantages may seem minor to some, they may turn others away from the notion of franchise ownership entirely. Read on to learn about the negatives of franchise ownership and decide if it is the path for you.

- Factors beyond your control: The value of a franchise lies in the value of the brand and the brand's reputation. When you purchase a franchise, you must take into account the reputation of the parent company and other branches of the franchise. If, over time, that reputation is damaged by factors beyond your control, the impact on your business can be catastrophic. And because your franchise agreement is a long-term contract, getting out of it may be more difficult than you thought.
- High costs: Many people who pursue franchise ownership do so because they believe the costs associated with franchises will be

lower than those of a traditional start-up business. And for some franchises, that is true; for many others, however, the costs can soar when franchise fees, capital requirements, marketing fees, royalties, and other expenses add up. In fact, one reason that new franchises fail is insufficient funding and a lack of working capital. There are hundreds of reputable, low-cost franchises, but you must know what to look for and be smart from the very beginning.

- Restrictions on business: If you are going into business to be independent, creative, and entrepreneurial, franchise ownership may not be right for you. Franchises are based on previously developed, successfully tested business ideas and plans. Most franchisors impose strict regulations on how individual franchises may operate, and deviations are rarely allowed. Franchise owners, for example, must sell a specific product or service and advertise with specific marketing materials and slogans. Although this may appeal to business owners who are eager for structure and support, others may find this too regimented for their individual business style.

- Reduced profits: One of the greatest appeals of business ownership is that you benefit personally from your hard work, and many people seek entrepreneurship as a way to increase their earnings and have greater control over their financial destiny. Franchise ownership is actually a middle step between the financial freedom of business ownership and the rigid pay structure of other jobs. As a franchise owner, you will see your hard work result directly in higher profits for your business, but most franchisors will require continuous monthly royalty payments equaling 5 to 10 percent of your profits.

FINDING A JOB OVERSEAS

Finding a job overseas can be even more challenging because of differences in language, in qualification requirements, and in general ways of doing things. Do your homework carefully to discover what is available and what you think you are qualified to do. Be flexible: if the job that you would like is not available, consider other options, such as a career change or going back to school. Talk to other spouses about what is available; join discussion groups and the spouses club if there is one. Remember that in some countries spouses of serving military are not allowed to work off the base.

Most overseas bases have commissaries or exchanges as well as civilian and defense contractors who may have open positions. Nearby US bases run by other branches of the military might also have job openings. Check out the Office of Personnel Management website (http://www.opm.gov). You'll be amazed how many federal jobs are posted and how many of them are overseas.

If you do get a job, make sure you comply with the country's tax laws. If employed by a US company, you might be paid in dollars that are exempt from federal taxes. If you are employed by a local company and paid in that country's currency, you will probably be subject to the local tax laws.

There may be opportunities for on-base work, and not necessarily on the base where your spouse is stationed. There are hundreds of civilian jobs on each base. Research which you are suitable for and how to apply if there are vacancies. These jobs fall into two categories: nonappropriated funds (NAF) positions and civil service or appropriated funds (AF) positions. NAF employees support the installation services through programs such as Morale, Welfare, and Recreation. Getting into the federal civil service system may be easier overseas than in the United States, but the process takes time. Almost all federal AF jobs are posted on the Office of Personnel Management site. Be sure to follow the announcement instructions carefully to apply.

Other options include working in the installation exchange or commissary or for a defense contractor working on base. Your installation's contracting office may have a list of contractors. Be sure to check with the installation's Family Employment Readiness Program for information too.

Keep in mind that contractors often offer many types of job opportunities. For example, a contractor who provides computer services may need software engineers as well as accounting clerks. Some defense contractors pay salaries in US dollars, which may be exempt from federal taxes. In other cases, the salaries are paid in host-nation currency, which can be subject to that country's taxes.

MILITARY SPOUSE PREFERENCE PROGRAM

The Military Spouse Preference (MSP) Program is derived from Title 10, USC, Section 1784, "Employment Opportunities for Military Spouses," and applies to spouses of active-duty military members of the US armed forces (including the coast guard) who relocate to accompany their sponsors on PCS moves. The program is intended to lessen the career interruption of spouses who relocate with their military sponsors. MSP is a DoD program. Consequently, it applies only to DoD vacancies. Military spouses are eligible to request MSP regardless of current employment status.

If you are the spouse of an active-duty military member, you may be eligible for MSP, which applies only under the following circumstances:

- The spouse was married to the military sponsor prior to the reporting date for the new assignment.
- The relocation was based on a PCS move and not for separation or retirement.
- The vacancy is within the commuting area of the sponsor's permanent new duty station.
- The spouse is among the "best qualified" and is within reach for selection.

MSP applies if you are ranked among the "best qualified" for a given vacancy, and vacancies are filled from those who make this list. To be rated "best qualified," MSP applicants must take an examination and attain an eligibility rating of eighty or higher, not including points for veterans' preference. MSP does not apply, however, when preference would violate statutes or regulations regarding veterans' preference or nepotism.

Note: Applicants claiming MSP will be required to produce a copy of their military sponsor's PCS orders to substantiate eligibility prior to appointment in the federal service. Failure to provide these orders may result in the cancellation of any pending appointment to a federal service position.

If you can't find employment, consider working from home, either for yourself or for an employer. You could give English-language lessons, or if you have the skills, you could offer music lessons or tutoring in math, science, computers, and so on. You could consider launching your own business, such as child-care or catering services. As mentioned above, there are also opportunities for home-based work for a company doing translation, transcription, data entry, and so on. Before embarking on any of these, however, make sure that you have the necessary permissions under both the installation's regulations and the host countries laws governing jobs, permits, and licenses.

14

COPING WITH LOSS AND DEATH

When military personnel are injured or killed, immediate and permanent disruptions in family life occur. As of March 2013, more than 50,550 American service members had been wounded in action, and more than 6,650 had lost their lives in Operation Enduring Freedom, Operation Iraqi Freedom, and Operation New Dawn. More than 44,700 children experienced a deployed parent's wounding, injury, illness, or death. Of these children, almost half were elementary-school-age; one in four were five years old or younger.

Each deployment-related death is unique. Special measures need to be taken to help a child cope successfully with the loss of a parent.

HELPING INFANTS AND TODDLERS COPE

During times of stress, caregivers can provide an emotional safety net for young children by offering ongoing support, love, and guidance that children need in order to feel safe during times of change. Based on age, gender, experiences, and developmental levels, children respond differently to the death of a parent. Research shows that children age five and younger may display increased behavioral problems and increased clinginess. Caregivers' responses play a critical role in helping children build skills to cope with the trauma and stress they may be experiencing.

Working with very young children comes with unique challenges due to their limited vocabulary and inability to identify and manage their own emotions. Infants and toddlers communicate stress through increased aggression, behavioral regression, sleep changes, withdrawal, whining, crying, and clinginess. Researchers say that changes in behavior are to be expected and may include anger, sadness, feelings of abandonment, anxiety, increased aggression, withdrawal, and confusion. The consistent presence of a caring adult expands opportunities to help the entire family through the changes that come with coping with a death.

Tips for working with infants include the following:

- Establish a secure and trusting relationship. Infants need to be surrounded by people they trust to build healthy relationships in the future.
- Maintain routines to allow for consistency. When everything else is changing in an infant's life, routines create a sense of security.
- Watch for signs of stress that you as parent or guardian may be exhibiting at home. Infants mirror the feelings of the important adults in their lives.

Tips for working with toddlers include the following:

- If toddlers become agitated or disruptive, remain calm and patient. Their behavior could be in response to stress or insecurity they are feeling in other areas of their lives.
- Maintain daily routines. Toddlers like to know what is coming next.
- Expect some regression, such as lapses in potty training. This is a normal response. Work with the child to grow through these setbacks.

Tips for working with preschoolers include the following:

- Help children express emotions in positive ways. Give them words to help them describe what they are feeling.
- Provide opportunities to express feelings through play.
- Display and read books that relate to parental separation and loss.

- Set clear expectations and limits. Children will attempt to test boundaries. It is important that they feel secure in familiar routines and know that the adult will protect them.

Signs to look out for include the following:

- Early school-age children (six to nine years):

  - Anger, fighting, bullying
  - Denial, irritability, self-blame
  - Fluctuating moods, withdrawal
  - Regression to earlier behavior
  - Fear of separation and being alone
  - Physical complaints (stomach-/headaches)
  - School problems (avoidance, academic difficulty, difficulty concentrating)

- Middle-school-age children (nine to twelve years):

  - Children in this age group exhibit the same signs as above but are better able to handle bad news; they should be told as soon as possible after the initial panic subsides
  - As soon as you have a clearer picture about what has happened
  - By you rather than someone else

- Early teens/adolescents (thirteen to eighteen years):

  - Numbing, avoidance of feelings
  - Resentment, loss of trust, guilt, shame
  - Depression, suicidal thoughts
  - Distancing, withdrawal, panic, anxiety
  - Mood swings, irritability, anger
  - Acting out (engaging in risky, antisocial, or illegal behavior), substance abuse
  - Appetite and/or sleep changes
  - Physical complaints or changes
  - Academic decline, refusal to attend school
  - Fear of similar events, illness, death, or the future

LOSS AND GRIEF

Grief is a normal and natural reaction to loss. It is also a natural and necessary part of healing after a loss. People usually grieve when someone they love dies. But a person can also feel grief after losing something meaningful or valuable.

People are often surprised by their reactions when they are grieving. For example, they may be in shock after first learning of the death of a loved one. They may be angry at God, themselves, the person who died, or someone whom they blame for the loss or death. They may also feel guilty about not having done something differently before the person died.

Major losses and death may cause some changes in life, sometimes very significant changes. These changes may include having to parent alone, getting used to single life after divorce, and going back to work. Going through these changes may add more stress, so it's important to have support from others. It's possible to find support by talking to a psychologist, chaplain, or other spiritual advisor, as well as to family members, friends, a health care professional, or other helpful people.

Losses can include the following:

- Divorce or the breakup of an important relationship
- Death of a loved one
- Death of a comrade (combat or noncombat related)
- Loss of a pet
- Loss of a sense of safety
- Loss of meaning and purpose in life
- Loss of physical health or a physical part of oneself
- Loss of ability to relate or connect with others
- Loss of identity
- Loss of self-esteem

Common thoughts, feelings, and reactions caused by loss and grief include

- Denial
- Disbelief or doubt
- Confusion
- Shock

- Sadness
- Yearning or longing
- Anger
- Shame
- Despair
- Guilt
- Regret
- Feelings of emptiness and/or depression
- Difficulty relating to or connecting with others
- Belief that a part of oneself has died
- Hopelessness about the future
- Belief that things aren't as important as they once were
- Tearfulness or a tendency to cry easily
- Restlessness or irritability
- Upset stomach, headaches, or other physical pains
- Worsening of existing health problems or appearance of new physical problems
- Loss of appetite
- Difficulty sleeping or sleeping much more than usual
- Low energy

The grieving period is different for everyone. Personality, as well as family, cultural, spiritual, and religious beliefs and practices, can influence how we respond to loss. It can take many months for the painful feelings and thoughts to ebb. Grief has its own time line. But, over time, grief will begin to abate. A grieving person will likely have good days and bad days. And it's normal and expected that the grief might return out of the blue; that's part of the process. Important dates, like anniversaries and birthdays, can bring back intense feelings of grief.

Grieving usually involves sadness and other feelings related to the loss. The process often entails talking about the loss with other people. However, sometimes people have a hard time grieving for the following reasons:

- It's uncomfortable.
- They were raised to believe that they should never be sad and were told that "crying is for babies."

- They believe that feelings are a sign of weakness or that grieving is only OK at funerals.
- Friends and family tell them, "You have to stay strong and move on with your life."

These mistaken beliefs get in the way of letting the grieving process happen naturally and may result in even worse grief from which it's then harder to recover.

Several warning signs may suggest that a person is having a severe grief reaction and needs help coping. Ignoring the warning signs may prolong the grief and/or make it more difficult. Professionals and groups with expertise can help. It is strongly recommended that a professional provider be contacted immediately if any of the following conditions or warning signs are present:

- Thoughts about or plans to commit suicide or engage in self-harm
- Neglect of self-care, such as eating and taking a shower
- Avoidance of grieving:

  - Not talking about the loss
  - Not being honest about the thoughts and feelings that are occurring since the loss
  - Not talking or thinking about memories related to the loss

- Inability to function for weeks to months after the loss
- Inability to perform work, school, or familial responsibilities

It is hard to accept and work through grief, but not dealing with it can lead to depression. Coping with loss and grief in healthy ways can prevent problems from getting worse. Here are some tips for allowing the grieving process to happen naturally, which will help avoid depression:

- People can be hard on themselves following a loss. In fact, it's OK to grieve. It takes courage to grieve following the loss of someone important.
- Be patient. Take time to grieve. It may not seem possible at first, but with time the pain will ease, and it will be easier to get on with normal activities.

- Join a support group where you can share personal stories with others. It is often helpful to spend time with people who have experienced a similar loss.
- Seek helpful people, such as family, friends, a chaplain, or another spiritual advisor.
- Consult a psychologist, social worker, or other health care professional if the grieving persists.

Even though it can be hard to ask for help, it's important to know that no one has to experience grief alone. It's easy to feel isolated and to think that no one else can possibly understand. However, often other people are going through the same thing or have had a similar experience coping with a loss. They may be having the same thoughts and dealing with the same issues.

Talking about feelings, although uncomfortable, is an important step toward getting past grief. Mental health professionals can offer a private, safe place to talk about grief and assist with the grieving process. It can be hard to ask for help, but health care professionals can provide a safe place to talk about feelings and help with the healing process. Here are a few resources:

- An installation's support services can provide information and support. Support services include a chaplain, a military treatment facility, family advocacy programs, and family centers. Phone numbers can be found in the installation's military directory.
- Talk to command. Check in with a leader about how to handle a stressful situation before it gets out of control. Keeping leadership informed is good practice.
- Make an appointment with a primary care provider to ask about available treatment options and for a referral to a mental health practitioner if that is indicated.
- Military OneSource (http://www.militaryonesource.com; 800-342-9647) provides grief counseling to active-duty military personnel and their families, including members of the Reserves and the National Guard.
- The Tragedy Assistance Program for Survivors (TAPS;http://www.TAPS.org; 800-959-TAPS [8277]) is a nonprofit Veterans Service

Organization providing a wide range of free services to all those affected by the death of a loved one in the armed forces.

- Veterans' centers (http://www.vetcenter.va.gov) offer readjustment counseling for veterans and their families. Staff is available toll-free at (800) 905-4675 (Atlantic) and (866) 496-8838 (Pacific).
- Veterans Administration (VA; http://www.va.gov) medical centers and veterans' centers provide veterans with affordable mental health services. Health insurance companies cover costs, or services cost little or nothing, according to a veteran's ability to pay. The Veterans Health Administration's specialized clinics and programs for posttraumatic stress disorder (PTSD) can provide educational information and diagnostic evaluations concerning PTSD to eligible veterans. Following discharge from a combat zone, veterans who have enrolled for VA services qualify for two years' worth of care for conditions potentially related to their service.
- Local community services can include crisis, mental health, and suicide-prevention centers.
- Find mental health providers locally. Check out http://www.goodtherapy.org/find-mental-health-counselors.html.
- The National Suicide Prevention Lifeline (http://www.suicidepreventionlifeline.org) is available twenty-four hours per day. Call (800) 273-TALK (8255) or (800) SUICIDE (784-2433). Both suicide hotlines will connect the caller to a certified crisis center nearest the location from which the call is placed.

CHILDHOOD GRIEF

Like adults, children and teens may feel intense sadness and loss when a person close to them dies. And like adults, children and teens express their grief in how they behave, what they think and say, and how they feel emotionally and physically. Each child and parent grieves differently, and there is no right or wrong way or correct length of time to grieve.

Some grief reactions cut across children's developmental levels, and children may show their grief in many different ways. For example, bereaved children or teens of any age may sleep or cry more than usual. They may regress and return to earlier behaviors, or they may develop new fears or problems in school. They may complain about aches and pains. They may be angry and irritable, or they may become withdrawn and isolate themselves from family and friends.

Bereaved children may also act in uncharacteristic ways that those around them may not recognize as grief reactions. For example, a quiet toddler may have more tantrums, an active child may lose interest in things he or she used to do, or a studious teen may engage in risky behavior. Whatever a child's age, he or she may feel unrealistic guilt about having caused the death. Sometimes bereaved children take on adult responsibilities and worry about their surviving parent, or they worry about who will care for them if they lose that parent as well. These worries can be especially acute if the surviving parent is also in the military.

TRAUMATIC GRIEF IN MILITARY CHILDREN

The reactions of some children and teens to the death of a parent or someone close to them may be more intense than the common deep sadness and upset of grief. In childhood traumatic grief, children can develop symptoms associated with PTSD. Children of military families may be more likely to experience these more intense reactions if, for example, the death was sudden or traumatic, if it occurred under terrifying circumstances, or if the child witnessed the death or learned of horrific details surrounding it. Also, although posttraumatic stress reactions may occur after a deployed parent has been killed in combat, symptoms can also appear when death comes weeks or months after an initial combat injury, even if the child or adults in the child's life have anticipated the death.

Not all children who experience the death of someone special under traumatic circumstances develop traumatic grief. However, in some cases, children may develop symptoms of PTSD that interfere with their ability to grieve and to call up comforting memories of the person who died. Traumatic grief may also interfere with everyday activities, such as being with friends and doing schoolwork. PTSD symptoms in children with traumatic grief can include the following:

- Reliving aspects of the person's death or having intrusive thoughts—for example, experiencing nightmares about the death, not being able to stop thinking about how the person died, imagining how much the person suffered, or imagining rescuing the person and reversing the outcome
- Avoiding reminders of the death or of the person who died—for example, by avoiding pictures of the deceased person or news about the military, by not visiting the cemetery or not wanting to remember or talk about the person, or by feeling emotionally numb
- Experiencing increased arousal—for instance, being nervous and jumpy, having trouble sleeping, having poor concentration, being irritable or angry, being "on alert," being easily startled, and developing new fears

In general, if it becomes apparent that your child or teen is having very upsetting memories, avoiding activities or feelings, or experiencing physical, emotional, or learning problems, he or she may be having a traumatic grief reaction. You may wish to seek help or counseling for your child or teen if grief reactions seem to continue without any relief, if they appear for the first time after an initial period of relative calm, if they get worse, or if they interfere with your child's spending time with friends, going to school, or enjoying activities.

Since 2001, thousands of military children have had parents killed in combat operations in Iraq and Afghanistan. Many other children have had siblings, cousins, and other relatives die in war. Children who lose military family members during wartime are similar to other grieving children in many ways. Like other American children, they come from families of varying diversity and configuration. However, those who care for or work with grieving military children should be aware of certain unique aspects of military family loss.

For one thing, many military parents may have been deployed for extended periods before dying. Because of this, children who have already been dealing with their parent's physical absence for some time may not experience any immediate changes in their day-to-day lives when they learn of the death. Their past experience with the person's absence may make it hard for some children to accept the permanence of their loss or to take part in their family's grieving.

Military deaths during wartime are also public events, which diminishes the privacy that families usually have when grieving. This lack of privacy can make it more difficult for family members and other caring adults to protect children from unexpected or unwanted intrusions into family mourning. A family may prefer that the death be kept private. In such circumstances, communities need to be mindful and respectful of the bereaved family's wishes.

However, even well-meaning individuals can encroach on desired privacy. Media can be particularly intrusive and sometimes even aggressive—for example, when they arrive unexpectedly at homes or funeral services where bereaved children are present. Responsible family members should be encouraged to set boundaries for intruders or well-intentioned individuals to protect children's interests.

Given the political nature of war and the public nature of military deaths, military children may feel confused by how the death is reported or framed within their families, at school, or in the community. A child who overhears others saying that a parent died "needlessly" in an "unnecessary" war may find it much harder to accept and integrate that death than a child whose parent's death is considered "noble" or "heroic." Also, older teenagers may have their own opinions and feelings about war, and these may either ease or complicate their grief over the loss of their loved one.

Depending on how they are perceived, military deaths may be experienced differently by families and communities. Many military children lose loved ones to combat, and in some cases, the body may be disfigured—for example, if death was caused by an improvised explosive device. Many other deaths occur as the result of accidents, risk-related behaviors, medical illnesses, or suicide. Any of these circumstances can further complicate children's reactions and affect their ability to integrate the loss.

From the arrival of the uniformed death-notification team through the funerary honors, military traditions and rituals surround the death of fallen service members. Because participation is voluntary, family members can decide to what degree to incorporate military ritual into their mourning process. Many children and families find these military ceremonies comforting.

However, even when families elect military funeral services, younger children may be confused or frightened by the events, so you should prepare them for what will happen. For example, they should be told in age-appropriate terms where the body will be (for example, in a casket), how people will react (for example, "People will be in uniform, and some will be crying"), and what the children may do (for example, "Your aunt will be there to keep you company and play with you if you get tired of sitting").

Bereaved families who live on military installations will likely be surrounded by community support and interest. Families typically appreciate this, but they should also feel free to choose what is most helpful for them. At the same time, the combination of sadness and fear brought about by a death can be challenging for bereaved military children when they are with other military classmates who are not bereaved. Conversely, Reserve and National Guard families or others who live outside military communities may find that their unique grief is less understood by others around them, and children who attend schools with few other military children may find themselves feeling isolated in their experience of loss. They may feel that others do not understand what they are going through.

After a parent dies, military children often experience additional stresses that further magnify the effects of their loss. For example, they may have to move from the military installation to a new community where those around them are unaware of their military identity or of the nature of their family member's death. In such circumstances, military children may find themselves suddenly no longer "military"; thus, they lose that identity in addition to having to leave behind friends and familiar activities, schools, and child-care providers. Once in their new community, children and families must also decide what they want to share with others about their lost loved one and their military-related experiences.

HELPING YOUR CHILD

The following are tactics for helping your child through the grieving process:

- Provide a sense of security. After a death, your child might cling to you more, have trouble separating, or be extra fearful of losing you too. When separating, reassure your child in concrete ways about when you will return. For example, you might say, "I will pick you up right after your lunch." Keep up with predictable, familiar, comforting, and reassuring routines and activities as much as possible. This helps children feel safer and more secure at a time when everything may feel different and unsettled. Be mindful that because children often react to stressful situations through their behavior rather than with words, discipline may need to be flexible. Rather than just punishing problem behaviors, explore the reasons for them and understand that they may be related to grief.

- Be patient. This may be hard. Your child's grief may make his or her behavior and needs more challenging, especially when you are managing your own grief at the same time. Remember that everyone is adjusting to lots of change in the household and daily life, so there may be ups and downs. Your child may need more frequent praise and positive reinforcement. Give extra hugs and comfort.
- Pay attention to what your child is communicating through his or her words and behaviors. Although some children will be able to verbalize what they are experiencing, others (especially the very young) might not know what they are feeling or how to express it in words. Be open to your child's reactions and questions. Listen to what your child is telling you in words but also note changes in behavior or physical complaints.
- Encourage expression of feelings. Drawing, writing, playing, acting, and talking can help your child get feelings out. Help your child identify the thoughts and feelings that go with his or her behavior.
- Know that it can be challenging to separate grief reactions from other feelings and behaviors. Children have their own styles and personalities and therefore have individualized ways of grieving. For example, some may hide their feelings; others may pick fights. In addition, as life continues, children face other life stresses, such as not getting picked for a team or worrying about tests. In general, if your child's reactions or behaviors become more intense or continue over time, consider seeking guidance to help distinguish grief reactions from other parenting and childhood difficulties.

- Watch out for reminders. Keep an eye out for military-related reminders that may be difficult for your child. A child who gets overly upset or angry at seeing another person in uniform or on hearing about a war may need additional support or professional help to learn how to cope with painful events or images.
- Support your child in maintaining a connection to the person who died. Sharing stories, photos, and memories can help your child keep the lost loved one as an ongoing part of his or her life and identity. As you share memories, follow and respect your child's lead. If he or she does not seem interested in talking or hearing about the person who died, don't push it. Try again another time. If your child becomes continually or intensely distressed when talking about the person who died or seems indifferent or shut down, consider talking to a professional for guidance.
- Provide explanations. Even the youngest child needs an explanation of what has happened. Use simple language and follow your child's cue as to how much information to offer at any given time. Be prepared to repeat the information. If your child is very young, it might take many years and many conversations for him or her to fully understand that the person who died is not coming back and that this is not the child's fault.
- Keep other important adults informed of what your child is experiencing. Partner with child-care and preschool providers, teachers, coaches, youth leaders, and other adults to support your child by helping them to understand the connection between grief and your child's feelings and behaviors.
- Be an advocate for your child at school. Discuss the impact of the death on the child with important school staff. Caregivers and teachers should work together to come up with an age-appropriate plan to help students who feel upset during the day or who worry about caregivers' safety when apart. Be aware if the school tries to diagnose your child with learning, emotional, and/or attention disabilities instead of recognizing the effects of grief. You may need to talk with school personnel about adjusting their expectations for schoolwork. You can refer school personnel to another fact sheet, "Traumatic Grief in Military Children: Information for School Personnel."

- Promote involvement. Participation in a project or organization that helps others will allow your child to feel needed and connected. Doing something as a family to honor the deceased's interests affirms life and can help counteract feelings of helplessness.
- Form peer support groups or play groups. Children want to feel normal and to know that they are not alone. Forming bonds with other children who are dealing and coping with similar situations can be extremely beneficial. There are often support groups around military bases, as well as TAPS seminars and Good Grief Camps held regionally across the country. These are a perfect place to meet others.
- If you have more than one child, be sure to spend one-on-one time with each so that no one feels left out and everyone feels special. This can be as simple as going to the park or baking together.
- Be sensitive to the changes in your child's life related to the death. Military deaths are associated with many other changes that can impact your child's grieving process. For example, if your family must now move from a military base to a civilian home, or if your child changes schools, it's important to help the child with his or her good-byes and to plan for the transition. Arranging and encouraging visits with old friends and working with a new community to get the child involved in activities and groups constitute important aspects of adjusting to the death.
- Be mindful of the interaction of grief and other issues. Consider the child's and the family's individual situation. For example, if a child had prior mental health problems or if the parents were divorced, the child may be experiencing additional feelings or encountering new living situations that need attention. Future relationships with extended family members of the person who died should also be handled with sensitivity to minimize additional loss for the child.
- Consider the differing needs of children who are bereaved at different ages. Children who were infants, toddlers, or even preschoolers at the time of the death will experience it differently than older children will. In particular, very young children will not have the same depth of relationship as an older child or spouse

and will not have a store of memories to draw upon. Surviving parents can help by telling stories and providing details in words and pictures to help establish the person's presence and give the child a sense of history. As your young child gets older, he or she may ask specific questions to help gather more memories.

- Help your child over time. As time goes by and your child becomes older, new situations will stir up grief reactions. For example, an older child who seemed to have been in good spirits may become upset when he or she realizes that the person who died will not be there to attend an important event, such as a sports competition or prom. Such reactions are normal and to be expected. Be prepared to revisit the loss with your child and seek professional support as needed.

TAKING CARE OF YOURSELF

The following are some tips for taking care of yourself:

- Get enough sleep, exercise, and time for yourself. You may believe that caring for your children is the only thing that matters now, but in order to do this, you also have to take care of yourself. Modeling self-care is one of the most important things you can do for your children. It assures them that you intend to stay healthy for a long time to come.
- Keep caring, familiar, and important adults around. They can provide support for you and your children. Grandparents, relatives, special friends, and neighbors can help provide caring stability and age-appropriate fun that your child may be craving.
- Model healthy coping. Children often take their cues for how to react from the important adults around them and use adults as models for their own feelings and behaviors. If you are sad or upset in front of your child, that's OK. Explain that grown-ups feel sad too. Show your child through words and actions that, even when you're upset, you are still able to manage your feelings and to take care of him or her. For example, you might say to your two-year-old, "I'm crying right now because I miss Daddy so

much, and I'm feeling a little sad. How about we just sit down and play with your blocks for a while? I love spending time with you."

- Seek professional support. Parents and caregivers sometimes feel as though they should handle everything on their own. Experiencing the death of a loved one can be extraordinarily painful—even overwhelming—and doesn't necessarily get better on its own. It makes sense to seek the advice, guidance, and support of people who know about grief and can answer your questions about what you are going through so that you can support your child in what he or she is experiencing. If you do seek counseling, you may want to talk with different clinicians until you find a good fit.

For more information, go to "Traumatic Grief in Military Children" on the website of the National Child Traumatic Stress Network (http://www.nctsn.org/trauma-types/traumatic-grief/traumatic-grief-military-children).

BLANKETING MILITARY CHILDREN WITH SECURITY

By Stephen J. Cozza, MD COL, US Army, Chief Department of Psychiatry, Walter Reed Army Medical Center

Military life is inherently one of great accomplishments and benefits, but it also presents significant risks and dangers to active-duty personnel. Injury and death are possibilities that can be faced by military personnel and their families at any time. If something does happen to a military service member, it affects everyone in his or her family; no family member is immune to the impact of such an incident. Even when children are too young to be able to speak and clearly reveal their thoughts and feelings, research and experience reveal that they are profoundly influenced by these significant events. Some experts refer to these as "transforming" experiences. Although we are powerless to protect military children from difficult life experiences, there are many ways we can work together to help children through these challenges and make transformations as positive as possible.

Below are some simple steps that might be taken by families facing uncertainty or grief:

- Keep lines of communication open. Parents and educators are both members of the child's support team. Since teamwork is more effective when communication is direct, talk and keeping talking about what is happening in the child's life. Every team member is responsible for this activity. Parents need to let educators know about changes that may affect their child. Teachers need to ask about any changes they observe in a child's understanding. Parents may be so overwhelmed by events and the critical decisions they have to make that they may forget to communicate important information to the school in a timely manner.
- Limit disruption to routines as much as possible. Continuity represents stability. A predictable schedule can be extremely comforting. Children know what to expect at school, making it a potential haven for children who feel that their life has been turned upside down. Keeping to a routine can also help adults see how a child is doing since they know how the child used to behave in the same situation.
- Talk about changes in the way that works best for your child. Children of different ages and abilities will require different amounts of information, explained in various ways. A thirteen-year-old will have more questions and want more information than a three-year-old. A child who has special needs may need to discuss or express his or her reactions to the changes in a different way. A verbal child may want to talk about what has happened more than a visual child, who would be better served by drawing pictures. Tailor your reactions and responses to the needs of that individual child.
- Discuss feelings. Just as children have to learn the names of colors and shapes, they also have to learn the names of feelings. They need to understand that everyone has all kinds of feelings and that even grown-ups feel scared or alone at times. Children are also incredibly perceptive. If they think an adult is sad or worried, it can be confusing if the adult denies those emotions and says that he or she is not. Talk about how the child feels, how you feel, and what you can each do to cope with those feelings. Show children that all feelings are OK; it is what you do about them that is most important.

- Tap into existing resources. The military has a host of resources to help military members and their spouses. Communities also have sources of support for families.
- Schools are a great place to learn about community resources. Remember that the Internet can link you to supportive people no matter where you live.
- Engage children in creating coping mechanisms. The most effective ways to support children are the ones that they take part in creating. Rather than pitying children, honor their sacrifices and their courage in expressing their feelings and involve them in creating coping mechanisms that work for them. In this way, you will be supporting their strength and encouraging their courage while helping them feel more in control.
- Provide extra time and support whenever possible. Children, just like adults, may not react to changes in the way that those around them may expect. Special events, such as Father's Day and Mother's Day, may reveal grief that had been hidden from view. Day-to-day activities may be abandoned because they are difficult to face at first—for example, the book that was always shared at bedtime may be shelved for a while. Since grief is such an intensely personal experience, make sure that those grieving have access to support for a while instead of confining your support to the period just after the change.

Knowing that someone else is thinking of their mother on her birthday may be just what a family needs. Support should be there any time grieving is detected or suspected.

Source: The above extract is from a fact sheet published by the US Army in its "Our Hero Handbook: A Guide for Families of Wounded Soldiers," issued in January 2008.

EMERGENCY COMMUNICATION SERVICES

When a military family experiences a crisis, the American Red Cross is there to help. Wherever their military service takes them, service members can rest assured that the Red Cross will deliver notification of an emergency, such as the death or serious illness of an immediate family member, as well as the good news of the birth of a service member's child or grandchild. Twenty-four hours per day, 365 days a year, the

Red Cross relays urgent messages containing accurate, factual, complete, and verified descriptions of the emergency to service members stationed anywhere in the world, including on ships at sea and at embassies and remote locations. Even if the service member receives an e-mail or phone call from home, Red Cross–verified information assists the member and his or her commanding officers in making a decision regarding emergency leave. Knowing in advance that communication links, access to financial assistance, and information and referral will be available in an emergency brings peace of mind to service members and to the families from whom they are separated.

The American Red Cross Emergency Communications Center is available to help twenty-four hours a day, seven days a week, 365 days a year. Call (877) 272-7337 (toll-free) if you are currently in the military or if you are calling about any of the following:

- Anyone on active duty in the army, marines, navy, air force, or coast guard
- An activated member of the National Guard or Reserve of any branch of the US armed forces
- An immediate family member or dependent of anyone in the above categories
- A civilian employed by or under contract with the Department of Defense and stationed outside the continental United States and any family residing with that person at that location
- A military retiree or the reiree's spouse or widow(er)
- A cadet or midshipman at a service academy or a Reserve Officers' Training Corps cadet on orders for training
- A merchant marine aboard a US naval ship

When calling the Red Cross, be prepared to provide as much of the following information about the service member as is known:

- Full legal name
- Rank/rating
- Branch of service (army, navy, air force, marines, coast guard)
- Social Security number
- Date of birth
- Military unit address

- Information about the deployed unit and home base unit (for deployed service members only)

15

HEALTH CARE AND INSURANCE

Dependents of active-duty members are covered by the TRICARE military medical system as of the very first day of active duty. During basic training in-processing, the recruit completes paperwork to enroll any dependents in the Defense Enrollment Eligibility Reporting System (DEERS) and apply for a military-dependent ID card. The ID card paperwork is mailed to the spouse, who can then take it to any military installation and obtain a military-dependent ID card. If medical care is needed before the ID card is obtained, the spouse can keep the medical receipts and file for reimbursement later, under the TRICARE Standard or TRICARE Extra program (depending on whether the medical provider is part of the TRICARE network).

All military spouses are entitled to medical benefits through DEERS. Enroll at the uniformed-services personnel office. You can find the one nearest to you at http://www.militaryinstallations.dod.mil.

DEERS ENROLLMENT

Proper DEERS registration is key to receiving timely and effective medical benefits. DEERS is a worldwide computerized database of uniformed-services members (sponsors), their dependents, and others who are eligible for military benefits, including TRICARE (for more information see below). All sponsors (active duty, retired, National Guard, and Reserve) are automatically registered in DEERS. However, the sponsor must register eligible family members. After family members are registered, they can update personal information such as addresses and phone numbers.

To use TRICARE benefits, you must have a valid uniformed-services or military ID card, which you can obtain from your nearest ID card office, and you must be listed in the DEERS database. The ID card states on the back, in the "Medical" block, whether you are eligible for medical care from military or civilian sources. When you are getting care, your provider will ask to see a copy of your ID card and will make copies for his or her records. Please ensure you have your ID card with you whenever you are getting care or having prescriptions filled.

Children

Children under age ten can generally use a parent or guardian's ID card, but they must be registered in DEERS. When a child reaches age ten, the sponsor must obtain an ID card for him or her. Children under age ten should have an ID card of their own when in the custody of a parent or guardian who is not eligible for TRICARE benefits or who is not the custodial parent after a divorce. If both parents are active-duty service members, then either may be listed as the child's sponsor in DEERS.

Step- and adopted children can also be enrolled, provided they live with the service member and spouse and are not already the dependent of another service member. You will need birth certificates and a final adoption decree in the case of an adopted child. If the child is from a former marriage, you will also need a copy of the divorce decree or a death certificate if your former spouse is deceased, as well as any custody documents.

Health Benefits

You may want to change to a family health-benefits enrollment. You may enroll, change enrollment from "self only" to "self and family" or from one plan or option to another, or make some combination of these changes during the period beginning thirty-one days before and ending sixty days after a change in your family status. Otherwise, you will have to wait until the next health-benefits open season to make the change.

If you want to provide immediate coverage for your new spouse, you may submit an enrollment request during the pay period before the anticipated date of your marriage. If the effective date of the change falls before your marriage, your new spouse does not become eligible for coverage until the actual day of your marriage.

Benefits Have Now Been Extended to All Military Spouses

On June 26, 2013, Defense Secretary Chuck Hagel announced steps to make benefits available to all military spouses. His statement was issued after the US Supreme Court struck down the Defense of Marriage Act. The law had prevented federal agencies from offering spouses in same-sex marriages all of the same benefits provided to other spouses. Hagel said,

> The Department of Defense [DoD] welcomes the Supreme Court's decision today on the Defense of Marriage Act. The Department will immediately begin the process of implementing the Supreme Court's decision in consultation with the Department of Justice and other executive branch agencies. The Department of Defense intends to make the same benefits available to all military spouses—regardless of sexual orientation—as soon as possible. That is now the law, and it is the right thing to do. Every person who serves our nation in uniform stepped forward with courage and commitment. All that matters is their patriotism, their willingness to serve their country and their qualifications to do so. Today's ruling helps ensure that all men and women who serve this country can be treated fairly and equally, with the full dignity and respect they so richly deserve.

The department immediately began to update the ID card issuance infrastructure and the applicable implementing guidance. For civilian employees, the department has looked to the Office of Personnel Management for guidance. For civilian employees eligible for ID-card-related benefits, the department intends to make ID cards available to same-sex spouses of civilian employees at the same time as for same-sex spouses of military members.

The Supreme Court's ruling means that the Department of Defense must extend all benefits to same-sex spouses of military personnel that are currently extended to opposite-sex spouses, including medical, dental, interment at Arlington National Cemetery, and with-dependent basic allowance for housing. The department will implement these benefit changes as soon as possible for same-sex spouses. The policies governing burial at Arlington National Cemetery will apply equally to same-sex and opposite-sex spouses.

Special Needs

The Extended Care Health Option (ECHO) is a supplemental program to the basic TRICARE program. It provides financial assistance for an integrated set of services and supplies to eligible active-duty family members (including family members of activated National Guard or Reserve members) who qualify, based on specific mental or physical disabilities, and offers services and supplies not available through the basic TRICARE program. ECHO supplements the benefits of the basic TRICARE program option that eligible family members use.

There is no enrollment fee for ECHO; however, family members must

- Have an ECHO-qualifying condition
- Enroll in the Exceptional Family Member Program (EFMP) as provided by the sponsor's branch of service
- Register in ECHO through ECHO case managers in each TRICARE region

OTHER BENEFITS UNDER ECHO

ECHO's additional components include respite care and ECHO Home Health Care (EHHC). ECHO also addresses the needs of the caregiver, which, in most cases, involve rest or time away from the "care environment."

Respite Care

Respite care provides relief for caregivers of special-needs dependents. ECHO beneficiaries qualify for sixteen hours of respite care per month, to be administered in the home by a TRICARE-authorized home health care agency. During respite hours, the caregiver may leave the home. Note that respite care is authorized only when the beneficiary is receiving some other ECHO benefit during the same month.

ECHO Home Health Care

ECHO also includes extended home health care and respite care for caregivers of special-needs dependents whose condition renders them homebound. EHHC allows for licensed or registered nurses to provide skilled home health care in excess of twenty-eight hours per week. Speak to your regional contractor or TRICARE area office to determine the maximum monthly cap for EHHC home health care benefits. Respite care under EHHC allows for a maximum of eight hours, five days per week of respite care, which may be used as a sleep benefit. Respite care under EHHC cannot be used in conjunction with ECHO's respite care. Finally, the monthly benefits maximum has increased from $1,000 to $2,500. In addition, the cost-share liability was not adjusted. Monthly cost shares range from $25 to $250, depending on the sponsor's pay grade.

ELIGIBILITY AND ENROLLMENT

Families are required to be enrolled in their service's EFMP in order to register for ECHO benefits. If you qualify for special-needs benefits, speak to an EFMP representative, who will ensure your proper enrollment in EFMP and provide appropriate ECHO contact information. In order to qualify for ECHO benefits, dependents of an active-duty service member must have a qualifying condition. Contact your regional managed-care support contractor to determine program eligibility and details.

ENHANCED ACCESS TO AUTISM SERVICES DEMONSTRATION

Several available treatments, therapies, and interventions, known as educational interventions for autism spectrum disorders (EIA), have been shown to reduce or eliminate specific problem behaviors and teach new skills to individuals with autism. These EIA services are not covered under basic TRICARE coverage (TRICARE Prime, Standard, Extra, etc.), and are only partially covered through ECHO. The Enhanced Access to Autism Services Demonstration allows eligible beneficiaries access to a greater range of existing evidence-based EIA services through an expanded network of educational intervention providers.

The Enhanced Access to Autism Services Demonstration began on March 15, 2008, and is only available in the fifty states and the District of Columbia. Visit the TRICARE Autism Services Demonstration website for additional information.

SELF AND FAMILY

A self-and-family enrollment provides benefits for you and your eligible family members. All of your eligible family members are automatically covered, even if you didn't list them on your Health Benefits Election Form (SF 2809) or other appropriate request. You cannot exclude any eligible family member, and you cannot provide coverage for anyone who is not an eligible family member.

You may enroll in self-and-family coverage before you have any eligible family members. Then, a new eligible family member (such as a newborn child or a new spouse) will be automatically covered by your family enrollment from the date he or she becomes a family member. When a new family member is added to your existing self-and-family enrollment, you do not have to complete a new SF 2809 or other appropriate request, but your carrier may ask you for information about your new family member. You will send the requested information directly to the carrier. Exception: if you want to add a foster child to your coverage, you must provide eligibility information to your employing office.

If both you and your spouse are eligible to enroll, one of you may enroll for self-and-family coverage for your entire family. If you have no eligible children to cover, each of you may enroll for self-only coverage through the same or different plans. Generally, you will pay lower premiums for two self-only enrollments.

TRICARE PROGRAMS

TRICARE Prime is a managed-care option, similar to a civilian health maintenance organization (HMO). Prime is for active-duty service members and available to other TRICARE beneficiaries. Active-duty service members are required to enroll in Prime and must take action to do so by filling out the appropriate enrollment form and submitting it to the regional contractor. There is no cost to the service member.

Other TRICARE beneficiaries may be eligible for Prime. The uniformed services determine eligibility for any kind of TRICARE coverage. TRICARE manages the military health care program, but the services decide who is or is not eligible to receive TRICARE coverage. Prime enrollees receive most of their health care at a military treatment facility (MTF), and a primary care manager coordinates their care. Prime is not available everywhere.

Prime enrollees must follow some well-defined rules and procedures, such as seeking care first from the MTF. For specialty care, the Prime enrollee must receive a referral from his or her primary care manager and authorization from the regional contractor. Failure to do so could result in costly point-of-service (POS) option charges. Emergency care is not subject to POS charges.

TRICARE Prime Remote is the program for service members and their families who are on remote assignment, typically fifty miles from an MTF. The TRICARE Overseas Program delivers the Prime benefit to active-duty service members and their families in Europe, the Pacific, Latin America, and Canada. The TRICARE Global Remote program delivers the Prime benefit to active-duty service members and families stationed in designated "remote" locations overseas.

TRICARE Standard is the basic TRICARE health care program, offering comprehensive health care coverage for beneficiaries (not to include active-duty members) not enrolled in TRICARE Prime. Standard does not require enrollment. It is a fee-for-service plan that gives beneficiaries the option to see any TRICARE-certified/-authorized provider (doctor, nurse-practitioner, lab, clinic, etc.). Standard offers the greatest flexibility in choosing a provider but will also involve greater out-of-pocket expenses for the insured. You also may be required to file your own claims. Standard requires that you satisfy a yearly deductible before TRICARE cost sharing begins, and you will be required to pay copayments or cost shares for outpatient care, medications, and inpatient care.

Any TRICARE-eligible beneficiary who is not on active duty, not otherwise enrolled in Prime, and not eligible for TRICARE for Life (TFL) can use TRICARE Extra, which goes into effect whenever a Standard beneficiary chooses to make an appointment with a TRICARE network provider. Extra, like Standard, requires no enrollment and involves no enrollment fee. TRICARE Extra is essentially an option for TRICARE Standard beneficiaries who want to save on out-of-pocket expenses by making an appointment with a TRICARE Prime network provider (doctor, nurse practitioner, lab, etc.). The appointment with the in-network provider will cost 5 percent less than it would with a doctor who is a TRICARE-authorized or -participating provider. The TRICARE Extra user can also expect that the network provider will file all claims forms for him. The Standard beneficiary might have claims filed for him, but the nonnetwork provider can decide to file on his behalf or not, on a case-by-case basis.

Under TRICARE Extra, because there is no enrollment, there is no identification card. Your valid uniformed-services ID card serves as proof of your eligibility to receive health care coverage from any TRICARE Prime provider.

TRICARE for Life is a Medicare wrap-around plan available to Medicare-entitled uniformed-service retirees, including retired Guard members and Reservists, Medicare-entitled family members and widow(er)s (excluding dependent parents and parents-in-law), Medicare-entitled Congressional Medal of Honor recipients and their family members, and certain Medicare-entitled nonremarried former spouses. To take advantage of TFL, you and your eligible family members' personal information and Medicare Part B status must be up to date in DEERS. You may update your information by phone (800-538-9552) or by visiting your nearest ID card issuing facility. Visit http://www.dmdc.osd.mil/rslto locate the nearest ID card facility.

SUPPORT SYSTEMS

Life in the military is challenging. When you have a special-needs child, it becomes even more so. However, families in the military have a vast array of available resources from within and beyond the military community. Help yourself and your family by learning about available support services and resources.

Military Community Resources

Family-support centers (FSC) are there to help military families. Most military installations have one or more FSCs that offer a variety of free services and support designed to assist service members and their families with the unique challenges of military life. Available offerings may vary due to the size and mission of the installation. Types of assistance may include the following:

- Relocation counseling and lending lockers
- Information and referrals for special needs
- Employment workshops
- Volunteer coordination
- Parenting classes
- Individual and family counseling
- Personal finance management
- Spouse education and support programs
- Deployment support
- Family-life education and workshops

FSCs can connect you with the EFMP. This will ensure that your child's medical and educational needs will be considered as a duty station is selected. Your FSC is also a good place to ask for information about local organizations and support groups concerned with specific disabilities. To find the FSC nearest you, go to http://www.militaryinstallations.dod.mil.

New Parent Support Program

The New Parent Support Program (http://www.militaryonesource.mil/parenting?content_id=266691) is a DOD-funded website that assists expectant and new parents by providing a variety of services matched to the needs of individual families. Services encompass home visits, education, counseling, and referrals to other resources, including special-needs organizations and services on the installation and within the local community. Parents who take advantage of the classes offered will gain hands-on training to help them make informed and responsible decisions for their children.

Family Advocacy Program

The military community is not immune to personal or family problems. Problems may range from stress arising from a deployment to domestic violence, including spousal or child abuse. Fortunately, vital services and support are available to military families. The Family Advocacy Program (FAP) sponsors activities and services to include public-awareness briefings, individual and couples counseling, crisis intervention, support groups, stress management, and other well-being workshops. FAP services may be found at military medical facilities or at installation FSCs.

Child, Youth, and Teen Development Programs

Military families face greater challenges than most other families. Shifting work schedules that are often longer than the typical eight-hour day and the obligation to be ready to deploy anywhere in the world on a moment's notice require a flexible child-development system that nonetheless maintains high standards. Add to these challenges a child with special needs, and finding quality child care can present a formidable challenge.

- Child development centers (CDCs): DoD CDCs provide care for children from six weeks to twelve years old. To help ensure that your exceptional child's needs are met in the day care setting, the army, navy, and marines offer special-needs resource teams. Contact information for all DoD CDCs is available at http://www.defense.gov/home/features/2005/Childcare/index_ChildCare.html.
- Family child care (FCC): FCC homes operated on base are certified by the military child development program. These providers deliver critical services to service members on shift work, those working extended hours or weekends, and those who prefer a

home-based environment for their children. An FCC home may be the best option for special-needs children who need the consistency of a single caregiver or require complex procedures that the caregiver must learn.

- Youth centers: Ask about available youth programs at your FSC. You will find an array of programs that will help your child become involved and make friends. Frequently available are sports leagues for soccer, basketball, and baseball and a center where your child can play Ping-Pong or video games. For information regarding child, youth, and teen services visit the Military One-Source website.
- Summer camps and recreation: Several bases have special camps and activities for children with special needs. Camp Lejeune offers Camp Special Time several weekends a year, giving parents some well-deserved time off. Fort Campbell offers Camp We Can. Ask about what is available on your base and in your community.

School Liaison Officers

The army sponsors a program providing a school liaison officer at each army installation to work with local schools in support of children from military families. School liaison officers are particularly helpful when students are transitioning from one school system to another. These officers may be able to advocate on behalf of parents who believe their child's special education needs are not being met. For more information about this program, go to http://www.militaryk12partners.dodea.edu/resources.cfm?colId=liaison.

Relief Societies

Military communities pride themselves on taking care of their own. Relief societies exist to help families with unexpected problems or financial emergencies. Help may be available for the following needs:

- Emergency transportation
- Funeral expenses
- Disaster-relief assistance

- Child-care expenses
- Essential vehicle repairs
- Unforeseen family emergencies
- Food, rent, and utilities
- Medical and dental bills (patient's share)

Each of the armed forces has established a relief society:

- Army Emergency Relief Society: www.aerhq.org, (866) 878-6378
- Navy/Marine Corps Relief Society: (703) 696-4904
- Air Force Aid Society: www.afas.org, (800) 769-8951
- Coast Guard Mutual Assistance: http://www.cgmahq.org

Service-Sponsored Websites

Each branch of the military sponsors a website that provides an overview of programs and support available to military personnel and family members. These websites also provide news articles and information relating to life in the military and online tutorials.

- US Army: Army OneSource (http://www.myarmyonesource.com)
- US Navy: LIFELines Services Network (www.lifelines.navy.mil)
- US Marine Corps: Marine Corps Community Services (www.usmc-mccs.org)
- US Air Force: Armed Forces Cross Roads (www.afcrossroads.com)

ADDITIONAL MILITARY RESOURCES

Military Homefront's Special Needs/EFMP Module

Military Homefront's (http://www.militaryhomefront.dod.mil/efm) Special Needs/EFMP module is the official DoD website designed to help troops and their special-needs family members. This site is packed with information. Military Homefront maintains a military community directory with a searchable list of family center addresses, websites, phone numbers, and e-mail addresses worldwide. You will also find tip sheets and resources regarding the following:

- Exceptional Family Member Program
- Parenting
- Relocation
- Military Spouse Resource Center
- Benefits and services
- Preseparation
- Military Teens on the Move
- General legal information
- Deployment connections
- Employment and transitioning

Military OneSource

Military OneSource (http://www.militaryonesource.com) provides information, referrals, and assistance to the military community. Accessed by telephone or the Internet, Military OneSource provides special-needs consultation, research, resources, and materials intended to enhance current military services available to families with special needs.

A military education specialist is available and devoted to military families who need assistance with issues related to educating their children. Services are provided on a scheduled-appointment basis via telephone and focus on special-needs children from birth to age twenty-one. Specialty services can be accessed through the main telephone number for Military OneSource, and an appointment with a military special-needs specialist should be requested.

Many tip sheets covering a wide range of topics of interest to military families with special needs are available. All services are free of charge.

Military Teens on the Move

Military Teens on the Move (http://apps.militaryonesource.mil/MOS/f?p=MYOM:HOME2:0) is a website specifically for military teens and kids facing yet another move. Here they will find age-appropriate information about how to deal with the feelings they have about moving, information about the new installation, and advice on handling the move and how to begin to fit in at their new home.

Plan My Move

Plan My Move (http://apps.militaryonesource.mil/MOS/f?p= PMM:ENTRY:0) includes comprehensive moving tools for military families with special needs. Users can create customized calendars, to-do lists, and arrival checklists, all intended to help them get organized and to make their next move as smooth as possible.

TRICARE

TRICARE offers several programs to assist families with special needs. The Extended Health Care Option offers financial assistance and additional benefits for services, equipment, and supplies beyond those available through TRICARE Prime, Extra, or Standard. Also available is ECHO Home Health Care, which provides home-bound family members with intensive home health care services.

FEDERAL, STATE, AND COMMUNITY RESOURCES

American Red Cross

Today's American Red Cross (http://www.redcross.org) is keeping pace with the changing military. The Red Cross sends communications on behalf of family members who are facing emergencies or other important events to members of the US armed forces serving all over the world. Both active-duty and community-based military can count on the Red Cross to provide access to financial assistance, counseling, aid to veterans, and emergency communications that link them with their families back home. To contact the Red Cross, visit the website or call (202) 303-4498.

Computer/Electronics Accommodations Program

The Computer/Electronic Accommodations Program (CAP) provides assistive technology and services to people with disabilities, federal managers, supervisors, IT professionals, and wounded service members. "We buy it, we pay for it, we get it to the users; it's just that simple," says CAP director Dinah Cohen. You can find additional information about CAP's EFMP initiatives at (703) 681-8813 or (703) 681-0881 (TTY).

Disabilityinfo.gov

This website (http://www.disabilityinfo.gov) exists to connect people with disabilities to the information and resources they need to pursue their personal and professional ambitions. Disabled individuals can look here for information about travel, workplace support, and fair housing.

Cadre (National Center on Dispute Resolution)

Cadre (http://www.directionservice.org) encourages the use of mediation and other collaborative strategies to resolve disagreements about special education and early-intervention programs. Cadre offers a spectrum of services, including promoting ways to prevent conflict, helping with early dispute assistance, and providing education about conflict-resolution options, mediation, resolution sessions, and due process hearings. To contact Cadre, visit the website, call (541) 686-5060 (voice) or (541) 284-4740 (TTY), or send a fax to (541) 686-5063.

Supplemental Nutrition Assistance Program and Family Subsistence Supplemental Allowance

The Supplemental Nutrition Assistance Program (SNAP; http://www.fns.usda.gov) serves as the first line of defense against hunger. It enables low-income families to buy nutritious food with Electronic Benefits Transfer (EBT) cards. SNAP recipients spend their benefits to buy eligible food in authorized retail food stores, including the commissary. To prequalify online, go to the website and click on the SNAP Pre-Screening Eligibility Tool (http://www.snap-step1.usda.gov/fns).

SNAP benefits are not available for military families stationed overseas. However, you can apply for the Family Subsistence Supplemental Allowance (FSSA). Although this allowance does target those families currently using SNAP, all service members may apply because eligibility is based on household income and family size, not whether one is currently receiving SNAP benefits. Nothing in the law prohibits service members from receiving both FSSA and SNAP benefits at the same time. However, the FSP will count any FSSA benefits as income, just like any other military income, in determining eligibility and allotment amounts under the FSP. For more information, visit the Defense Manpower Data Center website (http://www.dmdc.osd.mil).

Medicaid

Medicaid (http://www.cms.hhs.gov) is a program that pays for health care for some low-income individuals and families with few resources. Medicaid is a national program with broad guidelines, but each state sets its own eligibility rules and decides what services to provide. Be aware of this as you move from state to state. In most states, children who qualify for Supplemental Security Income will also qualify for Medicaid. States can also choose to cover other groups of children under age nineteen or those who live in higher-income families. Many states qualify children through programs that allow disabled children to qualify without considering their parents' income. To find information on Medicaid and Medicaid waivers in your state, go to http://www.medicaid.gov/Medicaid-CHIP-Program-Information/By-Topics/Waivers/Waivers.html.

National Center on Education, Disability, and Juvenile Justice

The National Center on Education, Disability, and Juvenile Justice (EDJJ; http://www.edjj.org) is concerned by the number of youth with disabilities at risk for contact with the courts or already involved the juvenile justice system. The EDJJ provides assistance, conducts research, and disseminates resources in three areas: prevention of school failure and delinquency, education and special education for detained and committed youth, and transition services for youth returning to schools and communities. For more information, visit the website or call (301) 405-6462.

National Dissemination Center for Children with Disabilities

The National Dissemination Center for Children with Disabilities (NICHCY;http://www.nichcy.org) has a wealth of information on disabilities. NICHCY serves the nation as a central source of information on the following:

- Disabilities in infants, toddlers, children, and youth
- Individuals with Disabilities Education Act, the law authorizing special education
- No Child Left Behind (as it relates to children with disabilities)
- Research based on effective educational practices

NICHCY is a valuable resource for all parents of disabled children, and its website links to the BrowseAloud text reader. This means all the information on the site can be read to you.

Shriners Hospitals for Children

Shriners hospitals are a network of twenty-two pediatric hospitals in the United States, Canada, and Mexico that provide specialized care for orthopedic conditions, burns, spinal cord injuries, and cleft lip and palate. All services are provided at no charge. If you know of a child in need, Shriners might be able to help. Please call the toll-free patient-referral line: in the United States: (800) 237-5055; in Canada: (800) 361-7256.

Specialized Training of Military Parents

Specialized Training of Military Parents (STOMP; http://www.stompproject.org) is the only national parent training and information center that provides support and advice to military parents regardless of the type of medical condition their child has. The STOMP Project hosts a list serve for military families and professionals to share ideas. The list serve enables military families all over the world to connect, learn, and help each other as they raise their special-needs children in military communities. On STOMP, parents can ask question and get answers about the resources available to them, as well as receive advice on educating their children and navigating the health care system. STOMP offers workshops addressing an array of topics. You can contact STOMP via the website or at (800) 5-PARENT (800-572-7368; voice and TTY).

Supplemental Security Income

Supplemental Security Income (SSI; http://www.ssa.gov) is a federal supplement program that can provide a monthly payment to those with low incomes and few resources who are sixty-five or older, blind, or disabled. Children may qualify. If you think you or your child might qualify, visit the nearest Social Security office or call the Social Security Administration at (800) 772-1213. If the application is denied, it is good practice to appeal the decision.

Women, Infants, and Children (WIC)

The Women, Infants, and Children (WIC) website (http://www.fns. usda.gov/wic) provides toll-free numbers across the country. If you can't access the Internet, call the state nutrition-counseling office or nearest military FSC. WIC offers nutritional help to low-income women and children who are nutritionally at risk. This includes women who are pregnant, postpartum, or breast-feeding and infants and children up to their fifth birthday. WIC provides nutrition education, nutritious foods, screening, and referrals to other health, welfare, and social services. Service members living overseas may be eligible to participate in the WIC Overseas program. For more information about this program, go to http://www.tricare.mil/Welcome/SpecialPrograms/WICOverseas. aspx.

Wrightslaw

Parents, educators, advocates, and attorneys go to Wrightslaw (http://www.wrightslaw.com) for reliable information about special education law and advocacy for children with disabilities. Wrightslaw includes thousands of articles, cases, and free resources on dozens of special education topics. This an excellent source for parents who are learning to navigate the special education system.

INSURANCE

Servicemembers' Group Life Insurance

Servicemembers' Group Life Insurance (SGLI) is a program of low-cost group life insurance for service members on active duty, ready Reservists, members of the National Guard, members of the Commissioned Corps of the National Oceanic and Atmospheric Administration and the Public Health Service, cadets and midshipmen of the four service academies, and members of the Reserve Officers' Training Corps. SGLI coverage is available in $50,000 increments up to the maximum of $400,000. SGLI premiums are currently $.065 per $1,000 of insurance, regardless of the member's age.

Family Servicemembers' Group Life Insurance

Family Servicemembers' Group Life Insurance (FSGLI) is a program extended to the spouses and dependent children of members insured under the SGLI program. FSGLI provides up to a maximum of $100,000 of insurance coverage for spouses, not to exceed the amount of SGLI the insured member has in force, and $10,000 for dependent children. Spousal coverage is issued in increments of $10,000, at a monthly cost ranging from $0.55 to $5.20 per increment. Service members should contact their personnel support center, personnel flight, payroll, and/or finance office for SGLI and FSGLI premium-payment information.

Traumatic Injury Protection under Servicemembers' Group Life Insurance

The Traumatic Injury Protection under Servicemembers' Group Life Insurance (TSGLI) program is a rider to SGLI. The TSGLI rider provides coverage to service members who are severely injured (on or off duty) as the result of a traumatic event and suffer a loss that qualifies for payment under TSGLI. TSGLI payments are designed to help traumatically injured service members and their families with financial burdens associated with recovering from a severe injury. TSGLI payments range from $25,000 to $100,000 based on the qualifying loss suffered.

TSGLI coverage is automatic for those insured under basic SGLI and cannot be declined. The only way to decline TSGLI is to decline basic SGLI coverage. The premium for TSGLI is a flat rate of $1 per month for most service members. Members who carry the maximum SGLI coverage of $400,000 will pay $29 per month for both SGLI and TSGLI.

To be eligible for TSGLI payment, you must meet all of the following requirements:

- You must be insured by SGLI when you experience a traumatic event.
- You must incur a scheduled loss, and that loss must be a direct result of a traumatic injury.
- You must have suffered the traumatic injury prior to midnight of the day that you separated from the uniformed services.
- You must suffer a scheduled loss within two years (730 days) of the traumatic injury.
- You must survive for a period of not less than seven full days from the date of the traumatic injury. (The seven-day period begins on the date and time of the traumatic injury, as measured by Zulu [Greenwich mean or zero meridian] time, and ends 168 full hours later).

Exceptional Family Member Program

The EFMP is a mandatory enrollment program, based on carefully defined rules. EFMP works with other military and civilian agencies to provide comprehensive and coordinated medical, educational, housing, community-support, and personnel services to families with special needs. EFMP enrollment works to ensure that needed services are available at the receiving command before an assignment is made. An exceptional family member is a dependent, regardless of age, who requires medical services for a chronic condition; receives ongoing services from a specialist; has behavioral health concerns, social problems, or psychological needs; receives education services provided through an individual education program; or receives services provided through an individual family service plan.

LIFE INSURANCE

If you already have a family plan, your personnel office can assist you in getting your spouse (and, if appropriate, your stepchildren) added to your enrollment. Changes must be made within sixty calendar days of your marriage. You must provide supporting documentation (e.g., marriage certificate) for any changes outside open season. Documentation should be submitted to your human resources or personnel office.

UPDATING BENEFICIARY DESIGNATIONS

You may want to change your beneficiary designations for life insurance or retirement benefits. New designations must be made in writing and witnessed. Your agency can provide the appropriate forms. There can be no erasures or cross-outs on these forms. If the forms are incomplete or have errant marks, they will not be processed and will be returned to you. When your beneficiary forms are filled in, be sure you have signed them. After obtaining witness signatures, submit your completed forms to the address or agency noted on the form.

Note: If you choose to complete beneficiary forms, it is your responsibility to keep them up to date. A marriage, divorce, or other change in family status does not automatically nullify a beneficiary form previously submitted; nor does it prevent the named beneficiary from receiving benefits.

16

COPING WITH STRESS

Recognizing the stresses military life and multiple deployments put on families, the services are stepping up their efforts to help their members strengthen family relationships and avoid the divorce courts. Stress also seriously impacts children and teens, so methods for reducing family stress are not only common but accessible and available. A full range of outreach programs—from support groups for spouses of deployed troops to weekend retreats for military couples—aim to help military families endure the hardships that military life often imposes.

The divorce rates for the army give a snapshot of a presumedly military-wide trend. The army divorce rate went down slightly in 2012, settling at 3.5 percent, according to Pentagon statistics, released in January 2013. Military officials and divorce experts are hopeful that the overall rate, which had crept slowly up from 2.6 percent in 2001 to 3.7 percent in 2011, is starting to move downward.

Between 2011 and 2012, the divorce rate went down slightly in every service among male and female service members of all ranks. Enlisted female soldiers and marines, however, continue to experience the highest rate of divorce: 9.4 and 9.3 percent, respectively. In the army, the female enlisted divorce rate is more than triple that of enlisted males. Still, those rates are down from the 2011 rates of 9.6 percent in the army and 9.8 percent in the marines.

These statistics reflect a general trend in American society, points out army chaplain Col. Glen Bloomstrom, director of ministry initiatives for the army's Office of the Chief of Chaplains. Of all first marriages, 45 to 50 percent end in divorce nationwide, he said, and the failure rate is even higher for second marriages: a whopping 60 to 70 percent.

Divorce rates run even higher in specific occupations, particularly those that expose people to traumatic events and danger, as well as heavy responsibilities and public scrutiny, army officials noted. Military police officers, for example, face divorce rates averaging between 66 and 75 percent, they said.

Nationwide trends aside, Bloomstrom was quick to point out that the numbers represent far more than just statistics. "These are people we're talking about," he said. "When a marriage ends, it's the end of a dream."

The toll encompasses more than human costs, affecting military operations as well, Bloomstrom said, adding that service members in happy marriages tend to be more focused on their jobs and less likely to become disciplinary problems. They're also more likely to remain in the military.

To help reverse the statistics, the services have introduced new programs and pumped up existing ones offered through their family-support, chaplain, and mental health counseling networks. For example, the army's offerings include the following:

- The new Deployment Cycle Support Program, which includes briefings for soldiers on how their absence and return may affect their family relationships and how they can cope with the inevitable changes
- A family support group system that provides both practical and emotional support for spouses of deployed soldiers
- The Building Strong and Ready Families program, a two-day program that helps couples develop better communication skills, reinforced by a weekend retreat
- The Strong Bonds marriage education program, which focuses specifically on issues that affect Reserve and National Guard couples, and the PICK a Partner program, which helps single soldiers make wise decisions when they choose mates

The army is not alone in offering programs to help its families survive the rigors of deployment and strengthen their relationships in the process. The Marine Corps' Prevention and Relationship Enhancement Program is a two-day workshop that teaches couples how to manage conflict, solve problems, communicate effectively, and preserve and enhance their commitment and friendship, Marine officials said. Participants begin the program by taking a marriage survey, developed by a retired navy chaplain, to help them evaluate their relationship and identify problems before they become serious. The four top problems generally involve communication, children and parenting, money, and sexual intimacy, according to a navy chaplain involved in the program. The Marine Corps program focuses on what the chaplain calls "the mother lode of all issues" that can affect marriages: communication. "If you don't have good communication skills, you can't talk about the rest of the issues," he said.

The navy has a similar program in its Marriage Enrichment Retreat. This weekend getaway is designed to give navy couples the tools they need to help strengthen their marriages, according to Rachelle Logan, public affairs director for Navy Installations Command. Participants begin the weekend session by getting a profile of their personalities, then attending sessions on marital communication, personality and family dynamics, and problems associated with military separation, Logan said.

Although the air force does not have servicewide marital-support programs, air force officials said individual bases offer a wide variety of programs to support military families and help them through separations, deployments, and the stresses relating to them.

Bloomstrom said he's optimistic about the emphasis the military services are putting on programs for married service members. The goal, he said, is to help couples recognize and address danger signs before they escalate. Another objective is to help military couples get more satisfaction out of their marriages by injecting a healthy dose of "fun and friendship" that, he said, builds up their "emotional bank account." "We're talking about investing in the relationship in the good times," he said. "That way, when you have to make a withdrawal—as you do during a deployment—you still have enough left in the bank to cover it."

STRESS AS A FACTOR

Stress is a response to signals called "stressors" that your brain interprets as a call to prepare for action. Adrenaline and stress hormones are released that activate your body ("fight or flight") and affect your actions, thoughts, and emotions. Stress helps to protect you, but it can be unhealthy if it continues for a long time. Too much stress can also interfere with your performance. Stress-related physical changes include the following:

- Increased blood pressure and heart rate
- Rapid breathing
- Sweating
- Stomach muscles contracting, causing "butterflies," cramps, diarrhea
- Muscle tension

Potential long-term effects of chronic stress include the following:

- Hypertension (high blood pressure)
- Heart disease
- Immune system suppression
- Increased risk of infectious disease
- Gastrointestinal disorders such as colitis
- Asthma
- Mental health problems

QUICK STRESS-REDUCTION TECHNIQUES

When you feel stressed, your breathing becomes fast and shallow and your muscles get tense. You can interrupt the stress response by doing the following:

- Slowing your breathing and taking deep, slow breaths from your belly
- Relaxing your muscles (e.g., by tensing and releasing muscles throughout your body)

Mental Reframing

Everyone has a stream of private thoughts running through his or her mind. Called self-talk, these thoughts reflect your beliefs and attitudes about the world, other people, and yourself, and they may be adding to your stress. To interrupt the automatic thought process, become aware; monitor your thoughts and self-talk. Recognize that thoughts cause feelings and motivate behavior. There is rarely a direct link between the stressful situation and your response. In fact, it's usually not the event or situation that leads to a stress reaction; it's your interpretation of the event or situation that causes you to respond in various ways.

The sequence of events that leads to feelings and behaviors in response to stressors is called the "ABCs":

You experience the *activating* event.
Your *beliefs* about the event lead to an interpretation of the event.
Your interpretation of the event either increases or decreases the
    stress you feel, that is, the *consequences*.

So,

$$A \text{ (activating event)} + B \text{ (beliefs)} = C \text{ (consequences)}$$

Check your thoughts and self-talk for these stress-promoting thinking patterns:

- All-or-nothing thinking: Judging things as all good or all bad, usually based on a single factor
- Exaggeration: Blowing the negative aspects of a situation or event way out of proportion
- Overgeneralization: Drawing conclusions about your whole life based on the negative outcome of a single incident
- Mind reading: Believing you know what another person or group of people is thinking about you (usually bad) when you have no evidence

Challenge your negative thoughts and self-talk by asking yourself whether there is evidence to support the way you are perceiving the situation. Replace negative or stressful self-talk with more positive, useful, and realistic self-talk.

Example: While on leave, you decide to take the bus to go visit your family and get stuck in traffic due to road construction. Change negative self-talk ("This will take forever. I will never get home. Why does this always happen to me?") to positive and useful self-talk ("I'm glad they are fixing this road. I can take this time to relax and listen to some music I enjoy").

CONTROLLING THE SOURCE OF STRESS BY SOLVING PROBLEMS

Take action on stressors that you can control (your own habits, behavior, environment, relationships) by using the problem-solving process:

1. Define the problem.
2. Set a goal (e.g., what would you like to see happen?).
3. Brainstorm possible solutions.
4. Evaluate the pros and cons of various possible solutions.
5. Choose the best solution (weigh the pros and cons).
6. Make a plan to implement the solution and try it.
7. Assess how well it went.
8. If the first solution doesn't work, try others.

If a source of stress is beyond your control, try an activity to distract or soothe yourself:

- Listen to music.
- Get together with a friend.
- Read a good book or watch a movie.
- Engage in physical exercise.
- Consider spiritual activity such as prayer.
- Perform yoga.
- Use humor (jokes or funny movies).
- Meditate.
- Take a nap.
- Write in a journal or diary.
- Take a hot bath or shower.
- Help others in need.
- Express your stress creatively.

- Take a mental holiday.

PLAN FOR FUTURE STRESSFUL EVENTS

To plan for future stressful events, do the following:

- Create a personalized "stress toolkit" by making a list of coping strategies that work for you when you're stressed, including deep breathing, muscle relaxation, and activities that you find soothing.
- Visualize potential stressful situations.
- Determine whether you will have some control in the situation.
- Decide how you will use the problem-solving process to reduce stressors.
- Plan to use various helpful activities to reduce the stress response.
- Remember to include friends and family for support.

HELPING CHILDREN COPE WITH STRESS

Stress in our lives is normal and natural, but too much can lead to serious physical and psychological problems. As adults we learn to handle stress by using control mechanisms to rationalize it and mitigate the effects. Children, however, often don't even understand that they are stressed. Instead their stress manifests as a headache, stomachache, trouble sleeping, or outburst of anger.

A child's ability to cope with stress is determined by his or her age and mental development, the intensity and duration of the stressor, and the level of support from family, friends, and others. Telltale signs in preschoolers are lack of self-control, bed-wetting, changes in eating and toilet habits, irritability, difficulty sleeping, and feeling unwell. Elementary-school-age children may have tantrums when things don't go their way, become aggressive, lack concentration, and have nightmares. They may become withdrawn and feel unloved, have headaches, and lose their appetite. Preteens and adolescents may become rebellious, have trouble sleeping, develop skin problems, skip school, or experiment with drugs. In all these cases, it is important to recognize the symptoms for what they are and to help the child cope with the stressors by being loving, sensitive, and supportive.

The best way to alleviate stress is to remove it. First, you must identify the stressor, and then you must find a way to eradicate it so that the child has as stress-free an environment as possible. Let your child know that he or she can talk to you at any time. And when your child does want to talk, listen to what he or she is saying and show that you care. A hug from a parent at this stage can be better than several hours of therapy.

One way to get children to open up is to have them to write down their fears. Even the act of putting anxieties down on paper can be cathartic. Once the fear has been put into words, you can discuss it by asking, "OK, so what are we going to do about it?"

Hundreds of children's books have been written specifically to help them understand stresses and fears. Select a book that deals with your child's particular fears and read it together. By identifying with the character, your child will realize that he or she is not alone and perhaps see that there is a solution.

Deep breathing, relaxation techniques, and yoga are other ways you can help your child cope. If the child is old enough, you can discuss conflict-resolution strategies to show him or her that there are always other ways to solve a problem.

If your child is unable to tell you what the problem is, you may need to consult a therapist of counselor. All branches of the military provide these support services.

17

SUBSTANCE ABUSE

Dependence on alcohol and drugs is our most serious national public health problem. It is prevalent among rich and poor, in all regions of the country, and among all ethnic and social groups. Millions of Americans misuse or depend on alcohol or drugs. Most of them have families who suffer the consequences, often serious, of living with this illness. If there is alcohol or drug dependence in your family, remember that you are not alone.

Substance abuse is a growing problem in the military because of the tremendous strains on military personnel themselves and their families. Alcohol abuse is the most prevalent problem, according to the National Institute on Drug Abuse (NIDA). A study of army soldiers screened three to four months after their return from deployment to Iraq showed that 27 percent met criteria for alcohol abuse and were at increased risk for related harmful behaviors (e.g., drinking and driving, using illicit drugs). And although soldiers frequently report alcohol concerns, few are referred for alcohol treatment.

Research findings highlight the need to improve screening and access to care for alcohol-related problems among service members returning from combat deployments. Some have experienced devastating consequences, including family disintegration and mental health disorders, and some even commit suicide. Research conducted by RAND has shown that 25 to 30 percent of Iraq and Afghanistan war veterans have reported symptoms of a mental disorder or cognitive impairment. Posttraumatic stress disorder (PTSD) is the most common, and traumatic brain injury may be a causal factor in some reported symptoms. Substance use is also a large concern, with aggregated data from the Substance Abuse and Mental Health Services Administration's annual household survey revealing that from 2004 to 2006, 7.1 percent of veterans (an estimated 1.8 million persons eighteen or older) met criteria for a past-year substance-use disorder.

Problems with alcohol and substance abuse pose a significant risk to the health of veterans as well as Reserve and National Guard soldiers. At greatest risk are deployed personnel with combat exposures, as they are more apt to engage in new-onset heavy weekly drinking and binge drinking and to suffer alcohol-related problems and relapse. Within this group, Reserve and National Guard personnel and younger service members are particularly vulnerable to subsequent drinking problems.

Service members today have a number of things working against them—combat, separation from loved ones, maiming or killing of comrades—causing them to return home addicted to drugs or alcohol or suffering from mental illness. The military now regularly prescribes medication to help ease stress and anxiety, to help with physical pain, or to keep service members alert when they need to be. These kinds of prescription drugs, although perhaps necessary in a combat situation, are addictive, and on their return to normal life, service members can't do without them. Many other members of the military self-medicate and become addicted in the process.

To gain a fuller understanding of these burgeoning issues, the Millennium Cohort Study, the largest prospective study in military history, is following a representative sample of US military personnel from 2001 to 2022. Early findings highlight the importance of prevention in this group, given the long-term effects of combat-related problems and the ensuing difficulties experienced in seeking or being referred for treatment, likely because of stigma and other real and perceived barriers. To fill this need, a host of government agencies, researchers, public health entities, and others are working together to adapt and test proven prevention interventions, as well as drug-abuse treatments, for potential use with military and veteran populations and their families.

To address the social problems both caused by and contributing to drug use, the Department of Defense and partners are developing and testing novel treatment approaches with veterans. For example, Dr. Marc Rosen's Money Management Intervention trains those in drug treatment to better manage their money by linking access to funds to treatment goal completion. For relapse prevention, James McKay's telephone treatment approach delivers counseling at home for several months once a veteran has completed an initial face-to-face treatment session.

Although NIDA is striving to expand its portfolio of research related to trauma, stress, and substance use and abuse among veterans and their families, a number of promising projects are already being funded. These include studies on smoking cessation and PTSD, behavioral interventions for the dually diagnosed, substance use and HIV progression, and virtual reality treatment of PTSD and substance abuse. Additionally, NIDA's National Drug Abuse Treatment Clinical Trials Network is developing, in conjunction with researchers from the Veterans Administration (VA), a protocol concept on the treatment of PTSD and substance-use disorder in veteran populations.

Efforts are under way to make it easier for veterans to access treatments. Research on drug courts, for example, is now being applied to developing courts for veterans, the former having demonstrated their effectiveness in addressing nonviolent crimes by drug abusers and ushering the perpetrators into needed treatment instead of prison. Because the criminal justice system is a frequent treatment referral source for veterans, such specialized courts may give them the opportunity to access services and support they may not otherwise receive. Although New York has the only court that exclusively handles nonviolent crimes committed by veterans, other states are considering establishing such courts.

It's common for troops to "self-medicate." They drink or abuse drugs to numb themselves and blot out the difficult thoughts, feelings, and memories related to war-zone experiences. Reactions to the stress of these experiences can range from mild to severe and may be either short-lived or persist for a very long time. One seemingly simple and easy solution to managing stress is to use alcohol or drugs. Military personnel, like civilians, may use these substances to relax or reduce anxiety and other bad feelings. In some cases, alcohol and drugs are used not only to decrease stress but also to manage severe symptoms that can arise from a traumatic experience in the war zone. Often stressed people use alcohol or drugs to help with the following:

- Falling asleep
- Decreasing sadness or emotional pain
- Relaxing
- Helping themselves be around others
- Increasing pleasure
- Drowning worries
- Keeping upsetting memories submerged
- Escaping present difficulties
- Shaking off stress
- Calming anxiety

Initially, alcohol and drugs may seem to make things better. They may help one sleep, forget problems, or feel more relaxed. But any short-term benefit can turn sour fast. In the long run, using alcohol and drugs to cope with stress will cause a whole new set of very serious problems, as well as worsen the original problems that led one to drink or use in the first place. Alcohol and drug abuse can cause problems with family life, physical health, mental well-being, relationships, finances, employment, spirituality, and sense of self-worth.

At the same time, the vast majority of people in American society drink. Sometimes it can be difficult to know if your drinking is actually a problem. Most individuals who abuse alcohol or drugs have jobs and are productive members of society, creating a false sense that "things are not that bad." The problem is that addiction tends to worsen over time, hurting both the addicted person and his or her family members. It is especially damaging to young children and adolescents.

Consider the family impact. It's difficult to create good relationships when you are regularly drunk or high. Being intoxicated decreases intimacy and creates an inability to communicate well. Family members can feel rejected by someone who is always under the influence. In addition, witnessing someone's behavior while under the influence can be distressing. Children may not understand the aggression, the shutting down, or the hiding out that can occur with substance use. The fallout from an accident or an arrest can have a long-lasting impact on a family. Alcohol and drug problems are also dangerous for loved ones because they are often linked with family violence and driving while intoxicated.

People who suffer from addiction really may believe that they drink normally or that "everyone" takes drugs. These false beliefs, called denial, are a part of the illness. Drug- and alcohol-dependence disorders are medical conditions that can be effectively treated. Millions of Americans and their families are in healthy recovery from this disease. If someone close to you misuses alcohol or drugs, it is critical to be honest about the problem and to seek help for yourself, your family, and your loved one.

Treatment can occur in a variety of settings, in many different forms, and for different lengths of time. Stopping the alcohol or drug use is the first step to recovery, and most people need help to stop. Often a person with alcohol or drug dependence will need treatment provided by professionals, as is the case with other diseases. Your doctor may be able to guide you.

ALCOHOL

Not all drinking is harmful, and moderate drinking might even be good for you. However, at-risk or heavy drinkers can face serious risks unless they take action.

- Injuries: Drinking too much increases your chances of being injured or even killed. Alcohol is a factor, for example, in about 60 percent of fatal burn injuries, drownings, and homicides, 50 percent of severe trauma injuries and sexual assaults, and 40 percent of fatal motor vehicle crashes, suicide attempts, and falls.
- Health problems: Heavy drinkers have a greater risk of liver disease, heart disease, sleep disorders, depression, stroke, bleeding from the stomach, sexually transmitted infections from unsafe sex, and several types of cancer. They may also have problems managing diabetes, high blood pressure, and other conditions.
- Birth defects in offspring: Drinking during pregnancy can cause brain damage and other serious problems in the baby. Because it is not yet known whether any amount of alcohol is safe for a developing fetus, women who are pregnant or who may become pregnant should not drink.

- Alcohol-use disorders: Generally known as alcoholism and alcohol abuse, alcohol-use disorders are medical conditions that doctors can diagnose when a patient's drinking causes distress or harm. In the United States, about 18 million people have an alcohol-use disorder.

Have you noticed any of the following symptoms in yourself or a loved one in the past year?

- Have you had times when you ended up drinking more or longer than you intended?
- Have you wanted more than once to cut down or stop drinking, or tried to but couldn't?
- Have you gotten into situations more than once, while drinking or afterward, that increased your chances of getting hurt (such as driving, swimming, using machinery, walking in a dangerous area, or having unsafe sex)?
- Have you had to drink much more than you once did to get the effect you want or found that your usual number of drinks had much less effect than before?
- Have you continued to drink even though it was making you feel depressed or anxious or adding to another health problem? Or after having had a memory blackout?
- Have you spent a lot of time drinking? Or being sick or getting over other aftereffects?
- Have you continued to drink even though doing so was causing trouble with your family or friends?
- Have you found that drinking—or being sick from drinking—has often interfered with taking care of your home or family or caused job troubles?
- Have you given up or cut back on activities that are important or interesting to you or that give you pleasure in order to drink?
- Have you more than once been arrested, been held at a police station, or had other legal problems because of your drinking?
- Have you found that when the effects of alcohol were wearing off, you had withdrawal symptoms, such as trouble sleeping, shakiness, restlessness, nausea, sweating, a racing heart, a seizure, or a hallucination?

If you or a loved one have any of these symptoms, then alcohol may already be a cause for concern. The more symptoms you have, the more urgent the need for change. A health professional can look at the number, pattern, and severity of symptoms to determine whether an alcohol-use disorder is present and help you decide the best course of action.

Alcoholism involves chronic alcohol abuse that results in a physical dependence on alcohol and an inability to stop or limit drinking. Warning signs of an alcohol problem include the following:

- Frequent excessive drinking
- Thoughts that you should cut down
- Guilt or remorse about your drinking
- Annoyance or criticism from others regarding how much you drink
- Drinking in the morning to calm your nerves
- Problems with work, family, school, or other regular activities caused by drinking

WHEN IS ALCOHOL USE A PROBLEM?

It is often hard to decide whether alcohol or drug use is becoming a problem. It can happen gradually and can sometimes be hard to notice for the person who is using. Here are things that people sometimes say to convince themselves that they do not have a problem. Do you recognize any?

- I just drink beer (wine).
- I don't drink every day.
- I don't use hard drugs.
- I've never missed a day of work.
- I'm not an alcoholic.
- I don't need help. I can handle it.
- I gave it up for three weeks last year.

Alcohol or drug use can be considered a problem when it causes difficulties, even in minor ways. Here are some questions that you can ask yourself to see if you are developing a problem:

- Have friends or family members commented on how much or how often you drink?
- Have you have found yourself feeling guilty about your drinking or drug use?
- Have you found yourself drinking (using) more over time?
- Have you tried to cut down your alcohol (drug) use?
- Does your drinking (drug use) ever affect your ability to fulfill personal obligations such as parenting or work?
- Do you put yourself in physically dangerous situations when you drink or use, such as driving or operating machinery while under the influence?
- Have you found that you need more alcohol (of the drug) to get the same effect?

If you find that you are answering yes to one or more of these questions, perhaps it is time to reevaluate your use, cut back, and seek help from friends, family, or a professional.

What Are the Treatment Options?

If you think that alcohol (drug) use has become (or is becoming) a problem for you, you can do a number of things. First, recognize that you are not alone and that others are available to lend support. Second, find help. Getting help is the most useful tool in decreasing or stopping problem drinking or drug use, even if you have doubts about being able to quit or if you are feeling guilty about the problem. Contact your health provider, a physician or therapist, your local VA hospital, or your local Alcoholics Anonymous chapter for guidance in your recovery.

CAGE is an acronym for the following questions:

C: Have you ever felt that you should *cut* down on your drinking?
A: Have people *annoyed* you by criticizing your drinking?
G: Have you ever felt bad or *guilty* about your drinking?
E: Have you ever had a drink first thing in the morning to steady your nerves or get rid of a hangover (i.e., as an *eye-opener*)?

Individuals answering yes to three or four of the CAGE questions over the past year are most likely alcohol dependent. An individual who endorses one or two of the CAGE questions may have alcohol-abuse issues. Combining the introductory screening comments with the quantity-frequency and CAGE questions can reliably predict 70 to 80 percent of individuals with alcohol-abuse or -dependence problems (Friedman et al., 2001).

The same screening tool can be adapted for illicit drug use. For example, initial questions about a person's response to notification of deployment might uncover marijuana use. The health care provider can then ask quantity-frequency questions followed by the adapted CAGE.

Family Intervention

Getting a loved one to agree to accept help and finding support services for all family members are the first steps toward healing for the addicted person and the entire family. When an addicted person is reluctant to seek help, sometimes family members, friends, and associates come together out of concern and love to confront the problem drinker. They strongly urge the person to enter treatment and list the serious consequences of not doing so, such as family breakup or job loss.

This is called "intervention." When carefully prepared with the guidance of a competent, trained specialist, the family, friends, and associates are usually able to convince their loved one—in a firm and loving manner—that the only choice is to accept help and begin the road to recovery. People with alcohol or drug dependence problems can and do recover. Intervention is often the first step.

Children in families experiencing alcohol or drug abuse need attention, guidance, and support. They may be growing up in homes in which the problems are either denied or covered up. These children need to have their experiences validated. They also need safe, reliable adults in whom to confide and who will support and reassure them and provide them with appropriate help for their age. They need to have fun and just be kids.

Families with alcohol and drug problems usually have high levels of stress and confusion. High-stress family environments are a risk factor for early and dangerous substance use, as well as mental and physical health problems. It is important to talk honestly with children about what is happening in the family and to help them express their concerns and feelings. Children need to trust the adults in their lives and to believe that they will support them.

Children living with alcohol or drug abuse in the family can benefit from participating in educational support groups in their school student-assistance programs. Those age eleven and older can join Alateen groups, which meet in community settings and provide healthy connections with others coping with similar issues. Associating with the activities of a faith community can also help.

If you're considering changing your drinking habits, you'll need to decide whether to cut down or to quit. It's a good idea to discuss different options with a doctor, a friend, or someone else you trust. Quitting is strongly advised if you

- Have tried cutting down but cannot stay within the limits you set
- Have had an alcohol-use disorder or now have symptoms
- Have a physical or mental condition that is caused or worsened by drinking
- Are taking a medication that interacts with alcohol
- Are or may become pregnant

If you do not have any of these conditions, talk with your doctor to determine whether you should cut down or quit, based on the following factors:

- Family history of alcohol problems
- Your age
- Whether you've had drinking-related injuries
- Symptoms such as sleep disorders and sexual dysfunction

Help is available on base and in your local community. Look in the yellow pages under alcoholism for treatment and self-help groups. Call your county health department and ask for licensed treatment programs in your community. Keep trying until you find the right help for your loved one, yourself, and your family. Ask a family therapist for a referral to a trained interventionist or call the Intervention Resource Center at (888) 421-4321.

Quitting Techniques

Several proven treatment approaches are available. One size doesn't fit all, however. It's a good idea to do some homework on the Internet or at the library to find social and professional support options that appeal to you, as you are more likely to stick with them. Chances are excellent that you'll pull together an approach that works for you.

Social Support

One potential challenge when people stop drinking is rebuilding a life without alcohol. It may be important to educate family and friends, to develop new interests and social groups, and to find rewarding ways to spend your time that don't involve alcohol. Ask for help from others. When asking for support from friends or significant others, be specific. This could include not offering you alcohol, not using alcohol around you, giving words of support and withholding criticism, not asking you to take on new demands right now, and going to a group like Al-Anon. Consider joining Alcoholics Anonymous or another mutual-support group. Recovering people who attend groups regularly do better than those who do not. Groups can vary widely, so shop around for one that's comfortable. You'll get more out of it if you become actively involved, get a sponsor, and reach out to other members for assistance.

Professional Support

Advances in the treatment of alcoholism mean that patients now have more choices and health professionals have more tools to help.

- Medications to treat alcoholism: Newer medications can make it easier to quit drinking by offsetting changes in the brain caused by alcoholism. These options (naltrexone, topiramate, and acamprosate) don't make you sick if you drink, as does an older medication (disulfiram). None of these medications are addictive, so it's fine to combine them with support groups or alcohol counseling. A major clinical trial recently showed that patients can now receive effective alcohol treatment from their primary care doctors or mental health practitioners by combining the newer medications with a series of brief office visits for support.

- Alcohol counseling: "Talk therapy" also works well. The various counseling approaches—twelve step, cognitive-behavioral, motivational enhancement, or a combination—are about equally effective. Getting help in itself appears to be more important than the particular approach used, as long as it offers empathy, avoids heavy confrontation, strengthens motivation, and provides concrete ways to change drinking behavior.
- Specialized, intensive treatment programs: Some people will need more intensive programs. If you need a referral to a program, ask your doctor.

Self-Help Groups

Adult Children of Alcoholics: http://www.adultchildren.org
Al-Anon Family Groups: http://www.al-anon.org
Alateen: http://www.alateen.org
Alcoholics Anonymous: http://www.aa.org

DRUGS

Each year, substance abuse contributes to more than 120,000 American deaths. According to the Office of National Drug Control Policy, it costs taxpayers more than $328 billion annually in preventable health care costs, extra law enforcement, auto crashes, crime, and lost productivity.

Drug abuse is the use of drugs to get "high." It is a voluntary act, unlike drug addiction, which is involuntary. The addict is not able to stop using drugs without intervention. Like alcoholism, drug addiction is a disease for which there is no cure.

Drug addiction can happen easily and quickly, leaving the addict suffering from either the severe effects of the drug or strong withdrawal effects. In order to conquer the addiction, the addict and those around him or her need a lot of support, help, and willpower.

The physical signs of a drug addiction can vary, depending on the drug used, the amount consumed, and the environment in which it is taken in. The early signs of a drug addiction can include mixed moods, sleepiness or excessive or unusual tiredness during the day, agitation, and paranoia. As the dependency develops, the signs can change to frequent distraction, depression, mixed mental states (including psychosis), and decreased ability to coordinate or perform tasks that are normally easy to complete. The degree of effect varies among users and substances. Other obvious signs are needle marks on the arms in those who have been injecting the drugs (although these "track marks" can appear on other area of the body once the veins in the arms have deteriorated and can no longer be used). People who are normally nonsmokers are likely to suffer from breathlessness or coughing if they have been smoking drugs for long periods.

Although cheaper than they were a few decades ago, drugs are still expensive, and most users struggle to keep up with the financial demands of their habit. As the drug addiction develops, the person is likely to become isolated from family and friends and may get quite agitated when confronted about this.

Commonly Abused Drugs

Marijuana

Effects: Euphoria, relaxation, slowed reaction time, distorted sensory perception, impaired balance and coordination, increased heart rate and appetite, impaired learning and memory, anxiety, panic attacks, psychosis

Health risks: Cough and frequent respiratory infections, possible mental health decline, addiction

Heroin and Opium

Effects: Euphoria, drowsiness, impaired coordination, dizziness, confusion, nausea, sedation, feeling of heaviness in the body, slowed or arrested breathing

Health risks: Constipation, endocarditis, hepatitis, HIV, addiction, fatal overdose

Cocaine, Amphetamines, and Methamphetamine

Effects: Increased heart rate, blood pressure, body temperature, and metabolism, feelings of exhilaration, increased energy and mental alertness, tremors, reduced appetite, irritability, anxiety, panic, paranoia, violent behavior, psychosis

Health risks: Weight loss, insomnia, cardiac or cardiovascular complications, stroke, seizures, addiction

Also, for cocaine: Nasal damage from snorting

Also, for methamphetamine: Severe dental problems

Club Drugs

Methylene-dioxy-methamphetamine (MDMA): Ecstasy, Adam, Clarity, Eve, lover's speed, peace, uppers

Flunitrazepam: Forget-me pill, Mexican valium, R2, roach, roche, roofies, roofinol, rope, rophies

Gamma hydroxybutyrate (GHB): G, Georgia homeboy, grievous bodily harm, liquid ecstasy, soap, scoop, goop, liquid X

Effects, for MDMA: Mild hallucinogenic effects, increased tactile sensitivity, empathic feelings, lowered inhibition, anxiety, chills, sweating, teeth clenching, muscle cramping

Also, for flunitrazepam: Sedation, muscle relaxation, confusion, memory loss, dizziness, impaired coordination

Also, for GHB: Drowsiness, nausea, headache, disorientation, loss of coordination, memory loss

Health risks, for MDMA: Sleep disturbances, depression, impaired memory, hyperthermia, addiction

Also, for flunitrazepam: Addiction

Also, for GHB: Unconsciousness, seizures, coma

Dissociative Drugs

Ketamine: Ketalar SV, cat valium, K, special K, vitamin K

PCP and analogs: Angel dust, boat, hog, love boat, peace pill

Salvia divinorum: Salvia, shepherdess's herb, Maria Pzastora, magin mint, Sally-D

Dextromethorphan (DXM): Found in some cough medications, robotripping, robo, triple C

Effects: Feelings of being separate from one's body and environment, impaired motor function

Also, for ketamine: Analgesia, impaired memory, delirium, respiratory depression and arrest, death

Also, for PCP and analogs: Analgesia, psychosis, aggression, violence, slurred speech, loss of coordination, hallucinations

Also, for DXM: Euphoria, slurred speech, confusion, dizziness, distorted visual perceptions

Health risks: Anxiety, tremors, numbness, memory loss, nausea

Hallucinogens

Lysergic acid diethylamide (LSD): Acid, blotter, cubes, microdot yellow sunshine, blue heaven

Mescaline: Buttons, cactus, mesc, peyote

Psilocybin: Magic mushrooms, purple passion, shrooms, little smoke

Effects: Altered states of perception and feeling, hallucinations, nausea

Also, for LSD and mescaline: Increased body temperature, heart rate, blood pressure, loss of appetite, sweating, sleeplessness, numbness, dizziness, weakness, tremors, impulsive behavior, rapid shifts in emotion

Also, for psilocybin: Nervousness, paranoia, panic

Health risks, for LSD: Flashbacks, hallucinogen persisting perception disorder

Other Compounds

Anabolic steroids: Roids, juice, gym candy, pumpers

Inhalants: Laughing gas, poppers, snappers, whippets

Effects, for anabolic steroids: No intoxication effects

Also, for inhalants (varies by chemical): Stimulation, loss of inhibition, headache, nausea or vomiting, slurred speech, loss of motor coordination, wheezing

Health risks, for anabolic steroids: Hypertension, blood clotting and cholesterol changes, liver cysts, hostility and aggression, acne, in adolescents—premature growth stoppage, in males—prostate cancer, reduced sperm production, shrunken testicles, breast enlargement; in females—menstrual irregularities, development of beard and other masculine characteristics

Also, for inhalants: Cramps, muscle weakness, depression, memory impairment, damage to cardiovascular and nervous systems, unconsciousness, sudden death

Abused Prescription Drugs

Barbiturates: Barbs, reds, red birds, phennies, tooies, yellows, yellow jackets

Benzodiazepines: Candy, downers, sleeping pills, tranks

Sleep medications: Forget-me pill, Mexican valium, R2, roche, roofies, roofinol, rope, rophies

Effects: Sedation/drowsiness, reduced anxiety, feelings of well-being, lowered inhibitions, slurred speech, poor concentration, confusion, dizziness, impaired coordination and memory

Health risks: Lowered blood pressure, slowed breathing, tolerance, withdrawal, addiction, increased risk of respiratory distress and death when combined with alcohol

Also, for barbiturates: Euphoria, unusual excitement, fever, irritability, life-threatening withdrawal in chronic users

Opioids and Morphine Derivatives and Opioid Pain Relievers

Codeine: Captain Cody, cody, schoolboy, with glutethimide—doors and fours, loads, pancakes and syrup

Morphine: M, Miss Emma, monkey, white stuff

Methadone: Fizzies, amidone, with MDMA—chocolate chip cookies

Fentanyl and analogs: Apache, China girl, China white, dance fever, friend, goodfella, jackpot, murder 8, TNT, Tango and Cash

Oxycodone HCL, hydrocodone bitartrate hydromorphone, oxymorphone, meperidine, propoxyphene: Hillbilly heroin, percs, juice, smack, D, footballs, dillies, biscuits, blue heaven, blues, Mrs. O, octagons, stop signs, O bomb, demmies, pain killers

Effects: Pain relief, euphoria, drowsiness, sedation, weakness, dizziness, nausea, impaired coordination, confusion, dry mouth, itching, sweating, clammy skin, constipation

Health risks: Slowed or arrested breathing, lowered pulse and blood pressure, tolerance, addiction, unconsciousness, coma, death, risk of death increased when combined with alcohol or other central nervous system depressants

Also, for fentanyl: Eighty to one hundred times more potent than
   morphine
Also, for oxycodone: Muscle relaxation, twice as potent as morphine,
   high abuse potential
Also, for codeine: Less analgesia, sedation, and respiratory depression than for morphine
Also, for methadone: Used to treat opioid addiction and pain, significant overdose risk when used improperly

Taking drugs by injection can increase the risk of infection through
needle contamination with staphylococci, HIV, hepatitis, and other organisms. Injection is a more common practice with opioids, but risks
apply to any medication taken by injection.

Stimulants

Amphetamines: Bennies, black beauties, crosses, hearts, LA turn-
   around, speed, truck drivers, uppers
Methylphenidate (MPH): JIF, R-ball, Skippy, the smart drug, vitamin R
Effects: Feelings of exhilaration, increased energy, mental alertness
Health risks: Increased heart rate, blood pressure, and metabolism;
   reduced appetite, weight loss; nervousness, insomnia, seizures,
   heart attack, stroke
Also, for amphetamines: Rapid breathing, tremor, loss of coordination, irritability, anxiousness, restlessness/delirium, panic, paranoia, hallucinations, impulsive behavior, aggressiveness, tolerance, addiction
Also, for methylphenidate: Increase or decrease in blood pressure,
   digestive problems, loss of appetite, weight loss

What Happens to Your Brain When You Take Drugs?

Drugs are chemicals that tap into the brain's communication system
and disrupt the way nerve cells normally send, receive, and process
information. Drugs are able to do this in at least two ways: (1) by
imitating the brain's natural chemical messengers, and/or (2) by over-
stimulating the reward circuit of the brain. Some drugs, such as marijuana and heroin, have a similar structure to chemical messengers,

called neurotransmitters, that are naturally produced by the brain. Because of this similarity, these drugs are able to fool the brain's receptors and activate nerve cells to send abnormal messages. Other drugs, such as cocaine or methamphetamine, can cause the nerve cells to release abnormally large amounts of natural neurotransmitters or prevent the normal recycling of these brain chemicals, which is needed to shut off the signal between neurons. This disruption produces a greatly amplified message that ultimately disrupts normal communication patterns.

Nearly all drugs, directly or indirectly, target the brain's reward system by flooding the circuit with dopamine. Dopamine is a neurotransmitter present in regions of the brain that control movement, emotion, motivation, and feelings of pleasure. The overstimulation of this system, which normally responds to natural behaviors linked to survival (e.g., eating, spending time with loved ones), produces euphoric effects. This reaction sets in motion a pattern that "teaches" people to repeat the drug use.

As a person continues to abuse drugs, the brain adapts to the overwhelming surges in dopamine by producing less dopamine or reducing the number of dopamine receptors in the reward circuit. As a result, dopamine's impact on the reward circuit is lessened, reducing the abuser's ability to enjoy the drugs and the things that previously brought pleasure. This decrease compels those addicted to drugs to keep abusing drugs in order to attempt to elevate their dopamine function. But they now require larger amounts of the drug than they first did to achieve the dopamine high—an effect known as tolerance.

Long-term abuse causes changes in other brain chemical systems and circuits as well. Glutamate is a neurotransmitter that influences the reward circuit and the ability to learn. When drug abuse alters the optimal concentration of glutamate, the brain attempts to compensate, which can impair cognitive function. Drugs of abuse facilitate nonconscious (conditioned) learning, which leads the user to experience uncontrollable cravings when they see a place or person associated with the drug experience, even when the drug itself is not available. Brain imaging studies of drug-addicted individuals show changes in areas of the brain critical to judgment, decision making, learning, memory, and behavior control. Together, these changes can drive an abuser to seek out and take drugs compulsively, despite adverse consequences—in other words, to become addicted to drugs.

Why Do Some People Become Addicted, Whereas Others Do Not?

No single factor can predict whether a person will become addicted to drugs. Biology, social environment, and age or stage of development all influence a person's risk of addiction.

- Biology: The genes that people are born with—in combination with environmental influences—account for about half of their addiction vulnerability. Additionally, gender, ethnicity, and the presence of other mental disorders may influence risk for drug abuse and addiction.
- Environment: A person's environment includes many different influences, from family and friends to socioeconomic status and quality of life in general. Factors such as peer pressure, physical and sexual abuse, stress, and parental involvement can greatly influence the course of drug abuse and addiction in a person's life.
- Development: Genetic and environmental factors interact with critical developmental stages in a person's life to affect addiction vulnerability, and adolescents experience a double challenge. Although taking drugs at any age can lead to addiction, the earlier that drug use begins, the more likely it is to progress to more serious abuse. And because adolescents' brains are still developing in the areas that govern decision making, judgment, and self-control, they are especially prone to risk-taking behaviors, including trying drugs of abuse.

The more risk factors an individual has, the greater the chance that taking drugs can lead to addiction.

Treatments

Before deciding on a program of drug treatment and support, the individual must be able to admit that he or she has an addiction and actually want to overcome it. Positive thinking, willpower, and determination are fundamental to the success of a drug-treatment plan.

Overcoming an addiction is a very individual experience, and a wide variety of resources may be needed to help break the drug addiction. Consider whether a support group, individual counseling, or a combination will be beneficial. These types of therapy are useful as the therapists know what addiction is about, will help determine the cause, and can give a vast amount of advice regarding craving control, withdrawal management, and restructuring life without the addiction. Also, find out about help lines and when they can be accessed, who runs them, and what they offer. Keep the list in close proximity at all times during the initial period of withdrawal and use these help lines when cravings are becoming too strong or anxieties are building up.

Allow for the "cold turkey" period. Warn family and close friends of what is happening and explain that it may cause distress to all concerned. Exercise helps to ease symptoms of withdrawal, so plan an exercise regime.

18

DOMESTIC VIOLENCE

Domestic violence happens so much in the military that the Department of Defense (DoD) has made it an item of specific concern. Accurate statistics of domestic abuse in the military are hard to come by, and it is acknowledged by the Pentagon that many cases go unreported. However, in 2002 there were more than eighteen thousand incidents of spousal abuse, 84 percent of which involved physical abuse. In 2011 (the latest data available), 19,277 cases were reported—the highest annual figure reported to date.

Risk factors for domestic violence are greater than among the general population. According to the Department of the Navy, a high percentage of military personnel have prior histories of family violence. Among navy recruits, 54 percent of women and 40 percent of men witnessed parental violence prior to enlistment. Other factors include the following:

- The military population is concentrated in the age range of highest risk for interpersonal violence (FBI, Crime in the United States, Defense Manpower Data Center).
- Constant moves and deployments may isolate victims by cutting them off from family and support systems (Family Advocacy Program, Military Community and Family Policy, Department of Defense).

- Higher-than-average unemployment and underemployment rates for military spouses leave them economically dependent on service members (Family Advocacy Program).
- Deployments and reunifications create unique stressors for military families (Family Advocacy Program).

First sergeants and military police hate domestic calls because the solutions are never clear-cut. More often than not, the victims of domestic violence refuse to cooperate because they perceive a threat to their spouse's career or further injury or danger to themselves or their loved ones.

In most cases, husbands abuse wives—but not always. If the abuser is a civilian, the military has no control over the matter. In most cases, the military can merely turn the information over the civilian authorities. If a child is involved, the civilian authorities must be notified immediately.

In the military, "domestic abuse" and "domestic violence" mean two different things. In both cases, the abuser and victim can be of the same or opposite sex, and the abuser must be one of the following:

- The victim's current or former spouse
- Co-parent with the victim of a child
- A current or former "intimate partner" whom the victim lives or has lived with

Domestic abuse is defined as a pattern of behavior resulting in emotional or psychological abuse, economic control, and/or interference with personal liberty. Physical violence need not be involved. *Domestic violence* in the military is a crime (under the United States Code, the Uniform Code of Military Justice (UCMJ), and/or state law) that involves the use, attempted use, or threatened use of force or violence or a violation of an order of protection.

In the military, the commanding officer has the authority to decide what behavior to address and whether to use judicial, administrative, or other means to deal with domestic abuse or violence. The civilian justice system makes decisions based on the state's laws. Courts will decide what punishment or other action to take based on testimony and evidence from both sides. In both the military and civilian justice systems, you can seek a protective order requiring the abuser to stay away from you and your children, your home, your workplace, or your school and not to engage in any violent conduct. Protective orders have different names in the various states, but the services consistently call them military protective orders (MPO). You can have both an MPO and a civil protective order at the same time. Installation commanders do have the power to bar civilians from military installations and will exercise that power to protect military members from abusive civilian spouses, if necessary.

If the abuser is a military member, domestic violence situations are handled on two separate tracks: the military justice system and the family advocacy system. It's important to realize that these are two separate, unconnected systems. Family advocacy is an identification, intervention, and treatment program—not a penal system. It's entirely possible for the Family Advocacy Committee to return a finding of "substantiated abuse" but for there to be insufficient legally admissible evidence to permit punishment under the provisions of military justice. On the other hand, one should realize that the family advocacy system does not enjoy the right of confidentiality provided under military law (such as with disclosures made to chaplains and attorneys), and evidence gathered and statements made during family advocacy investigations may be used in military justice proceedings.

If an incident happens off base, civilian agencies may be given jurisdiction on the legal side, but family advocacy should still be notified. Off base, local police may or may not report the incident to base officials. DoD officials are currently working to develop memoranda of understanding with civilian law enforcement authorities to establish such reporting procedures. Regulations require military and DoD officials to report any suspicion of family violence to Family Advocacy, no matter how small. These personnel include commanders, first sergeants, supervisors, medical personnel, teachers, and military police.

In many cases, when responding to a domestic situation, the commander or first sergeant will order the military individual to reside in the dormitory or barracks until the family advocacy investigation is completed. This may be accompanied by an MPO, which is a written order prohibiting the military member from having any contact with the alleged victim. Many bases have an "abused-dependent safeguard" system, whereby the first sergeant or commander places abused family members in billeting under an assumed name.

When domestic violence is reported to Family Advocacy, the agency will assign a caseworker to assess the victim's safety, develop a safety plan, and investigate the incident. Throughout the process, victims' advocates ensure that the victim's medical, mental health, and protection needs are being met. Family advocacy officials will also interview the alleged abuser. The alleged abuser is informed of his or her rights under the provisions of Article 31 of the UCMJ and does not have to speak to the investigation officials if he or she chooses not to. If child abuse is involved, regulations require that local child-protection agencies be notified and participate in the process.

After the investigation, the case is then presented to a multidisciplinary case-review committee with representatives from the Family Advocacy Program, law enforcement, staff judge advocate, medical staff, and chaplain. The committee decides whether the evidence indicates abuse occurred and arrives at one of the following findings:

- Substantiated: A case has been investigated, and the preponderance of available information indicates that abuse has occurred. This means that the information that supports the occurrence of abuse is of greater weight or more convincing than the information that indicates that abuse did not occur.
- Suspected: A case determination is pending further investigation. The duration for a case to be "suspected" and under investigation should not exceed twelve weeks.
- Unsubstantiated: An alleged case has been investigated, and the available information is insufficient to support the claim that child abuse and/or neglect or spousal abuse did occur. The family needs no family advocacy services.

In making these determinations, the committee uses the following definitions for abuse:

- Child abuse and/or neglect: Includes physical injury, sexual maltreatment, emotional maltreatment, deprivation of necessities, or any combination by an individual responsible for the child's welfare under circumstances indicating that the child's welfare is harmed or threatened. The term encompasses both acts and omissions on the part of a responsible person. A "child" is a person under eighteen years of age for whom a parent, guardian, foster parent, caretaker, employee of a residential facility, or any staff person providing out-of-home care is legally responsible. The term "child" means a natural child, adopted child, stepchild, foster child, or ward. The term also includes an individual of any age who is incapable of self-support because of a mental or physical incapacity and for whom treatment in a military treatment facility is authorized.

- Spousal abuse: Includes assault, battery, threat to injure or kill, other act of force or violence, or emotional maltreatment inflicted on a partner in a lawful marriage when one of the partners is a military member or is employed by the Department of Defense and is eligible for treatment in an military treatment facility. A spouse under eighteen years of age shall be treated in this category.

Based on the committee's recommendations, the commander decides what action to take regarding the abuser. The commander determines whether to order the individual into treatment and/or to seek to impose disciplinary procedures under the UCMJ. The commander may also seek to obtain the discharge of the service member from the military.

Stalking or other harassing behavior is often an integral part of domestic violence and is as prevalent in the military as it is in civilian life. According to *Workplace Violence: A Report to the Nation*, a 2001 study by the University of Iowa Injury Prevention Research Center, 5 percent of workplace homicides (that is, about one-third of homicides not associated with a robbery or other "stranger" crime) fall into this category.

Victims often hesitate to report abuse for many reasons. Some fear it will impact on their spouse's career. Many believe that their spouse will change and that the abuse will stop. Others fear that if they report the abuse, the violence might get worse or that their children could become victims as well. Unfortunately, many victims mistakenly think that the abuse is their fault—that they must have provoked it. Whatever the reason behind their hesitation, victims suffer both physical and psychological trauma and the decision of whether to report the abuse is very complex.

A recent DoD study found that service members reported for abuse are 23 percent more likely to be separated from the service than non-abusers and somewhat more likely to have other than honorable discharges. The majority who remain in the military are more likely to be promoted more slowly than nonabusers.

Many military spouses don't know that federal law gives financial protection to a spouse if a member is discharged for an offense that "involves abuse of the then-current spouse or a dependent child." It doesn't matter if the discharge is punitive, imposed by a court-martial, or administrative, initiated by the commander. The key is that the discharge must be the result of a "dependent-abuse" offense. The phrase "involves abuse of the then-current spouse or a dependent child" means that the criminal offense is against the person of that spouse or dependent child. Crimes that may qualify as "dependent-abuse offenses" include sexual assault, rape, sodomy, assault, battery, murder, and manslaughter.

You can check to see what the current authorized payment is. If the spouse has custody of a dependent child or children of the member, the amount of monthly compensation is increased for each child. If there is no eligible spouse, compensation is paid to a dependent child or to dependent children in equal shares to each child.

The duration of the payments cannot exceed thirty-six months. If the military member had less than thirty-six months of obligated military service at the time of the discharge or imposition of the court-martial sentence, then the duration of the payments will equal the length of the member's obligated service or twelve months, whichever is greater.

If a spouse receiving payments remarries, payments terminate as of the date of the remarriage. Payment shall not be renewed if such remarriage is terminated. If the payments to the spouse terminate due to remarriage and there is a dependent child not living in the same household as the spouse or member, payments shall be made to the dependent child.

If the military member who committed the abuse resides in the same household as the spouse or dependent child to whom compensation is otherwise payable, payment shall terminate as of the date the member begins residing in such household.

If the victim is a dependent child, and the spouse has been found by a competent authority designated by the secretary concerned to have been an active participant in the conduct constituting the criminal offense or to have actively aided or abetted the member in such conduct against that dependent child, the dependent child, if living with the spouse, shall not be paid transitional compensation.

In addition to the transitional benefits, if the military member was eligible for retirement but denied it because of the criminal offense, the spouse can still apply to a divorce court for a division of retired pay under the provisions of the Uniformed Services Former Spouse Protection Act, and the military will honor the payments. (*Note:* Under this provision, such payments terminate upon remarriage).

Even if a domestic violence case is handled off base via the civilian criminal court system, criminal conviction of even a misdemeanor involving domestic violence can end a service member's military career. The 1996 Lautenberg Amendment to the Gun Control Act of 1968 makes it unlawful for anyone convicted of a domestic violence misdemeanor to possess firearms. The law applies to law enforcement officers and military personnel.

The following observable behavior may suggest possible victimization:

- Tardiness or unexplained absences
- Frequent, often unplanned use of leave time
- Anxiety
- Lack of concentration
- Change in job performance
- A tendency to remain isolated from coworkers or reluctance to participate in social events
- Discomfort when communicating with others
- Disruptive phone calls or e-mails
- Sudden or unexplained requests to be moved from public locations in the workplace, such as sales or reception areas
- Frequent financial problems indicating lack of access to money
- Unexplained bruises or injuries
- Noticeable changes in makeup use (to cover up injuries)
- Inappropriate attire (e.g., sunglasses worn inside, turtleneck worn in the summer)
- Disruptive visits from a current or former intimate partner
- Sudden changes of address or reluctance to divulge current address
- Uncharacteristic moodiness, depression, or distractedness

- Undue anxiety during a breakup
- Court appearances
- Victimization by vandalism or threats

LONG-TERM EFFECTS OF DOMESTIC VIOLENCE

Battered women suffer physical and mental problems as a result of domestic violence. Battering is the primary cause of injury to women, more significant that auto accidents, rapes, or muggings. In fact, the emotional and psychological abuse inflicted by batterers may be more costly to treat in the long run than physical injury. Many of the physical injuries sustained by women seem to cause medical difficulties as women grow older. Battered women have identified arthritis, hypertension, and heart disease as being directly caused or aggravated by domestic violence suffered early in their adult lives. Depression remains the foremost response to battering, with 60 percent of battered women reporting. In addition, battered women are at greater risk for suicide attempts, with 25 percent of suicide attempts by Caucasian women and 50 percent by African American women who have been abused (Fischbach & Herbert, 1997).

Domestic violence victims may also experience posttraumatic stress disorder (PTSD), which is characterized by symptoms such as flashbacks, intrusive imagery, nightmares, anxiety, emotional numbing, insomnia, hypervigilance, and avoidance of traumatic triggers. Several empirical studies have explored the relationship between domestic violence and PTSD. In 1995, S. Vitanza, L. C. Vogel, and L. L. Marshall interviewed ninety-three women reporting to be in long-term, stressful relationships. The researchers looked at the relationships among psychological abuse, severity of violence in the relationship, and PTSD. The results of the study showed a significant correlation between domestic violence and PTSD. In each group in the study (psychological abuse only, moderate violence, and severe violence), women scored in the significant range for PTSD. Overall, 55.9 percent of the sample met diagnostic criteria for PTSD. In further support of the strong relationship between domestic violence and PTSD, P. Mertin and P. Mohr interviewed one hundred women in Australian shelters, each of whom had experienced domestic violence. They found that forty-five of the one hundred women met diagnostic criteria for PTSD.

Battered women lose their jobs because of absenteeism due to illness as a result of the violence. Absences occasioned by court appearances also jeopardize women's livelihoods. Battered women may have to move many times to avoid violence. Moving is costly and can interfere with continuity of employment. Battered women often lose family and friends as a result of the battering. First, the batterer isolates the victim from these individuals. Battered women then become embarrassed by the abuse inflicted upon them and withdraw from support persons. Some battered women are abandoned by their religions when separating from abusers, since some doctrines prohibit separation or divorce regardless of the severity of abuse.

Many battered women have had to forgo financial security during divorce proceedings to avoid further abuse. They are willing to accept almost any deal—no matter how bad—to get out of the marriage. As a result they become impoverished as they grow older. One-third of the children who witness the battering of their mothers demonstrate significant behavioral and/or emotional problems, including psychosomatic disorders, stuttering, anxiety and fear, sleep disruption, excessive crying, and school problems.

EFFECTS OF DOMESTIC VIOLENCE ON CHILDREN

When a mother is abused, a child may feel guilty about not being able to protect her or believe that he or she is the cause of the strife. Children may themselves be abused or neglected while their mothers attempt to deal with the trauma. The rate of child abuse is six to fifteen times higher in families where the mother is abused.

Children get hurt when they see their parents being yelled at, pushed, or hit. They may feel confusion, stress, fear, or shame. They grow up learning that it's OK to hurt other people or let other people hurt them. One-third of all children who see their mothers beaten develop emotional problems. Boys who see their fathers beat their mothers are ten times more likely to be abusive in their adult intimate relationships.

Children may exhibit emotional problems, cry excessively, or become withdrawn or shy. They may have difficulty making friends, fear adults, suffer from depression, and have excessive absences from school. They may use violence to solve problems at school and home. Children may be at greater risk of running away or committing suicide or criminal acts as juveniles and adults. Children experiencing stress may show it indifferent ways, including difficulty sleeping, bedwetting, overachieving, behavior problems, withdrawing, stomachaches, headaches, and/or diarrhea.

Children who grow up in violent homes have a much higher risk of becoming drug or alcohol abusers or being involved in abusive relationships, as a batterer or a victim. Children do not have to be abused themselves in order to be impacted by violence in the home. Children in homes where domestic violence occurs are physically abused or seriously neglected at a rate 1,500 percent higher than the national average (National Woman Abuse Prevention Project). Boys who witness family violence are more likely to batter their female partners as adults, and girls who witness their mother's abuse have a higher rate of being battered as adults (Georgia Department of Human Resources).

ACTIONS THAT REDUCE THE RISK OF HARM OR FUTURE VIOLENCE

- Seek an evaluation and advice from a qualified mental health professional or crisis intervention specialist if there are any critical risk factors.
- Review and familiarize yourself with the material on the Web that pertains to crisis intervention.
- Seek counseling or therapy from a qualified mental health professional for any emotional problems or difficulties associated with angry or violent behavior.
- Evaluate any alcohol and other drug use and treat as recommended by a qualified professional.
- Encourage a medical evaluation and treatment for any mental illness or other medical condition requiring medication or medical treatment.

- If appropriate, consider enrolling and participating in an educational or training group that will improve communication and interpersonal skills
- Develop a plan that will minimize and limit all communication that usually leads to conflict, aggression, or violence and take steps to resolve problems calmly. Establish a plan that supports communication that does not increase the risk of violence and supports actions that reduce the risk of violence.
- Ensure your own safety and provide for your basic emotional and physical needs while allowing the other person to do the same.
- If there is physical or sexual abuse, seek advice and further investigation from law enforcement or an attorney who has experience dealing with interpersonal violence, especially when violent or homicidal threats have been made. If appropriate, keep records of all contact, conversations, and threats made by the person, including dates, times, and witnesses.
- If appropriate, enroll in a personal-safety and self-defense course. Information regarding these courses can usually be obtained through local telephone crisis services, health care facilities, or the police or sheriff's department.

19

COPING WITH EMERGENCIES

Every year, millions of people around the world lose their lives or have them seriously disrupted because of floods, tsunamis, wildfires, earthquakes, blizzards, hurricanes, and other disasters. In today's troubled world, we face even greater threats from terrorism, civil unrest, explosions, and the possibility of chemical, biological, or even nuclear attack.

In the United States, the terrorist threat comes not only from overseas groups; domestic terrorism has been with us for decades, and violence in the workplace and schools is a serious concern. In the last twenty-five years, according to the FBI, there have been 327 confirmed or suspected domestic terrorist incidents—that averages out to more than one every month during this period. In the last eight years, more than forty students, teachers, and custodians have been shot dead at incidents in schools. The threat is real and growing. We must always be prepared for the unexpected, as the bombings at the Boston Marathon starkly remind us.

Being prepared and understanding what to do can reduce the fear, anxiety, and losses that accompany disasters. Communities, families, and individuals should know what to do in a fire and where to seek shelter from a tornado. They should be prepared to evacuate their homes, take refuge in public shelters, and care for their basic medical needs. People can also reduce the impact of disasters and sometimes avoid the danger altogether (e.g., by flood-proofing, elevating a home or moving it out of harm's way, securing items that could shake loose in an earthquake).

You should know how to respond to severe weather or any disaster that could occur in your area (e.g., hurricanes, earthquakes, extreme cold, or flooding). You should also be ready to be self-sufficient for at least three days. This may mean providing for your own shelter, first aid, food, water, and sanitation.

SOME BASICS

Immediately after an emergency, essential services may be cut off, and local disaster-relief and government responders may not be able to reach you right away. Even if they can reach you, knowing what to do to protect yourself and your household is essential. One of the most important steps you can take in preparing for emergencies is to develop a household disaster plan.

- Learn from your local emergency-management office or American Red Cross chapter about the natural disasters that could occur in your community. Find out whether hazardous materials are produced, stored, or transported near your area. Learn about possible consequences of deliberate acts of terror. Ask how to prepare for and respond to each potential emergency.
- Talk with employers and school officials about their emergency-response plans.
- Talk with your household about potential emergencies, how to respond to each, and what you would need to do in an evacuation.
- Plan how members of your household will stay in contact if separated. Identify two meeting places: the first should be near your home (perhaps a tree or a telephone pole); the second should be away from your neighborhood in case you cannot return home.
- Pick a friend or relative who lives out of the area for household members to call to say they are OK.
- Draw a floor plan of your home. Mark two escape routes from each room.
- Post emergency telephone numbers by telephones. Teach children how and when to call 911.

- Make sure everyone in your household knows how and when to shut off water, gas, and electricity at the main switches. Consult with your local utilities if you have questions.
- Take a first aid and CPR class. Local American Red Cross chapters can provide information. Official certification by the American Red Cross provides good Samaritan law protection for those giving first aid.
- Reduce the economic impact of disaster on your property and your household's health and financial well-being.
- Review property insurance policies before disaster strikes. Make sure policies are current and meet your needs (type and amount of coverage, hazards covered).
- Protect your household's financial well-being before a disaster strikes. Review life insurance policies and consider putting money in an emergency savings account for use in a crisis. It is advisable to keep a small amount of cash or traveler's checks at home in a safe place where you can access them quickly in case of an evacuation.
- Consider ways to help neighbors who may need special assistance, such as the elderly or the disabled.
- Make arrangements for pets. Pets are not usually allowed in public shelters. Service animals, for those who depend on them, are permitted. Most authorities allow small pets in main shelters, but large pets are generally not allowed. Some authorities provide one or two centers where large pets are allowed with their owners during a disaster.

DISASTER SUPPLY KITS

You and your family may need to survive on your own for three days or more. This means having your own water, food, and emergency supplies. Try using backpacks or duffel bags to keep the supplies together.

Assembling the supplies you might need following a disaster is an important part of your disaster plan. You should gather the following emergency supplies:

- Keep a disaster supply kit with essential food, water, and supplies for at least three days. Keep this kit in a designated place, ready to "grab and go" in case you have to leave your home quickly because of a disaster, such as a flash flood or major chemical emergency. Make sure all household members know where the kit is kept.
- Consider having additional supplies for up to two weeks for use in shelters or during home confinement.
- You should also have a disaster supply kit at work, kept in one container and ready to "grab and go" in case you have to evacuate the building.
- Keep a car kit of emergency supplies, including food and water, stored in your vehicle at all times. This kit should also include flares, jumper cables, and seasonal supplies.

The following checklists will help you assemble disaster supply kits that meet the needs of your household. The basic items that a disaster supply kit should include are water, food, first aid and emergency supplies, tools, clothing and bedding, and specialty items. You will need to change the stored water and food supplies every six months, so be sure to write the date you store these on all containers. You should also rethink your needs every year and update your kit as your household changes. Keep items in airtight plastic bags and put your entire disaster supply kit in one or two easy-to-carry containers, such as an unused trash can, camping backpack, or duffel bag.

Water: The Absolute Necessity

- Stocking water reserves should be a top priority. Drinking water should not be rationed in emergency situations. Therefore, it is critical to store adequate amounts of water for your household.
- Individual needs vary, depending on age, physical condition, activity, diet, and climate. A normally active person needs at least two quarts of water daily just for drinking. Children, nursing mothers, and ill people need more. Very hot temperatures can double the amount of water needed.

- Because you will also need water for sanitary purposes and possibly for cooking, you should store at least one gallon of water per person per day.
- Store water in thoroughly washed plastic, fiberglass, or enamel-lined metal containers. Don't use containers that can break, such as glass bottles. Never use a container that has held toxic substances. Sound plastic containers, such as soft drink bottles, are best. You can also purchase food-grade plastic buckets or drums.
- Containers for water should be rinsed with a diluted bleach solution (one part bleach to ten parts water) before use. Previously used bottles or other containers may be contaminated with microbes or chemicals. Do not rely on untested devices for decontaminating water.
- If your water is treated commercially by a water utility, you do not need to treat water before storing it. Additional treatments of treated public water will not increase storage life.
- If you have a well or public water that has not been treated, follow the treatment instructions provided by your public health service or water provider.
- If you suspect that your well may be contaminated, contact your local or state health department or agriculture extension agent for specific advice.
- Seal your water containers tightly, label them, and store them in a cool, dark place.
- It is important to change stored water every six months.

Food: Preparing an Emergency Supply

- If activity is reduced, healthy people can survive on half their usual food intake for an extended period or without any food for many days. Food, unlike water, may be rationed safely, except in the case of children and pregnant women.
- You don't need to go out and buy unfamiliar foods to prepare an emergency food supply. You can use the canned goods, dry mixes, and other staples on your cupboard shelves. Canned goods do not require cooking, water, or special preparation. Be sure to include a manual can opener.

- Keep canned goods in a dry place where the temperature is fairly cool. To protect boxed foods from pests and to extend their shelf life, store the food in tightly closed plastic or metal containers. Replace items in your food supply every six months. Throw out any canned good that becomes swollen, dented, or corroded. Use foods before they go bad and replace them with fresh supplies. Date each food item with a marker. Place new items at the back of the storage area and older ones in front.
- Food items that you might consider including in your disaster supply kit include ready-to-eat meats, fruits, and vegetables; canned or boxed juices, milk, and soup; high-energy foods like peanut butter, jelly, low-sodium crackers, granola bars, and trail mix; vitamins; foods for infants or people on special diets; cookies and hard candy; instant coffee, cereals, and powdered milk.

You may need to survive on your own after a disaster. Local officials and relief workers will be on the scene, but they cannot reach everyone immediately. Help could arrive in hours or might take days. Basic services, such as electricity, gas, water, sewage treatment, and telephones, may be cut off for a week or longer. Or you may have to evacuate at a moment's notice and take essentials with you. You probably won't have the opportunity to shop or search for the supplies you'll need. Your household will cope best by preparing for disaster before it strikes.

First Aid Supplies

Assemble a first aid kit for your home and for each vehicle. The basics for your first aid kit should include the following:

- First aid manual
- Sterile adhesive bandages in assorted sizes
- Assorted sizes of safety pins
- Cleansing agents (isopropyl alcohol, hydrogen peroxide, soap, germicide)
- Antibiotic ointment
- Latex gloves (two pairs)
- Petroleum jelly or other lubricant
- Two- and four-inch sterile gauze pads (four to six of each size)

- Triangular bandages (three)
- Two- and three-inch sterile roller bandages (three rolls each)
- Cotton balls
- Scissors
- Tweezers
- Needles
- Moistened towelettes
- Antiseptic
- Thermometer
- Tongue depressors (two)
- Sunscreen

It may be difficult to obtain prescription medications during a disaster because stores may be closed or supplies may be limited. Ask your physician or pharmacist about storing prescription medications and meet any storage instructions on the label. Be mindful of expiration dates; keep your stored medication up to date. Have an extra pair of prescription glasses or contact lenses.

Have the following nonprescription drugs in your disaster supply kit:

- Aspirin and nonaspirin pain reliever
- Antidiarrheal medication
- Antacid (for stomach upset)
- Syrup of ipecac (use to induce vomiting if advised by the poison-control center)
- Laxatives
- Vitamins

Tools and Emergency Supplies

It is important to assemble these items in a disaster supply kit in case you have to leave your home quickly. Even if you don't have to leave your home, if you lose power, having these item already assembled and in one place will make things easier.

Tools and Other Items

- A portable, battery-powered radio or television and extra batteries, as well as a National Oceanic and Atmospheric Administration (NOAA) weather radio (if appropriate for your area)
- Flashlight and extra batteries
- Signal flare
- Matches in a waterproof container (or waterproof matches)
- Shutoff wrench, pliers, a shovel, and other tools
- Duct tape and scissors
- Plastic sheeting
- Whistle
- Small-canister ABC-type fire extinguisher
- Tube tent
- Compass
- Work gloves
- Paper, pens, and pencils
- Needles and thread
- Battery-operated travel alarm clock

Kitchen Items

- Manual can opener
- Mess kits or paper or plastic cups and plates and plastic utensils
- All-purpose knife
- Household liquid bleach to treat drinking water
- Sugar, salt, and pepper
- Aluminum foil and plastic wrap
- Resealing plastic bags
- Small cooking stove and a can of cooking fuel

Sanitation and Hygiene Items

- Washcloth and towel
- Towelettes, soap, hand sanitizer, and liquid detergent
- Toothpaste, toothbrushes, shampoo, deodorant, comb and brush, razor, shaving cream, lip balm, sunscreen, insect repellent, contact lens solution, mirror, and feminine supplies
- Heavy-duty plastic garbage bags and ties for personal sanitation use

- Toilet paper
- Medium-size plastic bucket with tight lid
- Disinfectant and household chlorine bleach
- Dropper

Consider including a small shovel for digging a latrine

Household Documents and Contact Numbers

- Personal identification, cash (including change) or traveler's checks, and a credit card
- Copies of important documents (stored in a watertight container): birth certificates, marriage certificate, driver's licenses, Social Security cards, passports, wills, deeds, inventory of household goods, insurance papers, immunizations records, bank and credit card account numbers, stocks and bonds
- Emergency contact list and phone numbers
- Map of the area and phone numbers of places you could go
- An extra set of car keys and house keys

Clothes and Bedding

- One complete change of clothing and footwear for each household member
- Sturdy work shoes or boots
- Rain gear, hats and gloves, extra socks, extra underwear, thermal underwear, and sunglasses
- Blankets or sleeping bags and pillows for all household members

Specialty Items

Remember to consider the needs of infants, elderly people, disabled people, and pets and to include entertainment and comfort items (books, games, quiet toys, stuffed animals) for children.

It is important to be ready, wherever you may be, when disaster strikes. With the checklists provided you can now put together appropriate disaster supply kits for your household:

- A disaster supply kit kept in the home with supplies for at least three days (Although it is unlikely that food supplies would be cut off for so long, consider storing additional water, food, clothing, bedding, and other supplies to expand your supply kit to last up to two weeks.)
- A workplace disaster supply kit (It is important to store a personal supply of water and food at work; you will not be able to rely on water fountains or coolers. Women who wear high heels should be sure to have comfortable flat shoes at their workplace in case an evacuation requires walking long distances.)
- A car disaster supply kit (Keep a smaller disaster supply kit in the trunk of your car. If you become stranded or are not able to return home, having these items will help you stay more comfortable until help arrives. Add items for severe winter weather—salt, sand, shovels, and extra winter clothing, including hats and gloves—during months when heavy snow or icy roads are possible.)

SHELTER

Taking shelter is often a critical element in protecting yourself and your household in times of disaster. Sheltering can take several forms. In-place sheltering is appropriate when conditions require that you seek protection in your home, place of employment, or other location where you are located when disaster strikes. In-place sheltering may either be short term, such as going to a safe room for a fairly short period while a tornado warning is in effect or while a chemical cloud passes. It may also be longer term, such as when you stay in your home for several days without electricity or water services following a winter storm. We also use the term "shelter" for mass-care facilities that provide a place to stay, along with food and water, for people who evacuate following a disaster.

The appropriate steps to take in preparing for and implementing short-term in-place sheltering depend entirely on the emergency situation. For instance, during a tornado warning you should go to an underground room, if such a room is available. During a chemical release, on the other hand, you should seek shelter in a room above ground level.

Long-Term In-Place Sheltering

Sometimes disasters make it unsafe for people to leave their homes for extended periods. Winter storms, floods, and landslides may isolate individual households and make it necessary for each to take care of its own needs until the disaster abates (e.g., snows melt and temperatures rise) or until rescue workers arrive. Your household should be prepared to be self-sufficient for three days when cut off from utilities and outside supplies of food and water.

1. Stay in your shelter until local authorities say it's OK to leave. The length of your stay can range from a few hours to two weeks.
2. Maintain a twenty-four-hour communications and safety watch. Take turns listening for radio broadcasts. Watch for fires.

   - Assemble an emergency toilet, if necessary.
   - Use a garbage container, pail, or bucket with a snug-fitting cover. If the container is small, use a larger container with a cover for waste disposal. Line both containers with plastic bags.
   - After each use, pour or sprinkle a small amount of regular household disinfectant, such as chlorine bleach, into the container to reduce odors and germs.

MANAGING WATER SUPPLIES

Water is critical for survival. Plan to have about one gallon of water per person per day for drinking, cooking, and personal hygiene. You may need more for medical emergencies.

1. Allow people to drink according to their need. The average person should drink between 2 and 2.5 quarts of water or other liquids per day, but many people need more. This will depend on age, physical activity, physical condition, and time of year.
2. Never ration water unless ordered to do so by authorities. Drink the amount you need today and try to find more for tomorrow. Under no circumstances should a person drink less than one

quart of water each day. You can minimize the amount of water your body needs by reducing activity and staying cool.

3. Drink water that you know is not contaminated first. If necessary, suspicious water, such as cloudy water from regular faucets or muddy water from streams or ponds, can be used after it has been treated. If water treatment is not possible, put off drinking suspicious water as long as possible, but do not become dehydrated.

4. In addition to stored water, other sources include the following:

   • Melted ice cubes
   • Water drained from the water heater tap, if the water heater has not been damaged
   • Water dipped from the flush tanks (not the bowls) of home toilets (though bowl water can be used for pets)
   • Liquids from canned goods, such as fruit and vegetable juices

5. Carbonated beverages do not meet drinking-water requirements. Drinks containing caffeine and alcohol dehydrate the body, increasing the need for drinking water.

6. If water pipes are damaged or if local authorities advise you to do so, turn off the main water valves to prevent water from draining away in case the water main breaks.

   • The pipes will be full of water when the main valve is closed.
   • To use this water, turn on the faucet at the highest point in your house (which lets air into the system).
   • Then draw water, as needed, from the lowest point in your house, either a faucet or the hot water tank.

7. Unsafe drinking-water sources include the following:

   • Radiators
   • Hot water boilers (home heating system)
   • Water beds (due to fungicides added to the water or chemicals in the vinyl)

- Swimming pools and spas (due to chemicals to kill germs, though the water can be used for personal hygiene, cleaning, and related uses)

WATER TREATMENT

Treat all water of uncertain purity before using it for drinking, food washing or preparation, washing dishes, brushing teeth, or making ice. In addition to having a bad odor and taste, contaminated water can contain microorganisms that cause diseases such as dysentery, cholera, typhoid, and hepatitis.

There are many ways to treat water. None is perfect. Often the best solution is a combination of methods. Before treatment, let any suspended particles settle to the bottom or strain the water through layers of clean cloth. Following are four treatment methods. The first three methods—boiling, chlorination, and water-treatment tablets—will kill microbes but will not remove other contaminants, such as heavy metals, salts, most other chemicals, and radioactive fallout. The final method—distillation—will remove microbes, as well as most other contaminants, including radioactive fallout.

Boiling is the safest method of treating water. Doing so kills harmful bacteria and parasites. Bringing water to a rolling boil for one minute will kill most organisms. Let the water cool before drinking. Boiled water will taste better if you put oxygen back into it by pouring it back and forth between two containers. This will also improve the taste of stored water.

Chlorination uses liquid chlorine bleach to kill microorganisms, such as bacteria. Use regular household liquid bleach that contains no soap or scent. Some containers warn, "Not for Personal Use." You can disregard these warnings if the label lists sodium hypochlorite as the only active ingredient and if you use only the small quantities mentioned in these instructions.

Add sixteen drops of unscented bleach per gallon of water stir and let stand for thirty minutes. If the water does not taste and smell of chlorine at that point, add another dose and let stand for another fifteen minutes. This treatment will not kill parasitic organisms.

If you do not have a dropper, use a spoon and a square-ended strip of paper or thin cloth about a 1/4 inch by 2 inches. Put the strip in the spoon with an end hanging down about a 1/2 inch below the scoop of the spoon. Place bleach in the spoon and carefully tip it. Drops the size of those from a medicine dropper will drip off the end of the strip.

Water-treatment "purification" tablets release chlorine or iodine. They are inexpensive and available at most sporting goods stores and some drugstores. Follow the package directions carefully.

Note: People with hidden or chronic liver or kidney disease may be adversely affected by iodized tablets and may experience worsened health problems as a result of ingestion. Iodized tablets are safe for healthy, physically fit adults and should be used only if you lack the supplies for boiling, chlorination, and distillation.

Distillation involves boiling water and collecting the vapor, which condenses back into water. The condensed vapor may include salt or other impurities.

- Fill a pot halfway with water.
- Tie a cup to the handle on the pot's lid so that the cup hangs right side up when the lid is upside down (make sure the cup is not dangling into the water).
- Boil for twenty minutes. The water that drips from the lid into the cup is distilled.

MANAGING FOOD SUPPLIES

1. It is important to be sanitary when storing, handling, and eating food:

   - Keep food in covered containers.
   - Keep cooking and eating utensils clean.
   - Keep garbage in closed containers and dispose of it outside. Bury garbage, if necessary. Avoid letting garbage accumulate inside, both for fire and sanitation reasons.
   - Keep hands clean. Wash frequently with soap and boiled or disinfected water. Be sure to wash in the following instances:

- Before preparing or eating food
- After toilet use
- After participating in flood cleanup activities
- After handling articles contaminated with floodwater or sewage

2. Carefully ration food for everyone except children and pregnant women. Most people can remain relatively healthy with about half as much food as usual and can survive without any food for several days.
3. Try to avoid foods high in fat and protein, since they will make you thirsty. Try to eat salt-free crackers, whole-grain cereals, and canned foods with high liquid content.
4. For emergency cooking, heat food with candle warmers, chafing dishes, and fondue pots or use a fireplace. Charcoal grills and camp stoves are for outdoor use only.
5. Commercially canned food can be eaten out of the can without warming. Before heating food in a can, remove the label, thoroughly wash the can, and then disinfect it with a solution consisting of one cup of bleach in five gallons of water, and open before heating.

   - Do not eat foods from cans that are swollen, dented, or corroded, even if the product looks OK.
   - Do not eat any food that looks or smells abnormal, even if the can looks normal.
   - Discard any food not in a waterproof container if there is any chance that it has come into contact with contaminated floodwater.
   - Discard food containers with screw caps, snap lids, crimped caps (soda pop bottles), twist caps, flip tops, or snap-open tops, as well as home-canned foods, if they have come into contact with floodwater because they cannot be disinfected. For infants, use only preprepared canned baby formula. Do not use powdered formulas with treated water.

6. Your refrigerator will keep foods cool for about four hours without power if it is left unopened. Add block or dry ice to your refrigerator if the electricity will be off longer than four hours.

Thawed food usually can be eaten if it is still "refrigerator cold" or refrozen if it still contains ice crystals. To be safe, remember, when in doubt, throw it out. Discard any food that has been at room temperature for two hours or more and any food that has an unusual odor, color, or texture.

If you are without power for a long period, do the following:

- If friends have electricity, ask them to store your frozen foods in their freezers.
- Inquire if freezer space is available in a store, church, school, or commercial establishment that has electrical service.
- Use dry ice, if available. Twenty-five pounds of dry ice will keep a ten-cubic-foot freezer below freezing for three to four days. Use care when handling dry ice. Wear dry, heavy gloves to avoid injury.

HELPING CHILDREN COPE WITH A DISASTER

Disasters can leave children feeling frightened, confused, and insecure. Whether a child has personally experienced trauma, has seen the event on television, or has heard adults discussing it, it is important for parents and teachers to be informed and ready to help if stress reactions begin to occur.

Children respond to trauma in many different ways. Some may have reactions very soon after the event; others may seem to be doing fine for weeks or months and then begin to show worrisome behavior. Knowing the common signs at different ages can help parents and teachers recognize problems and respond appropriately.

Reassurance is the key to helping children through a traumatic time. Very young children need a lot of cuddling, as well as verbal support. Answer questions about the disaster honestly, but don't dwell on frightening details or allow the subject to dominate family or classroom time indefinitely. Encourage children of all ages to express emotions through conversation, drawing, or painting and to find a way to help others affected by the disaster. Also limit the amount of disaster-related material (e.g., television) your children see or hear and pay careful attention to how graphic it is. Try to maintain a normal household or classroom routine and encourage children to participate in recreational activity. Reduce your expectations temporarily about performance in school or at home, perhaps by substituting less demanding responsibilities for normal chores.

Additional information about how to communicate with children can be found on the Federal Emergency Management Agency (FEMA) for Kids website (http://www.fema.gov/kids).

FLOODS

Floods are among the most common hazards in the United States. However, all floods are not alike. Riverine floods develop slowly, sometimes over a period of days. Flash floods can develop quickly, sometimes in just a few minutes, without any visible signs of rain. Flash floods often bring a dangerous wall of roaring water that carries a deadly cargo of rocks, mud, and other debris and can sweep away most things in its path. Overland flooding occurs outside a defined river or stream, such as when a levee is breached, but still can be destructive. Flooding can also occur from a dam break, producing effects similar to flash floods.

Flood effects can be very local, impacting a neighborhood or community, or very widespread, affecting entire river basins and multiple states. Be aware of flood hazards no matter where you live, but especially if you live in a low-lying area, near water, or downstream from a dam. Even very small streams, gullies, creeks, culverts, dry streambeds, and low-lying ground that appear harmless in dry weather can flood. Every state is at risk of this hazard.

What to Do before a Flood

1. Know the terms used to describe flooding:

   • Flood watch: Flooding is possible. Stay tuned to NOAA Weather Radio or commercial radio or television for information. Watches are issued twelve to thirty-six hours in advance of a possible flooding event.

- Flash flood watch: Flash flooding is possible. Be prepared to move to higher ground. A flash flood could occur without any warning. Listen to NOAA Weather Radio or commercial radio or television for additional information.
- Flood warning: Flooding is occurring or will occur soon. If advised to evacuate, do so immediately.
- Flash flood warning: A flash flood is occurring. Seek higher ground on foot immediately.

2. Ask local officials whether your property is in a flood-prone or high-risk area. (Remember that floods often occur outside high-risk areas.) Ask about official flood warning signals and what to do when you hear them. Also ask how you can protect your home from flooding.

3. Identify dams in your area and determine whether they pose a hazard to you.

4. Purchase a NOAA Weather Radio with battery backup and a tone-alert feature that automatically alerts you when a watch or warning is issued (tone alert is not available in some areas). Purchase a battery-powered commercial radio and extra batteries.

5. Be prepared to evacuate. Learn your community's flood evacuation routes and where to find high ground.

6. Talk to your household about flooding. Plan a place to meet members of your household in case you are separated in a disaster and cannot return home. Choose an out-of-town contact for everyone to call to say they are OK. In some emergencies, calling out-of-state is possible even when local phone lines are down.

7. Determine how you will care for household members who may live elsewhere but might need your help in a flood. Determine any special needs your neighbors might have.

8. Prepare to survive on your own for at least three days. Assemble a disaster supply kit. Keep a stock of food and extra drinking water.

9. Know how to shut off electricity, gas, and water at main switches and valves. Know where gas pilot lights are located and how the heating system works.

10. Consider purchasing flood insurance:

- Flood losses are not covered under homeowners' insurance policies.
- FEMA manages the National Flood Insurance Program, which makes federally backed flood insurance available in communities that agree to adopt and enforce floodplain management ordinances to reduce future flood damage.
- Flood insurance is available in most communities through insurance agents.
- There is a thirty-day waiting period before flood insurance goes into effect, so don't delay.
- Flood insurance is available whether the building is in or out of the identified flood-prone area.

11. Consider options for protecting your property:

- Make a record of your personal property. Take photographs or videotapes of your belongings. Store these documents in a safe place.
- Keep insurance policies, deeds, property records, and other important papers in a safe place away from your home.
- Avoid building in a floodplain unless you elevate and reinforce your home.
- Elevate the furnace, water heater, and electric panel to higher floors or the attic if your home is susceptible to flooding.
- Install check valves in sewer traps to prevent floodwater from backing up through your drains into your home.
- Construct barriers, such as levees, berms, and floodwalls, to stop floodwater from entering the building.
- Seal walls in basements with waterproofing compounds to avoid seepage.
- Call your local building department or emergency-management office for more information.

What to Do during a Flood

1. Be aware of flash flooding. If there is any possibility of a flash flood, move immediately to higher ground. Do not wait for instructions to move.
2. Listen to radio or television stations for local information.
3. Be aware of streams, drainage channels, canyons, and other areas known to flood suddenly. Flash floods can occur in these areas with or without such typical warning signs as rain clouds or heavy rain.
4. If local authorities issue a flood watch, prepare to evacuate:

   • Secure your home. If you have time, tie down or bring outdoor equipment and lawn furniture inside. Move essential items to the upper floors.
   • If instructed, turn off utilities at the main switches or valves. Disconnect electrical appliances. Do not touch electrical equipment if you are wet or standing in water.
   • Fill the bathtub with water in case water becomes contaminated or services are cut off. Before filling the tub, sterilize it with a diluted bleach solution.

5. Do not walk through moving water. Six inches of moving water can knock you off your feet. If you must walk in a flooded area, walk where the water is not moving. Use a stick to check the firmness of the ground in front of you.
6. Do not drive into flooded areas. Six inches of water will reach the undercarriage of most passenger cars, causing loss of control and possible stalling. A foot of water will float many vehicles. Two feet of water will wash away almost all vehicles. If floodwaters rise around your car, abandon the car and move to higher ground if you can do so safely. You and your vehicle can be swept away quickly as floodwaters rise.

What to Do after a Flood

1. Avoid floodwaters. The water may be contaminated by oil, gasoline, or raw sewage. The water may also be electrically charged from underground or downed power lines.
2. Avoid moving water. Moving water only six inches deep can sweep you off your feet.
3. Be aware of areas where floodwaters have receded. Roads may have weakened and could collapse under the weight of a car.
4. Stay away from downed power lines and report them to the power company.
5. Stay away from designated disaster areas unless authorities ask for volunteers.
6. Return home only when authorities indicate that doing so is safe. Stay out of buildings if they are surrounded by floodwaters. Use extreme caution when entering buildings. There may be hidden damage, particularly in foundations.
7. Consider your family's health and safety needs:

   - Wash hands frequently with soap and clean water if you come in contact with floodwaters.
   - Throw away food that has come in contact with floodwaters.
   - Listen for news reports to learn whether the community's water supply is safe to drink.
   - Listen to news reports for information about where to get assistance for housing, clothing, and food.
   - Seek necessary medical care at the nearest medical facility.

8. Service damaged septic tanks, cesspools, pits, and leaching systems as soon as possible. Damaged sewage systems are serious health hazards.
9. Contact your insurance agent. If your policy covers your situation, an adjuster will be assigned to visit your home. To prepare, do the following:

   - Take photos of or videotape your belongings and your home.
   - Separate damaged and undamaged belongings.
   - Locate your financial records.

• Keep detailed records of cleanup costs.

10. If your residence has been flooded, obtain a copy of "Repairing Your Flooded Home" from the local American Red Cross chapter.

HURRICANES

A hurricane is a type of tropical cyclone, the generic term for a low-pressure system that generally forms in the tropics. The ingredients for a hurricane include a preexisting weather disturbance, warm tropical oceans, moisture, and relatively light winds aloft. A typical cyclone is accompanied by thunderstorms and, in the Northern Hemisphere, a counterclockwise circulation of winds near the Earth's surface. Tropical cyclones are classified as follows:

• Tropical depression: An organized system of clouds and thunderstorms with a defined surface circulation and maximum sustained winds of thirty-eight miles per hour (thirty-three knots) or less. Sustained winds are defined as one-minute average wind speed measured at about thirty-three feet (ten meters) above the surface.
• Tropical storm: An organized system of strong thunderstorms with a defined surface circulation and maximum sustained winds of thirty-nine to seventy-three miles per hour (thirty-four to sixty-three knots).
• Hurricane: An intense tropical weather system of strong thunderstorms with a well-defined surface circulation and maximum sustained winds of seventy-four miles per hour (sixty-four knots) or higher. All Atlantic and Gulf of Mexico coastal areas are subject to hurricanes and tropical storms. Although rarely struck by hurricanes, parts of the southwestern United States and the Pacific Coast experience heavy rains and floods each year from hurricanes spawned off Mexico. The Atlantic hurricane season lasts from June through November, with the peak season from mid-August to late October.

As we all have seen, hurricanes can cause catastrophic and deadly damage to coastlines and reach several hundred miles inland. Winds can exceed 155 miles per hour. Hurricanes and tropical storms can also spawn tornadoes and microbursts, create a surge along the coast, and cause extensive damage due to inland flooding from trapped water.

Tornadoes most often occur in thunderstorms embedded in rain bands well away from the center of the hurricane; however, they also occur near the eyewall. Typically, tornadoes produced by tropical cyclones are relatively weak and short-lived, but they still pose a threat.

A storm surge is a huge dome of water pushed onshore by hurricane and tropical storm winds. Storm surges can reach twenty-five feet in height and fifty to one hundred miles in width. A storm tide is a combination of the storm surge and the normal tide (i.e., a fifteen-foot storm surge combined with a two-foot normal high tide over the mean sea level creates a seventeen-foot storm tide). These phenomena cause severe erosion and extensive damage to coastal areas.

Despite improved warnings and a decrease in the loss of life, property damage continues to rise because an increasing number of people are living or vacationing near coastlines. Those in hurricane-prone areas need to be prepared for hurricanes and tropical storms.

Hurricanes are classified into five categories based on their wind speed, central pressure, and damage potential. Category 3 storms and higher are considered major hurricanes, though category 1 and 2 storms are still extremely dangerous and warrant your full attention.

Inland/Freshwater Flooding from Hurricanes

Hurricanes can produce widespread torrential rains. Floods are the deadly and destructive result. Excessive rain can also trigger landslides or mudslides, especially in mountainous regions. Flash flooding can occur due to the intense rainfall. Flooding on rivers and streams may persist for several days or more after the storm.

The speed of the storm and the geography beneath it are the primary factors determining the amount of rain produced. Slow-moving storms and tropical storms moving into mountainous regions tend to produce more rain. Between 1970 and 1999, more people lost their lives from freshwater flooding associated with land-falling tropical cyclones than from any other weather hazard related to tropical cyclones.

What to Do before a Hurricane

1. Know the difference between watches and warnings:

   • Hurricane/tropical storm watch: Hurricane/tropical storm conditions are possible in the specified area, usually within thirty-six hours.
   • Hurricane/tropical storm warning: Hurricane/tropical storm conditions are expected in the specified area, usually within twenty-four hours.
   • Short-term watches and warnings: Warnings provide detailed information on specific hurricane threats, such as flash floods and tornadoes.

2. Listen for local radio or television weather forecasts. Purchase a NOAA Weather Radio with battery backup and a tone-alert feature that automatically alerts you when a watch or warning is issued (tone alert is not available in some areas). Purchase a battery-powered commercial radio and extra batteries because the media will be broadcasting information on other events as well.
3. Ask your local emergency-management office about community evacuation plans relating to your neighborhood. Learn evacuation routes. Determine where you will go and how you will get there if you need to evacuate. Sometimes alternate routes are desirable.
4. Talk to your household about hurricane issues. Create a household disaster plan. Plan to meet at a place away from your residence in case you are separated. Choose an out-of-town contact for everyone to call to say they are safe.
5. Determine the needs of your household members who may live elsewhere but need your help in a hurricane. Consider the special needs of neighbors, such as people who are disabled or those with limited sight or vision problems.
6. Prepare to survive on your own for at least three days. Assemble a disaster supply kit. Keep a stock of food and extra drinking water.

7. Make plans to secure your property. Permanent storm shutters offer the best protection for windows. A second option is to board up windows with 5/8-inch marine plywood, cut to fit and ready to install. Tape does not prevent windows from breaking.

8. Learn how to shut off utilities and where gas pilots and water mains are located.

9. Have your home inspected for compliance with local building codes. Many of the roofs destroyed by hurricanes have not been constructed or retrofitted according to building codes. Installing straps or additional clips to securely fasten your roof to the frame structure will substantially reduce roof damage.

10. Be sure trees and shrubs around your home are well trimmed. Dead limbs or trees could cause personal injury or property damage. Clear loose and clogged rain gutters and downspouts.

11. If you have a boat, determine where to secure it in an emergency.

12. Consider flood insurance. Purchase insurance well in advance as there is a thirty-day waiting period before flood insurance takes effect.

13. Make a record of your personal property. Take photographs or make videotapes of your belongings. Store these documents in a safe place.

What to Do during a Hurricane Threat

1. Listen to radio or television newscasts. If a hurricane watch is issued, you typically have twenty-four to thirty-six hours before the hurricane hits land.

2. Talk with household members. Make sure everyone knows where to meet and whom to call in case you are separated. Consider the needs of relatives and neighbors with special needs.

3. Secure your home. Close storm shutters. Secure outdoor objects or bring them indoors. Moor your boat if time permits.

4. Gather several days' supply of water and food for each household member. Water systems may become contaminated or damaged. Sterilize (with diluted bleach solution of one part bleach to ten parts water) and fill the bathtub to ensure a supply of safe water in case you are unable or told not to evacuate.

5. If you are evacuating, take your disaster supply kit with you to the shelter. Remember that alcoholic beverages and weapons are prohibited within shelters. Also, pets are not usually allowed in a public shelter due to health reasons. Contact your local humane society for additional information.

6. Prepare to evacuate. Fuel your car; service stations may be closed after the storm. If you do not have a car, make arrangements for transportation with a friend or relative. Review evacuation routes. If instructed, turn off utilities at the main valves.

7. Evacuate to an inland location under the following circumstances:

    • Local authorities announce an evacuation, and you live in an evacuation zone.
    • You live in a mobile home or temporary structure. They are particularly hazardous during hurricanes, no matter how well fastened to the ground.
    • You live in a high-rise. Hurricane winds are stronger at higher elevations.
    • You live on the coast or on a floodplain near a river or inland waterway.
    • You feel you are in danger.

8. When authorities order an evacuation, do the following:

    • Leave immediately.
    • Follow evacuation routes announced by local officials.
    • Stay away from coastal areas, riverbanks, and streams.
    • Tell others where you are going.

9. If you are not required or are unable to evacuate, stay indoors during the hurricane and away from windows and glass doors. Keep curtains and blinds closed. Do not be fooled if there is a lull; it could be the eye of the storm—winds will pick up again.

    • Turn off utilities if told to do so by authorities.
    • If not instructed to turn off power, turn the refrigerator to its coldest setting and keep closed.
    • Turn off propane tanks.

10. In strong winds, follow these rules:

- Take refuge in a small interior room, closet, or hallway.
- Close all interior doors. Secure and brace external doors.
- In a two-story residence, go to a small interior first-floor room, such as a bathroom or closet.
- In a multiple-story building, go to the first or second floor and stay in interior rooms away from windows.
- Lie on the floor under a table or another sturdy object.

11. Avoid using the phone except in serious emergencies. Local authorities need first priority to telephone lines.
12. If you do not have a backup generator, consider buying one. Hurricanes can take out power lines that may not be restored for days or weeks.
13. Be sure you have gas in portable tanks to feed the generator and extension cords to hook it up to appliances, lamps, and so forth.
14. If you have a cell phone, be sure it's charged.
15. If you have time and flooding is a threat, remove or secure irreplaceable valuables from lower levels of your home—furniture can be replaced but photo albums, report cards, and other memorabilia cannot.

What to Do after a Hurricane

1. Stay where you are, if you are in a safe location, until local authorities say it is OK to leave. If you evacuated the community, do not return to the area until authorities say it is safe to return.
2. Keep tuned to local radio or television stations for information about caring for your household, where to find medical help, how to apply for financial assistance, and so forth.
3. Drive only when necessary. Streets will be filled with debris. Roads may have weakened and could collapse. Do not drive on flooded or barricaded roads or bridges. Closed roads are for your protection. As little as six inches of water may cause you to lose control of your vehicle; two feet of water will carry most cars away.

4. Do not drink or prepare food with tap water until notified by officials that it is safe to do so.
5. Consider your family's health and safety needs. Be aware of symptoms of stress and fatigue. Keep your household together and seek crisis counseling if needed.
6. Talk with your children about what has happened and how they can help during the recovery. Being involved will help them deal with the situation. Consider the needs of your neighbors. People often become isolated during hurricanes.
7. Stay away from disaster areas unless local authorities request volunteers. If you are needed, bring your own drinking water, food, and sleeping gear.
8. Stay away from riverbanks and streams until potential flooding has passed. Do not allow children, especially under the age of thirteen, to play in flooded areas. There is a high risk of injury or drowning in areas that may appear safe.
9. Stay away from moving water. Moving water only six inches deep can sweep you off your feet. Standing water may be electrically charged from underground or downed power lines.
10. Stay away from downed power lines and report them to the power company. Report to local officials any broken gas, sewer, or water mains.
11. Don't use candles or other open flames indoors. Use a flashlight to inspect damage.
12. Set up a manageable schedule to repair property.
13. Contact your insurance agent. An adjuster will be assigned to visit your home. To prepare, do the following:

- Take photos of or videotape your belongings and your home.
- Separate damaged and undamaged belongings.
- Locate your financial records.
- Keep detailed records of cleanup costs.

14. Consider building a safe room or shelter to protect your household.

THUNDERSTORMS

Thunderstorms are very common and affect great numbers of people each year. Despite their small size in comparison to hurricanes and winter storms, all thunderstorms are dangerous. Every thunderstorm produces lightning. Other associated dangers of thunderstorms include tornadoes, strong winds, hail, and flash flooding. Flash flooding is responsible for more fatalities—more than 140 annually—than any other thunderstorm-associated hazard.

Some thunderstorms do not produce rain that reaches the ground. These are generically referred to as dry thunderstorms and are most prevalent in the western United States. Known to spawn wildfires, these storms occur when there is a large layer of dry air between the base of the cloud and the ground. The falling raindrops evaporate, but lightning can still reach the ground.

What to Do before Thunderstorms Approach

1. Know the terms used by weather forecasters:

   - Severe thunderstorm watch: This tells you when and where severe thunderstorms are likely to occur. Watch the sky and stay tuned to radio or television to know when warnings are issued.
   - Severe thunderstorm warning: This is issued when severe weather has been reported by spotters or indicated by radar. Warnings indicate imminent danger to life and property for those in the path of the storm.

2. Know thunderstorm facts:

   - Thunderstorms may occur singly, in clusters, or in lines.
   - Some of the most severe weather occurs when a single thunderstorm affects one location for an extended time.
   - Thunderstorms typically produce heavy rain for a brief period, anywhere from thirty minutes to an hour.
   - Warm, humid conditions are very favorable for thunderstorm development.

- A typical thunderstorm is fifteen miles in diameter and lasts an average of thirty minutes.
- Of the estimated one hundred thousand thunderstorms each year in the United States, about 10 percent are classified as severe.
- A thunderstorm is classified as severe if it produces hail at least three-quarters of an inch in diameter, has winds of fifty-eight miles per hour or higher, or produces a tornado.

3. Know the calculation to determine how close you are to a thunderstorm. Count the number of seconds between a flash of lightning and the next clap of thunder. Divide this number by five to determine the distance to the lightning in miles.
4. Remove dead or rotting trees and branches that could fall and cause injury or damage during a severe thunderstorm.
5. When a thunderstorm approaches, secure outdoor objects that could blow away or cause damage. Shutter windows, if possible, and secure outside doors. If shutters are not available, close window blinds, shades, or curtains.

LIGHTNING

The ingredient that defines a thunderstorm is lightning. Since lightning creates thunder, a storm producing lightning is called a thunderstorm. Lightning occurs during all thunderstorms. It results from the buildup and discharge of electrical energy between positively and negatively charged areas. The unpredictability of lightning increases the risk to individuals and property. On average, in the United States, three hundred people are injured and eighty people are killed each year by lightning. Although most survive, people struck by lightning often report a variety of long-term, debilitating symptoms, including memory loss, attention deficits, sleep disorders, numbness, dizziness, stiffness in joints, irritability, fatigue, weakness, muscle spasms, depression, and an inability to sit for a long period.

When thunderstorms threaten your area, get inside a home, building, or hard-top automobile (not a convertible), and stay away from metallic objects and fixtures.

1. If you are inside a home, do the following:

   - Avoid showering or bathing. Plumbing and bathroom fix-
     tures can conduct electricity.
   - Avoid using a corded telephone, except in emergencies.
     Cordless and cellular telephones are safe to use.
   - Unplug appliances and other electrical items, such as com-
     puters, and turn off air conditioners. Power surges from
     lightning can cause serious damage.
   - Use your battery-operated NOAA Weather Radio for up-
     dates from local officials.

2. If you are outside with no time to reach a safe location, follow
   these recommendations:

   - In a forest, seek shelter in a low area under a thick growth
     of small trees.
   - In open areas, go to a low place, such as a ravine or valley.
     Be alert for flash floods.
   - Do not stand under a natural lightning rod, such as a tall,
     isolated tree in an open area.
   - Do not stand on a hilltop, in an open field, on the beach, or
     in a boat on the water.
   - Avoid isolated sheds or other small structures in open areas.
   - Get away from open water. If you are boating or swimming,
     get to land and find shelter immediately.
   - Get away from anything metal (e.g., tractors, farm equip-
     ment, motorcycles, golf carts, golf clubs, bicycles).
   - Stay away from wire fences, clotheslines, metal pipes, rails,
     and other metallic paths that could carry lightning to you
     from some distance away.
   - If you feel your hair stand on end (which indicates that
     lightning is about to strike), squat low to the ground on the
     balls of your feet. Place your hands over your ears and your
     head between your knees.

3. Make yourself the smallest target possible and minimize your
   contact with the ground. Do not lie flat on the ground.
4. Remember the following facts and safety tips about lightning:

- Lightning often strikes outside heavy rain and may occur as far as ten miles away from any rainfall.
- Lightning-strike victims carry no electrical charge and should be attended to immediately. If breathing has stopped, begin mouth-to-mouth resuscitation. If the heart has stopped, a trained person should administer CPR. If the victim has a pulse and is breathing, look for other possible injuries. Check for burns where the lightning entered and left the body. Be alert also for nervous system damage, broken bones, and loss of hearing or eyesight. Contact your local emergency-management office or American Red Cross chapter for information on CPR and first aid classes.
- "Heat lightning" is actually lightning from a thunderstorm too far away for thunder to be heard. However, the storm may be moving in your direction.
- Most lightning deaths and injuries occur when people are caught outdoors in the summer months during the afternoon and evening.
- Lightning starts many fires in the western United States and Alaska.
- Lightning can occur within a cloud or move from cloud to cloud, cloud to ground, or cloud to air.

5. Your chances of being struck by lightning are estimated to be one in six hundred thousand but could be minimized if you follow these safety tips:

- Postpone outdoor activities if thunderstorms are likely.
- Remember the thirty/thirty lightning-safety rule: go inside if, after seeing lighting, you cannot count to thirty before hearing thunder. Stay indoors for thirty minutes after hearing the last clap of thunder.
- Rubber-soled shoes and rubber tires provide no protection from lightning. However, the steel frame of a hard-topped vehicle provides increased protection if you are not touching metal. Although you may be injured if lightning strikes your car, you are much safer inside a vehicle than outside.

TORNADOES

Tornadoes are nature's most violent storms. Spawned by powerful thunderstorms, tornadoes can uproot trees, destroy buildings, and turn harmless objects into deadly missiles. They can devastate a neighborhood in seconds. A tornado appears as a rotating, funnel-shaped cloud that extends to the ground with whirling winds that can reach three hundred miles per hour. Damage paths can be in excess of one mile wide and fifty miles long. Every state is at some risk for this hazard.

Tornado Facts

1. A tornado is a violently rotating column of air extending from a thunderstorm to the ground.
2. Tornadoes are capable of destroying homes and vehicles and can cause fatalities.
3. Tornadoes may strike quickly, with little or no warning.
4. Tornadoes may appear nearly transparent until dust and debris are picked up or a cloud forms in the funnel. The average tornado moves southwest to northeast, but they have been known to move in any direction.
5. The average forward speed is thirty miles per hour but may vary from stationary to seventy miles per hour, with rotating winds that can reach three hundred miles per hour.
6. Tornadoes can accompany tropical storms and hurricanes as they move onto land.
7. Waterspouts are tornadoes that form over water.
8. Tornadoes are most frequently reported east of the Rocky Mountains during spring and summer months but can occur in any state at any time of year.
9. In the southern states, peak tornado season is March through May, while peak season in the northern states is during the late spring and early summer.
10. Tornadoes are most likely to occur between 3 and 9 p.m. but can occur at any time of the day or night.

What to Do before Tornadoes Threaten

1. Know the terms used to describe tornado threats:

   • Tornado watch: Tornadoes are possible. Remain alert for approaching storms. Listen to your battery-operated NOAA Weather Radio or local radio or television outlets for updated reports.
   • Tornado warning: A tornado has been sighted or indicated by weather radar. Take shelter immediately.

2. Ask your local emergency-management office or American Red Cross chapter about the tornado threat in your area. Ask about community warning signals.
3. Purchase a NOAA Weather Radio with a battery backup and tone-alert feature that automatically alerts you when a watch or warning is issued (tone alert is not available in some areas). Purchase a battery-powered commercial radio and extra batteries as well.
4. Know which county or parish you live in. Counties and parishes are used in watches and warnings to identify the location of tornadoes.
5. Determine places to seek shelter, such as a basement or storm cellar. If an underground shelter is not available, identify an interior room or hallway on the lowest floor.
6. Practice going to your shelter with your household.
7. Know the locations of designated shelters in places where you and your household spend time, such as public buildings, nursing homes, and shopping centers. Ask local officials whether a registered engineer or architect has inspected your children's schools for shelter space.
8. Ask your local emergency manager or American Red Cross chapter if there are any public safe rooms or shelters nearby.
9. Assemble a disaster supply kit. Keep a stock of food and extra drinking water.
10. Make a record of your personal property. Take photographs or videotapes of your belongings. Store these documents in a safe place.

What to Do during a Tornado Watch

1. Listen to NOAA Weather Radio or to commercial radio or television newscasts for the latest information.
2. Be alert for approaching storms. If you see any revolving funnel-shaped clouds, report them immediately by telephone to your local police department or sheriff's office.
3. Watch for tornado danger signs:

   - Dark, often greenish sky
   - Large hail
   - A large, dark, low-lying cloud (particularly if rotating)
   - Loud roar, similar to a freight train

   Caution:

   - Some tornadoes are clearly visible, while rain or nearby low-hanging clouds obscure others.
   - Occasionally, tornadoes develop so rapidly that little, if any, advance warning is possible.
   - Before a tornado hits, the wind may die down, and the air may become very still.
   - A cloud of debris can mark the location of a tornado even if a funnel is not visible.
   - Tornadoes generally occur near the trailing edge of a thunderstorm. It is not uncommon to see clear, sunlit skies behind a tornado.

4. Avoid places with wide-span roofs, such as auditoriums, cafeterias, large hallways, supermarkets, and shopping malls.
5. Be prepared to take shelter immediately. Gather household members and pets. Assemble supplies to take to the shelter, such as flashlight, battery-powered radio, water, and first aid kit.

What to Do during a Tornado Warning

When a tornado has been sighted, go to your shelter immediately.

1. In a residence or small building, move to a predesignated shelter, such as a basement, storm cellar, safe room, or shelter.
2. If there is no basement, go to an interior room on the lower level (closet, interior hallway). Put as many walls as possible between you and the outside. Get under a sturdy table and use your arms to protect your head and neck. Stay there until the danger has passed.
3. Do not open windows. Use the time to seek shelter.
4. Stay away from windows, doors, and outside walls. Go to the center of the room. Stay away from corners because they attract debris.
5. In a school, nursing home, hospital, factory, or shopping center, go to predetermined shelter areas. Interior hallways on the lowest floor are usually safest. Stay away from windows and open spaces.
6. In a high-rise building, go to a small, interior room or hallway on the lowest floor possible.
7. Get out of vehicles, trailers, and mobile homes immediately and go to the lowest floor of a sturdy nearby building or to a storm shelter. Mobile homes, even if tied down, offer little protection from tornadoes.
8. If caught outside with no shelter, lie flat in a nearby ditch or depression and cover your head with your hands. Be aware of potential for flooding.
9. Do not get under an overpass or bridge. You are safer in a low, flat location.
10. Never try to outrun a tornado in urban or congested areas in a car or truck; instead, leave the vehicle immediately for safe shelter. Tornadoes are erratic and move swiftly.
11. Watch out for flying debris. Flying debris from tornadoes causes most fatalities and injuries.

What to Do after a Tornado

1. Look out for broken glass and downed power lines.
2. Check for injuries. Do not attempt to move seriously injured people unless they are in immediate danger of death or further injury. If you must move an unconscious person, first stabilize the neck and back and then call for help immediately.

- If the victim is not breathing, carefully position the victim for artificial respiration, clear the airway, and commence mouth-to-mouth resuscitation.
- Maintain body temperature with blankets. Be sure the victim does not become overheated.
- Never try to feed liquids to an unconscious person.

3. Use caution when entering a damaged building. Be sure that walls, ceiling, and roof are in place and that the structure rests firmly on the foundation. Wear sturdy work boots and gloves.

Wind Shelter or Safe Room

Extreme windstorms in many parts of the country pose a serious threat to buildings and their occupants. Your residence may be built "to code," but that does not mean that it can withstand winds from extreme events like tornadoes or major hurricanes. The purpose of a wind shelter or safe room is to provide a space where you and your household can seek refuge that provides a high level of protection. You can build a shelter in one of several places in your home:

- In your basement
- Beneath a concrete slab-on-grade foundation or garage floor
- In an interior room on the first floor

Shelters built below ground level provide the greatest protection, but a shelter built in a first-floor interior room can also provide the necessary protection. Below-ground shelters must be designed to avoid accumulating water during the heavy rains that often accompany severe windstorms.

To protect its occupants, an in-house shelter must be built to withstand high winds and flying debris, even if the rest of the residence is severely damaged or destroyed. Therefore,

- The shelter must be adequately anchored to resist overturning and uplift.

- The walls, ceiling, and door of the shelter must withstand wind pressure and resist penetration by windborne objects and falling debris.
- The connections between all parts of the shelter must be strong enough to resist the wind.
- If sections of either interior or exterior residence walls are used as walls of the shelter, they must be separated from the structure of the residence so that damage to the residence will not cause damage to the shelter.

If you are concerned about wind hazards where you live, especially if you live in a high-risk area, you should consider building a shelter. Publications are available from FEMA to assist in determining if you need a shelter and how to construct one. Contact the FEMA distribution center for a copy of "Taking Shelter from the Storm" (L-233 for the brochure and FEMA-320 for the booklet with complete construction plans).

WINTER STORMS AND EXTREME COLD

Heavy snowfall and extreme cold can immobilize an entire region. Even areas that normally experience mild winters can be hit with a major snowstorm or extreme cold. The impacts include flooding, storm surges, closed highways, blocked roads, downed power lines, and hypothermia. You can protect yourself and your household from the many hazards of winter by planning ahead.

What to Do before a Winter Storm Threatens

1. Know the terms used by weather forecasters:

   - Freezing rain: Rain freezes when it hits the ground, creating a coating of ice on roads, walkways, trees, and power lines.
   - Sleet: Rain turns into ice pellets before reaching the ground (sleet also causes roads to freeze and become slippery).
   - Winter storm watch: A winter storm is possible in your area.

- Winter storm warning: A winter storm is occurring, or will soon occur, in your area.
- Blizzard warning: Sustained winds or frequent gusts up to thirty-five miles per hour or greater and considerable falling or blowing snow (reducing visibility to less than a quarter mile) are expected to prevail for a period of three hours or longer.
- Frost/freeze warning: Below-freezing temperatures are expected.

2. Prepare to survive on your own for at least three days. Assemble a disaster supply kit. Be sure to include winter-specific items, such as rock salt to melt ice on walkways, sand to improve traction, snow shovels, and other snow-removal equipment. Keep a stock of food and extra drinking water. Prepare for possible isolation in your home:

- Have sufficient heating fuel; regular fuel sources may be cut off.
- Have emergency heating equipment and fuel (a gas fireplace or a wood-burning stove or fireplace) so that you can keep at least one room in your residence livable. (Be sure the room is well ventilated.) If a thermostat controls your furnace and your electricity is cut off by a storm, you will need emergency heat. Kerosene heaters are another emergency-heating option.
- Store a good supply of dry, seasoned wood for your fireplace or wood-burning stove.
- Keep fire extinguishers on hand and make sure your household knows how to use them.
- Never burn charcoal indoors.

3. Winterize your home to extend the life of your fuel supply:

- Insulate walls and attics.
- Caulk and weather-strip doors and windows.
- Install storm windows or cover windows with plastic.

4. Maintain several days' supply of medicines, water, and food that needs no cooking or refrigeration.

What to Do during a Winter Storm

1. Listen to the radio or television for weather reports and emergency information.
2. Eat regularly and drink ample fluids, but avoid caffeine and alcohol.
3. Dress for the season:

   - Wear several layers of loose fitting, lightweight, and warm clothing rather than one layer of heavy clothing. The outer garments should be tightly woven and water repellent.
   - Mittens are warmer than gloves.
   - Wear a hat; most body heat is lost through the top of the head if the head is uncovered.
   - Cover your mouth with a scarf to protect your lungs.

4. Be careful when shoveling snow. Overexertion can bring on a heart attack—a major cause of death in the winter. If you must shovel snow, stretch before going outside and don't overexert yourself.
5. Watch for signs of frostbite: loss of feeling and white or pale appearance in extremities, such as fingers, toes, ear lobes, or the tip of the nose. If symptoms are detected, get medical help immediately.
6. Watch for signs of hypothermia: uncontrollable shivering, memory loss, disorientation, incoherence, slurred speech, drowsiness, and apparent exhaustion. If symptoms of hypothermia are detected, get the victim to a warm location, remove any wet clothing, warm the center of the body first, and give warm, nonalcoholic beverages if the victim is conscious. Get medical help as soon as possible.
7. When at home, do the following:

   - Conserve fuel if necessary by keeping your residence cooler than normal. Temporarily close off heat to some rooms.

- When using kerosene heaters, maintain ventilation to avoid buildup of toxic fumes. Refuel kerosene heaters outside and keep them at least three feet from flammable objects.

WINTER DRIVING

About 70 percent of winter deaths related to snow and ice occur in automobiles. Consider public transportation if you must travel. If you travel by car, travel in the day, don't travel alone, and keep others informed of your schedule. Stay on main roads; avoid back-road short-cuts.

1. Winterize your car. This includes checking the battery, anti-freeze, windshield wipers and washer fluid, ignition system, thermostat, lights, hazard lights, exhaust system, heater, brakes, defroster, oil, and tires. Consider using snow tires, snow tires with studs, or chains. Keep your car's gas tank full.
2. Carry a winter car kit in the trunk of your car. The kit should include the following:

- Shovel
- Windshield scraper
- Battery-powered radio
- Flashlight
- Extra batteries
- Water
- Snack food
- Mittens
- Hat
- Blanket
- Tow chain or rope
- Tire chains
- Bags of road salt and sand
- Fluorescent distress flag
- Booster cables
- Road maps
- Emergency flares

- Cellular telephone or two-way radio

3. If a blizzard traps you in your car, do the following:

- Pull off the highway. Turn on hazard lights and hang a distress flag from the radio aerial or window.
- Remain in your vehicle, where rescuers are most likely to find you. Do not set out on foot unless you can see a building close by where you know you can take shelter. Be careful: distances are distorted by blowing snow. A building may seem close but be too far to walk to in deep snow.
- Run the engine and heater for about ten minutes each hour to keep warm. When the engine is running, open a window slightly for ventilation. This will protect you from possible carbon monoxide poisoning. Periodically clear snow from the exhaust pipe.
- Exercise to maintain body heat, but avoid overexertion. In extreme cold, use road maps, seat covers, and floor mats for insulation. Huddle with passengers and use your coat for a blanket.
- Take turns sleeping. One person should be awake at all times to look for rescue crews.
- Drink fluids to avoid dehydration.
- Be careful not to waste battery power. Balance electrical energy needs—for lights, heat, and radio—with supply.
- At night, turn on the inside light so work crews or rescuers can see you.
- If stranded in a remote area, spread a large cloth over the snow to attract the attention of rescue personnel who may be surveying the area by airplane.
- Once the blizzard passes, you may need to leave the car and proceed on foot.

EXTREME HEAT (HEAT WAVE)

Heat kills by pushing the human body beyond its limits. Under normal conditions, the body's internal thermostat produces perspiration that evaporates and cools the body. However, in extreme heat and high humidity, evaporation is slowed, and the body must work extra hard to maintain a normal temperature. Most heat disorders occur because the victim has been overexposed to heat or has overexercised for his or her age and physical condition. The elderly, young children, and the ill or overweight are more likely to succumb to extreme heat. Heat exhaustion leads to heat stroke, which kills.

Conditions that can induce heat-related illnesses include stagnant atmospheric conditions and poor air quality. Consequently, people living in urban areas may be at greater risk for the effects of a prolonged heat wave than those living in rural areas. Also, asphalt and concrete store heat longer and gradually release heat at night, which can produce higher nighttime temperatures, known as the "urban heat island effect."

What to Do before an Extreme Heat Emergency

1. Know the terms associated with extreme heat:

   - Heat wave: Heat wave refers to a prolonged period of excessive heat, often combined with excessive humidity.
   - Heat index: This number of degrees Fahrenheit (F) tells how hot it feels when relative humidity is added to the air temperature. Exposure to direct sunlight can increase the heat index by fifteen degrees.
   - Heat cramps: Heat cramps are muscular pains and spasms due to heavy exertion. Although the least severe, heat cramps are often the first signal that the body is having trouble with the heat.
   - Heat exhaustion: Heat exhaustion typically occurs when people exercise heavily or work in a hot, humid place where body fluids are lost through heavy sweating. Blood flow to the skin increases, causing blood flow to decrease to the vital organs, resulting in a form of mild shock. If not treated, the victim's condition will worsen. Body temperature will keep rising, and the victim may suffer heat stroke.
   - Heat stroke: Heat stroke is life threatening. The victim's temperature-control system, which produces sweating to cool the body, shuts down. The body's temperature can

increase to the point that brain damage and death may result if the body is not cooled quickly.

- Sun stroke: This is another term for heat stroke.

2. Consider the following preparedness measures when faced with the possibility of extreme heat:

   - Install window air conditioners snugly; insulate if necessary.
   - Close any floor heat registers nearby and use a circulating or box fan to spread cool air.
   - Check air-conditioning ducts for proper insulation.
   - Install temporary reflectors, such as aluminum foil covered cardboard, to reflect heat back outside and be sure to weather-strip doors and sills to keep cool air in.
   - Cover windows that receive morning or afternoon sun with drapes, shades, awnings, or louvers.
   - Outdoor awnings or louvers can reduce the heat that enters a home by up to 80 percent. Consider keeping storm windows up all year.

What to Do during Extreme Heat or a Heat Wave Emergency

1. Stay indoors as much as possible. If air conditioning is not available, stay on the lowest floor out of the sunshine. Remember that electric fans do not cool; they just blow hot air around.
2. Eat well-balanced, light, and regular meals. Avoid using salt tablets unless directed to do so by a physician.
3. Drink plenty of water regularly, even if you do not feel thirsty. People who have epilepsy or heart, kidney, or liver disease, are on fluid-restrictive diets, or have a problem with fluid retention should consult a doctor before increasing liquid intake.
4. Limit intake of alcoholic beverages. Although beer and alcoholic beverages appear to satisfy thirst, they actually cause further body dehydration.
5. Never leave children or pets alone in closed vehicles.
6. Dress in loose clothes that cover as much skin as possible. Lightweight, light-colored clothing reflects heat and sunlight and helps maintain normal body temperature.

7. Protect your face and head by wearing a wide-brimmed hat.
8. Avoid too much sunshine. Sunburn slows the skin's ability to cool itself. Use a sunscreen lotion with a high sun-protection factor (SPF) rating (i.e., fifteen or greater).
9. Avoid strenuous work during the warmest part of the day. Use a buddy system when working in extreme heat and take frequent breaks.
10. Spend at least two hours per day in an air-conditioned place. If your home is not air conditioned, consider spending the warmest part of the day in public buildings, such as libraries, schools, movie theaters, shopping malls, and other community facilities.
11. Check on family, friends, and neighbors who do not have air conditioning and who spend much of their time alone.

First Aid for Heat-Induced Illnesses

1. Sunburn

   - Signs and symptoms include skin redness and pain, possible swelling, blisters, fever, and headaches.
   - First aid: Take a shower, using soap, to remove oils that may block pores, preventing the body from cooling naturally. If blisters occur, apply dry, sterile dressings and get medical attention.

2. Heat cramps

   - Signs and symptoms include painful spasms, usually in leg and abdominal muscles, and heavy sweating.
   - First aid: Get the victim to a cooler location. Lightly stretch and gently massage affected muscles to relieve spasm. Give sips of up to half a glass of cool water every fifteen minutes. Do not give liquids with caffeine or alcohol. If the victim becomes nauseated, discontinue liquids.

3. Heat exhaustion

- Signs and symptoms include heavy sweating; cool, pale, or flushed skin; and weak pulse. Normal body temperature is possible, but temperature will likely rise. Fainting, dizziness, nausea, vomiting, exhaustion, and headaches are possible.
- First aid: Get the victim to lie down in a cool place. Loosen or remove clothing. Apply cool, wet cloths. Fan or move the victim to an air-conditioned place. Give sips of water if the victim is conscious. Be sure water is consumed slowly. Give half a glass of cool water every fifteen minutes. If nausea occurs, discontinue. If vomiting occurs, seek immediate medical attention.

4. Heat stroke (sun stroke)

- Signs and symptoms include high body temperature (105°F or higher); hot, red, dry skin; a rapid, weak pulse; rapid, shallow breathing; and possible unconsciousness. The victim will likely not sweat unless from recent strenuous activity.
- First aid: Heat stroke is a severe medical emergency. Call 911 or emergency medical services or get the victim to a hospital immediately. Delay can be fatal. Move the victim to a cooler environment. Remove clothing. Try a cool bath, sponging, or wet sheet to lower body temperature. Watch for breathing problems. Use extreme caution. Use fans and air conditioners.

EARTHQUAKES

An earthquake is a sudden shaking of the earth caused by the breaking and shifting of rock beneath the earth's surface. Earthquakes can cause buildings and bridges to collapse and telephone and power lines to fall; they can result in fires, explosions, and landslides. Earthquakes can also cause huge ocean waves, called tsunamis, which travel long distances over water until they crash into coastal areas.

The following information includes general guidelines for earth-quake preparedness and safety. Because injury-prevention techniques may vary from state to state, it is recommended that you contact your local emergency-management office, health department, or American Red Cross chapter.

What to Do before an Earthquake

1. Know the terms associated with earthquakes.

   - Earthquake: An earthquake is a sudden slippage or move-ment of a portion of the earth's crust accompanied and followed by a series of vibrations.
   - Aftershock: An aftershock is an earthquake of similar or lesser intensity that follows the main earthquake.
   - Fault: The earth's crust slips along a fault, an area of weak-ness where two sections of crust have separated. The crust may move only a few inches or, in a severe earthquake, up to a few feet.
   - Epicenter: The epicenter refers to the area of the earth's surface directly above the origin of an earthquake.
   - Seismic waves: These are vibrations that travel outward from the center of the earthquake at speeds of several miles per second. The waves can shake some buildings so rapidly that they collapse.
   - Magnitude: This measure indicates how much energy an earthquake has released. It is gauged on a recording device and graphically displayed through lines on the Richter scale. A magnitude of 7.0 on the Richter scale indicates a very strong earthquake. Each whole number on the scale represents an increase of about thirty times the energy re-leased. Therefore, an earthquake measuring 6.0 is about thirty times more powerful than one measuring 5.0.

2. Look for items in your home that could become a hazard in an earthquake:

- Repair defective electrical wiring, leaky gas lines, and inflexible utility connections.
- Bolt down water heaters and gas appliances (install an automatic gas shutoff device that is triggered by an earthquake).
- Place large or heavy objects on lower shelves. Fasten shelves to walls. Brace high and top-heavy objects.
- Store bottled foods, glass, china, and other breakables on low shelves or in cabinets that can fasten shut.
- Anchor overhead lighting fixtures.
- Check and repair deep plaster cracks in ceilings and foundations. Get expert advice, especially if there are signs of structural defects.
- Be sure the residence is firmly anchored to its foundation.
- Install flexible pipe fittings to avoid gas or water leaks. Flexible fittings are more resistant to breakage.

3. Know where and how to shut off electricity, gas, and water at main switches and valves. Check with your local utilities for instructions.
4. Hold earthquake drills with your household:

- Locate safe spots in each room under a sturdy table or against an inside wall. Test out these safe spots in advance by placing yourself and your household in these locations.
- Identify danger zones in each room—near windows where glass can shatter, next to bookcases or furniture that can fall over, or under ceiling fixtures that could fall down.

5. Develop a plan for reuniting your household after an earthquake. Establish an out-of-town telephone contact for household members to call to let others know that they are OK.
6. Review your insurance policies. Some damage may be covered even without specific earthquake insurance. Protect important home and business papers.
7. Prepare to survive on your own for at least three days. Assemble a disaster supply kit. Keep a stock of food and extra drinking water.

What to Do during an Earthquake

1. Drop, cover, and hold on! Minimize your movements during an earthquake to a few steps to a nearby safe place. Stay indoors until the shaking has stopped and you are sure exiting is safe.
2. If you are indoors, take cover under a sturdy desk, table, or bench or against an interior wall, and hold on. Stay away from glass, windows, exterior doors and walls, and anything that could fall, such as lighting fixtures or furniture. If you are in bed, stay there, hold on, and protect your head with a pillow, unless you are under a heavy light fixture that could fall.
3. If there isn't a table or desk near you, cover your face and head with your arms and crouch in an interior corner of the building. Use doorways for shelter only if they are in close proximity to you and you know that they are located in a strongly supported load-bearing wall.
4. If you are outdoors, stay there. Move away from buildings, street-lights, and utility wires.
5. If you live in an apartment building or other multihousehold structure with many levels, consider the following:

   - Get under a desk and stay away from windows and outside walls.
   - Be aware that the electricity may go out and sprinkler systems may come on.
   - Do not use the elevators.

6. If you are in a crowded indoor public location, consider the following:

   - Stay where you are. Do not rush for the doorways.
   - Move away from tall shelves, cabinets, and bookcases containing objects that may fall.
   - Take cover and grab something to shield your head and face from falling debris and glass.
   - Be aware that the electricity may go out or sprinkler systems or fire alarms may turn on.
   - Do not use elevators.

7. In a moving vehicle, stop as quickly as safety permits and stay in the vehicle. Avoid stopping near or under buildings, trees, overpasses, or utility wires. Then, proceed cautiously, watching for road and bridge damage.

8. If you become trapped in debris, remember the following:

   - Do not light a match.
   - Do not move about or kick up dust.
   - Cover your mouth with a handkerchief or clothing.
   - Tap on a pipe or wall so rescuers can locate you. Use a whistle if one is available. Shout only as a last resort—shouting can cause you to inhale dangerous amounts of dust.

9. Stay indoors until the shaking has stopped and you are sure exiting is safe. Most injuries during earthquakes occur when falling objects hit people as they enter or exit buildings.

What to Do after an Earthquake

1. Be prepared for aftershocks. These secondary shock waves are usually less violent than the main quake but can be strong enough to do additional damage to weakened structures.

2. Check for injuries. Do not attempt to move seriously injured people unless they are in immediate danger of further injury or death. If you must move an unconscious person, first stabilize the neck and back and then call for help immediately.

   - If the victim is not breathing, carefully position the victim for artificial respiration, clear the airway, and start mouth-to-mouth resuscitation.
   - Maintain body temperature with blankets. Be sure the victim does not become overheated.
   - Never try to feed liquids to an unconscious person.

3. If the electricity goes out, use flashlights or battery-powered lanterns. Do not use candles, matches, or open flames indoors after an earthquake because of possible gas leaks.

4. In areas covered with fallen debris and broken glass, wear sturdy shoes.

5. Check your home for structural damage. If you have any doubts about safety, have your home inspected by a professional before entering.

6. Check chimneys for visual damage; have a professional inspect the chimney for internal damage before lighting a fire.

7. Clean up spilled medicines, bleaches, gasoline, and flammable liquids. Evacuate the building if gasoline fumes are detected and the building is not well ventilated.

8. Visually inspect utility lines and appliances for damage.

- If you smell gas or hear a hissing or blowing sound, open a window and leave. Shut off the main gas valve. Report the leak to the gas company from the nearest working phone or cell phone.
- Stay out of the building. If you shut off the gas supply at the main valve, you will need a professional to turn it back on.
- Switch off electrical power at the main fuse box or circuit breaker if electrical damage is suspected or known.
- Shut off the water supply at the main valve if water pipes are damaged.
- Do not flush toilets until you know that sewage lines are intact.

9. Open cabinets cautiously. Beware of objects that can fall off shelves.

10. Use the phone only to report life-threatening emergencies.

11. Listen to news reports for the latest emergency information.

12. Stay off the streets. If you must go out, watch for fallen objects, downed electrical wires, and weakened walls, bridges, roads, and sidewalks.

13. Stay away from damaged areas unless your assistance has been specifically requested by police, fire, or relief organizations.

14. If you live in coastal areas, be aware of possible tsunamis, sometimes mistakenly called tidal waves. When local authorities issue a tsunami warning, assume that a series of dangerous waves is on

the way. Stay away from the beach. See the "Tsunamis" section for more information.

VOLCANOES

A volcano is a vent through which molten rock escapes to the earth's surface. When pressure from gases within the molten rock becomes too great, an eruption occurs. Some eruptions are relatively quiet, producing lava flows that creep across the land at two to ten miles per hour.

Explosive eruptions can shoot columns of gases and rock fragments tens of miles into the atmosphere, spreading ash hundreds of miles downwind. Lateral blasts can flatten trees for miles. Hot, sometimes poisonous gases may flow down the sides of the volcano.

Lava flows are streams of molten rock that either pour from a vent quietly through lava tubes or lava fountains. Because of their intense heat, lava flows are also great fire hazards. Lava flows destroy everything in their path, but most move slowly enough that people can move out of the way.

Fresh volcanic ash, made of pulverized rock, can be harsh, acidic, gritty, glassy, and odorous. Although not immediately dangerous to most adults, the combination of acidic gas and ash can cause lung damage in small infants, very old people, and those suffering from severe respiratory illnesses. Volcanic ash can also damage machinery, including engines and electrical equipment. Ash accumulations mixed with water become heavy and can collapse roofs.

Other natural hazards can accompany volcanic eruptions: earthquakes, mudflows, flash floods, rock falls, landslides, acid rain, fire, and (under special conditions) tsunamis. Active volcanoes in the United States are found mainly in Hawaii, Alaska, and the Pacific Northwest.

What to Do before an Eruption

1. Make evacuation plans. If you live in a known volcanic-hazard area, plan a route out and have a backup route in mind.
2. Develop a household disaster plan. In case household members are separated from one another during a volcanic eruption (a real possibility during the day when adults are at work and children

are at school), have a plan for getting back together. Ask an out-of-town relative or friend to serve as the household contact because, after a disaster, it's often easier to call long-distance. Make sure everyone knows the name, address, and phone number of the contact person.

3. Assemble a disaster supply kit.
4. Get a pair of goggles and a throwaway breathing mask for each member of the household in case of ashfall.
5. Do not visit an active volcano site unless officials designate a safe-viewing area.

What to Do during an Eruption

1. If you are close to the volcano, evacuate immediately to avoid flying debris, hot gases, lateral blast, and lava flow.
2. Avoid areas downwind from the volcano to avoid volcanic ash.
3. Be aware of mudflows. The danger from a mudflow increases as you approach a stream channel and decreases as you move away from a stream channel toward higher ground. In some parts of the world (Central and South America, Indonesia, the Philippines), this danger also increases with prolonged heavy rains. Mudflows can move faster than you can walk or run. Look upstream before crossing a bridge, and do not cross if the mudflow is approaching. Avoid river valleys and low-lying areas.
4. Stay indoors until the ash has settled unless there is danger of the roof collapsing.
5. During an ashfall, close doors, windows, and all ventilation in the house (chimney vents, furnaces, air conditioners, fans, and other vents).
6. Avoid driving in heavy dust unless absolutely necessary. If you do drive in dense dust, keep speed to thirty-five miles per hour or less.
7. Remove heavy ash from flat or low-pitched roofs and rain gutters.
8. Volcanic ash is actually fine, glassy fragments and particles that can severely injure breathing passages, eyes, and open wounds and irritate skin. Follow these precautions to keep yourself safe from ashfall:

- Wear long-sleeved shirts and long pants.
- Use goggles and wear eyeglasses instead of contact lenses.
- Use a dust mask or hold a damp cloth over your face to help with breathing.
- Keep car or truck engines off. Driving can stir up volcanic ash, which can clog engines and stall vehicles. Moving parts can be damaged from abrasion, including bearings, brakes, and transmissions.

What to Do after the Eruption

1. Avoid ashfall areas if possible. If you are in an ashfall area, cover your mouth and nose with a mask, keep skin covered, and wear goggles to protect the eyes.
2. Clear roofs of ashfall because it is very heavy and can cause buildings to collapse. Exercise great caution when working on a roof.
3. Avoid driving through ashfall, which is easily stirred up and can clog engines, causing vehicles to stall.
4. If you have a respiratory ailment, avoid contact with any amount of ash. Stay indoors until local health officials advise it is safe to go outside.

LANDSLIDES AND DEBRIS FLOW (MUDSLIDE)

Landslides occur in all US states and territories and occur when masses of rock, earth, or debris move down a slope. Landslides may be small or large and can move at slow or very high speeds. They are activated by storms, earthquakes, volcanic eruptions, fires, and human modification of the land.

Debris- and mudflows are rivers of rock, earth, and other debris saturated with water. They develop when water rapidly accumulates in the ground, during heavy rainfall or rapid snowmelt, changing the earth into a flowing river of mud or slurry. They can flow rapidly down slopes or through channels and can strike with little or no warning at avalanche speeds. They can also travel several miles from their source, growing in size as they pick up trees, boulders, cars, and other materials along the way.

Landslide, mudflow, and debris-flow problems are occasionally caused by land mismanagement. Improper land-use practices on ground of questionable stability, particularly in mountain, canyon, and coastal regions, can create and accelerate serious landslide problems. Land-use zoning, professional inspections, and proper design can minimize many landslide, mudflow, and debris-flow problems.

What to Do before a Landslide or Debris Flow

1. Contact your local emergency-management office or American Red Cross chapter for information on local landslide and debris-flow hazards.
2. Get a ground assessment of your property. County or state geological experts, local planning departments, or departments of natural resources may have specific information on areas vulnerable to landslides. Consult an appropriate professional expert for advice on corrective measures you can take.
3. Minimize home hazards by having flexible pipe fittings installed to avoid gas or water leaks. Flexible fittings are more resistant to breakage. Only the gas company or its professionals should install gas fittings.
4. Familiarize yourself with your surrounding area:

   - Small changes in your local landscape could alert you to the potential for greater future threat.
   - Observe the patterns of storm-water drainage on slopes and especially the places where runoff water converges.
   - Watch for any sign of land movement, such as small slides, flows, or progressively leaning trees, on the hillsides near your home.

5. Be particularly observant of your surrounding area before and during intense storms that could heighten the possibility of landslide or debris flow from heavy rains. Many debris-flow fatalities occur when people are sleeping.
6. Talk to your insurance agent. Debris flow may be covered by flood insurance policies from the National Flood Insurance Program.

7. Learn to recognize landslide warning signs.

- Doors or windows stick or jam for the first time.
- New cracks appear in plaster, tile, brick, or foundations.
- Outside walls, walks, or stairs begin pulling away from the building.
- Slowly developing, widening cracks appear on the ground or on paved areas, such as streets or driveways.
- Underground utility lines break.
- Bulging ground appears at the base of a slope.
- Water breaks through the ground surface in new locations.
- Fences, retaining walls, utility poles, or trees tilt or move.
- You hear a faint rumbling sound that increases in volume as the landslide nears.
- The ground slopes downward in one specific direction and may begin shifting in that direction under your feet.

What to Do during a Heightened Threat (Intense Storm) of Landslide or Debris Flow

1. Listen to radio or television for warnings of intense rainfall:

   - Be prepared to evacuate if so instructed by local authorities or if you feel threatened.
   - Should you remain at home, move to a second story, if possible, to distance yourself from the direct path of debris flow and landslide debris.

2. Be alert when intense, short bursts of rain follow prolonged heavy rains or damp weather, which increases the risk of debris flows.
3. Listen for any unusual sounds that might indicate moving debris, such as trees cracking or boulders knocking together. A trickle of flowing or falling mud or debris may precede larger landslides. Moving debris can flow quickly and sometimes without warning.
4. If you are near a stream or channel, be alert for sudden increases or decreases in water flow and for a change from clear to muddy water. Such changes may indicate landslide activity upstream. Be prepared to move quickly.

5. Be especially alert when driving. Embankments along roadsides are particularly susceptible to landslides. Watch for collapsed pavement, mud, fallen rocks, and other indications of possible debris flows.
6. Evacuate when ordered to do so by local authorities.

What to Do during a Landslide or Debris Flow

1. Quickly move away from the path of a landslide or debris flow.
2. The following areas are generally considered safe:

   - Areas that have not moved in the past
   - Relatively flat-lying areas away from drastic changes in slope
   - Areas at the top of or along ridges set back from the tops of slopes

3. If escape is not possible, curl into a tight ball and protect your head.

What to Do after a Landslide or Debris Flow

1. Stay away from the slide area. There may be danger of additional slides.
2. Check for injured and trapped people near the slide, without entering the direct slide area, and direct rescuers to them.
3. Help neighbors who may require special assistance—large families, children, elderly people, and people with disabilities.
4. Listen to local radio or television stations for the latest emergency information.
5. Landslides and flows can provoke associated dangers, such as broken electrical, water, gas, and sewage lines, and disrupt roadways and railways:

   - Look for and report broken utility lines to the appropriate authorities. Reporting potential hazards will get the utilities turned off as quickly as possible, preventing further hazard and injury.

- Check building foundations, chimneys, and surrounding land for damage. Damage to foundations, chimneys, or surrounding land may help you assess the safety of the area.

6. Watch for flooding, which may occur after a landslide or debris flow and be started by the same event.
7. Replant damaged vegetation as soon as possible since erosion caused by loss of ground cover can lead to flash flooding and additional landslides in the near future.
8. Seek the advice of a geotechnical expert for evaluating landslide hazards or designing corrective techniques to reduce landslide risk. A professional will be able to advise you of the best ways to eradicate or reduce landslide risk, without creating further hazard.

TSUNAMIS

A tsunami (pronounced tsoo-na-mee), sometimes mistakenly called a tidal wave, is a series of enormous waves created by an underwater disturbance, such as an earthquake. A tsunami can move hundreds of miles per hour in the open ocean and smash into land with waves as high as one hundred feet or more, although most waves are less than eighteen feet high.

From the area where the tsunami originates, waves travel outward in all directions, much like the ripples caused by throwing a rock into a pond. In deep water, the tsunami wave is not noticeable. Once the wave approaches the shore, it builds in height. All tsunamis are potentially dangerous, even though they may not damage every coastline they strike. A tsunami can strike anywhere along most of the US coastline. The most destructive tsunamis have occurred along the coasts of California, Oregon, Washington, Alaska, and Hawaii.

Earthquake-induced movement of the ocean floor most often generates tsunamis. Landslides, volcanic eruptions, and even meteorites can also generate tsunamis. If a major earthquake or landslide occurs close to shore, the first wave in a series could reach the beach in a few minutes, even before a warning is issued.

Areas are at greater risk if less than twenty-five feet above sea level and within a mile of the shoreline. Drowning is the most common cause of death associated with tsunamis. Tsunami waves and the receding waters are very destructive to structures in the run-up zone. Other hazards include flooding, contamination of drinking water, and fires from ruptured gas lines or tanks.

What to Do before a Tsunami

1. Know the terms used by the West Coast/Alaska Tsunami Warning Center (WC/ATWC), responsible for tsunami warnings for California, Oregon, Washington, British Columbia, and Alaska) and the Pacific Tsunami Warning Center (PTWC), responsible for tsunami warnings to international authorities, Hawaii, and the US territories within the Pacific basin.

   • Advisory: An earthquake has occurred in the Pacific basin, which might generate a tsunami. WC/ATWC and PTWC will issue hourly bulletins advising of the situation.
   • Watch: A tsunami was or may have been generated but is at least two hours away from the area in watch status.
   • Warning: A tsunami was or may have been generated, which could cause damage; people in the warning area are strongly advised to evacuate.

2. Listen to radio or television for more information and follow the instructions of your local authorities.
3. Immediate tsunami warnings sometimes come in the form of a noticeable recession in water away from the shoreline. This is nature's tsunami warning, and you should heed it by moving inland to higher ground immediately.
4. If you feel an earthquake in a coastal area, turn on your radio to learn if there is a tsunami warning.
5. Know that a small tsunami at one beach can be a giant wave a few miles away. The topography of the coastline and the ocean floor will influence the size of the wave.

6. A tsunami may generate more than one wave. Do not let the modest size of one wave allow you to forget how dangerous a tsunami is. The next wave may be bigger.
7. Prepare for possible evacuation. Learn evacuation routes. Determine where you will go and how you will get there if you need to evacuate.

What to Do during a Tsunami

1. If you are advised to evacuate, do so immediately.
2. Stay away from the area until local authorities say it is safe. Do not be fooled into thinking that the danger is over after a single wave—a tsunami is not a single wave but a series of waves that can vary in size.
3. Do not go to the shoreline to watch for a tsunami. When you can see the wave, it is too late to escape.

What to Do after a Tsunami

1. Avoid flooded and damaged areas until officials say it is safe to return.
2. Stay away from debris in the water; it may pose a safety hazard to boats and people.

FIRE

Each year more than four thousand Americans die and more than twenty-five thousand are injured in fires, many of which could have been prevented. Direct property loss due to fires is estimated at $8.6 billion annually.

To protect yourself, it's important to understand the basic characteristics of fire. Fire spreads quickly. There is no time to gather valuables or make a phone call. In just two minutes a fire can become life threatening; in five minutes a residence can be engulfed in flames.

Heat and smoke from fire can be more dangerous than the flames. Inhaling the superhot air can sear your lungs. Fire produces poisonous gases that make you disoriented and drowsy. Instead of being awakened by a fire, you may fall into a deeper sleep. Asphyxiation is the leading cause of fire deaths, exceeding burns by a three-to-one ratio.

What to Do before Fire Strikes

1. Install smoke alarms. Working smoke alarms decrease your chances of dying in a fire by half:

    - Place smoke alarms on every level of your residence: outside bedrooms on the ceiling or high on the wall, at the top of open stairways or at the bottom of enclosed stairs, and near (but not in) the kitchen.
    - Test and clean smoke alarms once a month and replace batteries at least once a year. Replace smoke alarms once every ten years.

2. With your household, plan two escape routes from every room in the residence. Practice escaping from each room with your household:

    - Make sure windows are not nailed or painted shut.
    - Consider escape ladders if your home has more than one level and ensure that burglar bars and other anti-theft mechanisms that block outside window entry are easily opened from inside.
    - Teach household members to stay low to the floor (where the air is safer) when escaping from a fire.
    - Pick a place outside your home for the household to meet after escaping from a fire.

3. Clean out storage areas. Don't let trash, such as old newspapers and magazines, accumulate.
4. Check the electrical wiring in your home:

    - Inspect extension cords for frayed or exposed wires or loose plugs.
    - Outlets should have cover plates and no exposed wiring.

- Make sure wiring does not run under rugs, over nails, or across high-traffic areas.
- Do not overload extension cords or outlets. If you need to plug in two or three appliances, get a UL-approved unit with built-in circuit breakers to prevent sparks and short circuits.
- Make sure home insulation does not touch electrical wiring.
- Have an electrician check the electrical wiring in your home.

5. Never use gasoline, benzene, naptha, or similar liquids indoors:

   - Store flammable liquids in approved containers in well-ventilated storage areas.
   - Never smoke near flammable liquids.
   - After use, safely discard all rags or materials soaked in flammable material.

6. Check heating sources. Many home fires are started by faulty furnaces or stoves, cracked or rusted furnace parts, and chimneys with creosote buildup. Have chimneys, woodstoves, and all home-heating systems inspected and cleaned annually by a certified specialist.
7. Insulate chimneys and place spark arresters on top. The chimney should be at least three feet higher than the roof. Remove branches hanging above and around the chimney.
8. Take care when using alternative heating sources, such as wood, coal, and kerosene heaters and electrical space heaters:

   - Check with your local fire department on the legality of using kerosene heaters in your community. Be sure to fill kerosene heaters outside after they have cooled.
   - Place heaters at least three feet away from flammable materials. Make sure the floor and nearby walls are properly insulated.
   - Use only the type of fuel designated for your unit and follow manufacturer's instructions.
   - Store ashes in a metal container outside and away from the residence.

- Keep open flames away from walls, furniture, drapery, and flammable items. Keep a screen in front of the fireplace.
- Have chimneys and woodstoves inspected annually and cleaned, if necessary.
- Use portable heaters only in well-ventilated rooms.

9. Keep matches and lighters up high, away from children, and, if possible, in a locked cabinet.
10. Do not smoke in bed or when drowsy or medicated. Provide smokers with deep, sturdy ashtrays. Douse cigarette and cigar butts with water before disposal.
11. Safety experts recommend that you sleep with your door closed.
12. Know the locations of the gas valve and electric main and how to turn them off in an emergency. If you shut off your main gas line for any reason, allow only a gas company representative to turn it on again.
13. Install ABC-type fire extinguishers in the home and teach household members how to use them (type A: wood or paper fires only; type B: flammable liquid or grease fires; type C: electrical fires; type ABC: rated for all fires and recommended for the home).
14. Consider installing an automatic fire-sprinkler system in your home.
15. Ask your local fire department to inspect your residence for fire safety and prevention.
16. Teach children how to report a fire and when to use 911.
17. To support insurance claims in case you do have a fire, conduct an inventory of your property and possessions and keep the list in a separate location. Photographs are also helpful.

What to Do during a Fire

1. Use water or a fire extinguisher to put out small fires. Do not try to put out a fire that is getting out of control. If you're not sure if you can control it, get everyone out of the residence and call the fire department from a neighbor's residence.
2. Never use water on an electrical fire. Use only a fire extinguisher approved for electrical fires.

3. Smother oil and grease fires in the kitchen with baking soda or salt, or put a lid over the flame if it is in a pan. Do not attempt to take the pan outside.
4. If your clothes catch fire, stop, drop, and roll until the fire is extinguished. Running only makes the fire burn faster.
5. If you are escaping through a closed door, use the back of your hand to feel the surface of the door, the doorknob, and the crack between the door and doorframe before you open it. Never use the palm of your hand or fingers to test for heat—burning those areas could impair your ability to escape a fire (i.e., climb down ladders, crawl):

   • If the door is cool, open slowly and ensure fire or smoke is not blocking your escape route. If your escape route is blocked, shut the door immediately and use an alternate escape route, such as a window. If the route is clear, leave immediately through the door. Be prepared to crawl. Smoke and heat rise. The air is clearer and cooler near the floor.
   • If the door is warm or hot, do not open. Escape through a window. If you cannot escape, hang a white or light-colored sheet outside the window, alerting firefighters to your presence.

6. If you must exit through smoke, crawl low under the smoke to your exit; heavy smoke and poisonous gases collect first along the ceiling.
7. Close doors behind you as you escape to delay the spread of the fire.
8. Once you are safely out, stay out and call 911.

What to Do after a Fire

1. Give first aid where needed. After calling 911 or your local emergency number, cool and cover burns to reduce the chance of further injury or infection.
2. Do not enter a fire-damaged building unless authorities say it is OK.

3. If you must enter a fire-damaged building, be alert for heat and smoke. If you detect either, evacuate immediately.

4. Have an electrician check your household wiring before the current is turned on.

5. Do not attempt to reconnect any utilities yourself. Leave this to the fire department and other authorities.

6. Beware of structural damage. Roofs and floors may be weakened and in need of repair.

7. Contact your local disaster-relief service, such as the American Red Cross or Salvation Army, if you need housing, food, or a place to stay.

8. Call your insurance agent:

   - Make a list of damage and losses. Pictures are helpful.
   - Keep records of cleanup and repair costs. Receipts are important for both insurance and income tax claims.
   - Do not throw away any damaged goods until an official inventory has been taken. Your insurance company takes all damages into consideration.

9. If you are a tenant, contact the landlord. It's the property owner's responsibility to prevent further loss or damage to the site.

10. Secure personal belongings or move them to another location.

11. Discard food, beverages, and medicines that have been exposed to heat, smoke, or soot. Refrigerators and freezers left closed hold their temperature for a short time. Do not attempt to refreeze food that has thawed.

12. If you have a safe or strong box, do not try to open it. It can hold intense heat for several hours. If the door is opened before the box has cooled, the contents could burst into flames.

13. If a building inspector says the building is unsafe and you must leave your home, do the following:

   - Ask local police to watch the property during your absence.
   - Pack identification, medicines, glasses, jewelry, credit cards, checkbooks, insurance policies, and financial records, if you can reach them safely.
   - Notify friends, relatives, police and fire departments, your insurance agent, the mortgage company, utility companies,

delivery services, employers, schools, and the post office of your whereabouts.

14. See the "Shelter" section for more information.

WILDLAND FIRES

If you live on a remote hillside or in a valley, prairie, or forest where flammable vegetation is abundant, your residence could be vulnerable to wildland fire. These fires are usually triggered by lightning or accidents.

1. Fire facts about rural living include the following:

    - Once a fire starts outdoors in a rural area, it is often hard to control. Firefighters dealing with such fires are trained to protect natural resources, not homes and buildings.
    - Many homes are located far from fire stations. The result is longer emergency-response times. Within a matter of minutes, fire may destroy an entire home.
    - Limited water supply in rural areas can make fire suppression difficult.
    - Homes may be secluded and surrounded by woods, dense brush, and combustible vegetation, which fuel fires.

2. Ask fire authorities for information about wildland fires in your area. Request that they inspect your residence and property for hazards.
3. Be prepared and have a fire safety and evacuation plan:

    - Practice fire escape and evacuation plans.
    - Mark the entrance to your property with address signs visible clearly from the road.
    - Know which local emergency services are available and have those numbers posted near telephones.
    - Provide emergency-vehicle access through roads and driveways at least twelve feet wide with adequate turnaround space.

4. Follow these tips for making your property fire resistant:

- Keep lawns trimmed, leaves raked, and the roof and gutters free of debris, such as dead limbs and leaves.
- Stack firewood at least thirty feet away from your home.
- Store flammable materials, liquids, and solvents in metal containers outside the home, at least thirty feet away from structures and wooden fences.
- Create defensible space by thinning trees and brush within thirty feet of your home. Beyond thirty feet, remove dead wood, debris, and low tree branches.
- Landscape your property with fire-resistant plants and vegetation to prevent fire from spreading quickly. For example, hardwood trees are more fire resistant than pine, evergreen, eucalyptus, or fir trees.
- Make sure water sources, such as hydrants, ponds, swimming pools, and wells, are accessible to the fire department.

5. Protect your home as follows:

- Use fire-resistant, protective roofing and materials like stone, brick, and metal to protect your home. Avoid using wood materials; they offer the least fire protection.
- Cover all exterior vents, attics, and eaves with metal mesh screens no larger than 6 mm or 1/4 inch to prevent debris from collecting and to help keep sparks out.
- Install multipane windows, tempered safety glass, or fireproof shutters to protect large windows from radiant heat.
- Use fire-resistant draperies for added window protection.
- Have chimneys, woodstoves, and all home-heating systems inspected and cleaned annually by a certified specialist.
- Insulate chimneys and cap them with spark arresters. Chimney should be at least three feet above the roof.
- Remove branches hanging above and around chimneys.

6. Follow local burning laws:

- Do not burn trash or other debris without proper knowledge of local burning laws, techniques, and the safest times of day and year to burn.
- Before burning debris in a wooded area, make sure you notify local authorities and obtain a burning permit.
- Use an approved incinerator with a safety lid or covering with holes no larger than 3/4 inch.
- Create at least a ten-foot clearing around the incinerator before burning debris.
- Have a fire extinguisher or garden hose on hand when burning debris.

7. If wildfire threatens your home and time permits, consider the following:

- Inside

  - Shut off gas at the meter. Turn off pilot lights.
  - Open fireplace damper. Close fireplace screens.
  - Close windows, vents, doors, blinds, and noncombustible window coverings and heavy drapes.
  - Remove flammable drapes and curtains.
  - Move flammable furniture into the center of the home away from windows and sliding-glass doors.
  - Close all interior doors and windows to prevent drafts.
  - Place valuables that will not be damaged by water in a pool or pond.
  - Gather pets into one room. Make plans to care for your pets if you must evacuate.
  - Back your car into the garage or park it in an open space facing in the direction of escape. Shut doors and roll up windows. Leave the key in the ignition and the car doors unlocked. Close garage windows and doors, but leave them unlocked. Disconnect automatic garage door openers.

- Outside

- Seal attic and ground vents with precut plywood or commercial sealants.
- Turn off propane tanks.
- Place combustible patio furniture inside.
- Connect a garden hose to outside taps. Place lawn sprinklers on the roof and near aboveground fuel tanks. Wet the roof.
- Wet or remove shrubs within fifteen feet of the home.
- Gather fire tools, such as a rake, axe, handsaw or chainsaw, bucket, and shovel.

8. If advised to evacuate, do so immediately. Choose a route away from the fire hazard. Watch for changes in the speed and direction of fire and smoke.

NUCLEAR POWER PLANTS

Nuclear power plants operate in most US states and produce about 20 percent of the nation's power. Nearly 3 million Americans live within ten miles of an operating nuclear power plant. Although the Nuclear Regulatory Commission regulates and closely monitors the construction and operation of these facilities, accidents at these plants are possible. An accident could result in dangerous levels of radiation, which could in turn affect the health and safety of those living near the nuclear power plant.

Local and state governments, federal agencies, and the electric utilities have emergency-response plans in the event of an incident at a nuclear power plant. The plans define two "emergency planning zones." One covers an area within a ten-mile radius of the plant, where direct radiation exposure could harm people. The second zone covers a broader area, usually up to a fifty-mile radius from the plant, in which radioactive materials could contaminate water supplies, food crops, and livestock.

Understanding Radiation

Radioactive materials consist of atoms that are unstable. An unstable atom gives off its excess energy until it becomes stable. The energy emitted is called radiation. Each of us is exposed to radiation daily from natural sources, including the sun and earth. Small traces of radiation are present in food and water. Radiation is also released from man-made sources such as X-ray machines, television sets, and microwave ovens. Nuclear power plants use the heat generated from nuclear fission in a contained environment to convert water to steam, which powers generators to produce electricity.

The potential danger in a nuclear power plant accident is exposure to radiation. Radiation has a cumulative effect. The longer a person is exposed to it, the greater the risk. A high exposure to radiation can cause serious illness or death. This exposure could come from the release of radioactive material from the plant into the environment, usually characterized by a plume (cloud-like) formation of radioactive gases and particles. The area that the radioactive release may affect is determined by the amount released from the plant, wind direction and speed, and weather conditions. The major hazards to people in the vicinity of the plume are radiation exposure to the body from the cloud and particles deposited on the ground and inhalation and ingestion of radioactive materials.

If an accident at a nuclear power plant were to release radiation in your area, local authorities would activate warning sirens or another approved alert method. They would also instruct you, through the Emergency Alert System on local television and radio stations, as to how to protect yourself.

The three ways to minimize radiation exposure are distance, shielding, and time:

- Distance: The more distance between you and the source of the radiation, the better. In a serious nuclear power plant accident, local authorities will call for an evacuation to increase the distance between you and the radiation.
- Shielding: As with distance, the heavier and denser the material between you and the source of the radiation, the better. This is why local authorities might advise you to remain indoors if an

accident occurs at a nearby nuclear power plant. In some cases, the walls in your home will be sufficient shielding to protect you.

- Time: Usually radioactivity loses its strength fairly quickly. In a nuclear power plant accident, local authorities will monitor any release of radiation and determine when the threat has passed.

What to Do before a Nuclear Power Plant Emergency

1. Know the terms used to describe a nuclear emergency:

   - Notification of unusual event: A small problem has occurred at the plant. No radiation leak is expected. Federal, state, and county officials will be told right away. No action on your part will be necessary.
   - Alert: A small problem has occurred, and small amounts of radiation could leak inside the plant. This will not affect you. You should not have to do anything.
   - Site area emergency: A more serious problem has occurred. Small amounts of radiation could leak from the plant. If necessary, state and county officials will act to ensure public safety. Area sirens may be sounded. Listen to your radio or television for safety information.
   - General emergency: This is the most serious problem. Radiation could leak outside the plant and off the plant site. The sirens will sound. Tune to your local radio or television station for reports. State and county officials will act to protect the public. Be prepared to follow instructions promptly.

2. Learn your community's warning system. Nuclear power plants are required to install sirens and other warning systems (flash warning lights) to cover a ten-mile area around the plant.

   - Find out when the warning systems will be tested next.
   - When the systems are tested in your area, determine whether you can hear and/or see sirens and flash warning lights from your home.

3. Obtain public emergency information materials from the power company that operates your local nuclear power plant or your local emergency services office. If you live within ten miles of the power plant, you should receive these materials yearly from the power company or your state or local government.

4. Learn about the emergency plans for schools, day-care centers, nursing homes, and other places that members of your household frequent. Learn where people will go in case of evacuation. Stay tuned to your local radio and television stations.

5. Be prepared to evacuate:

   • Prepare an emergency evacuation supply kit.
   • Consider your transportation options. If you do not own or drive a car, ask your local emergency manager about plans for people without private vehicles.

What to Do during a Nuclear Power Plant Emergency

1. Listen to the warning. Not all incidents result in the release of radiation. The incident could be contained inside the plant and pose no danger to the public.

2. Stay tuned to local radio or television. Local authorities will provide specific instructions and information:

   • The advice given will depend on the nature of the emergency, how quickly it is evolving, and how much radiation, if any, is likely to be released.
   • Local instructions should take precedence over any advice given in this handbook.
   • Review the public information materials you have received from the power company or government officials.

3. Evacuate if you are advised to do so:

   • Close and lock doors and windows.
   • Keep car windows and vents closed; use recirculating air.
   • Listen to radio for evacuation routes and other instructions.

4. If you are not advised to evacuate, remain indoors:

   • Close doors and windows.
   • Turn off the air conditioner, ventilation fans, furnace, and other air intakes.
   • Go to a basement or other underground area, if possible.
   • Keep a battery-powered radio with you at all times.

5. Shelter livestock and give them stored feed, if time permits.
6. Do not use the telephone unless absolutely necessary. Lines will be needed for emergency calls.
7. If you suspect exposure, take a thorough shower:

   • Change clothes and shoes.
   • Put exposed clothing in a plastic bag.
   • Seal the bag and place it out of the way.

8. Put food in covered containers or in the refrigerator. Food not previously covered should be washed before being put into containers.

What to Do after a Nuclear Power Plant Emergency

1. If told to evacuate, do not return home until local authorities say it is safe.
2. If advised to stay in your home, do not go outside until local authorities indicate it is safe.
3. Seek medical treatment for any unusual symptoms, such as nausea, that may be related to radiation exposure.
4. See the "Shelter" section for more information.

NATIONAL SECURITY EMERGENCIES

In addition to the natural and technological hazards described above, Americans face threats posed by hostile governments or extremist groups. These threats to national security include acts of terrorism and acts of war. The following is general information about national security emergencies.

Terrorism

Terrorism entails the use of force or violence against people or property in violation of the criminal laws of the United States for purposes of intimidation, coercion, or ransom. Terrorists often use threats to create fear among the public, to try to convince citizens that their government is powerless to prevent terrorism, and to get immediate publicity for their causes. Acts of terrorism can range from threats of terrorism to assassinations, kidnappings, hijackings, cyberattacks (computer based), bomb scares and bombings, and the use of chemical, biological, and nuclear weapons. High-risk targets include military and civilian government facilities, international airports, large cities, and high-profile landmarks. Terrorists might also target large public gatherings, water and food supplies, utilities, and corporate centers. Further, they are capable of spreading fear by sending explosives or chemical and biological agents through the mail.

In the immediate area of a terrorist event, you will need to rely on police, fire, and other officials for instructions. However, you can prepare in much the same way as you would prepare for other crises.

Preparing for Terrorism

1. Wherever you are, be aware of your surroundings. The very nature of terrorism suggests there may be little or no warning.
2. Take precautions when traveling. Be aware of suspicious or unusual behavior. Do not accept packages from strangers. Do not leave luggage unattended. Report unusual behavior, suspicious packages, and strange devices promptly to police or security personnel.
3. Do not be afraid to move or leave if you feel uncomfortable or if something does not seem right.
4. Learn where emergency exits are located in buildings you frequent. When you enter unfamiliar buildings, notice where exits and staircases are located. Plan how to get out of a building,

subway, congested public area, or traffic. Notice heavy or breakable objects that could move, fall, or break in an explosion.

5. Assemble a disaster supply kit at home and learn first aid. Separate the supplies you would take if you had to evacuate quickly and put them in a backpack or container, ready to go.

6. Be familiar with different types of fire extinguishers and how to locate them. Know the location and availability of hard hats in buildings in which you spend a lot of time.

You never know when a disaster will strike or what form it will take. However, if you stock up, plan ahead, and learn what to do in an emergency, you will minimize your risk and help keep your family safe.

RESOURCES

FAMILIES

Army Families Online: http://www.armyfamiliesonline.org—The well-being liaison office assists the army leadership with ensuring the effective delivery of well-being programs in the army.

Army Morale Welfare and Recreation: http://www.armymwr.com—This site lists army recreation programs.

Army OneSource: http://www.myarmyonesource.com—This website of choice for army families provides accurate, updated articles and information on various topics.

Azalea Charities: http://www.azaleacharities.com/about/mission.shtml—Azalea Charities provides comfort and relief items for soldiers, sailors, airmen, and marines who are sick, injured, or wounded due to service in Iraq and Afghanistan. It purchases specific items requested by military medical centers, Veterans Administration medical centers, and Fisher House rehabilitation facilities each week. It also provides financial support to Crisis-Link, a hotline for wounded soldiers and their families, and Hope for the Warriors, which undertakes special projects for wounded soldiers.

Blue Star Mothers of America: http://www.bluestarmothers.org—This nonprofit organization comprises mothers who now have, or have had, children honorably serving in the military. Their mission is "supporting each other and our children while promoting patriotism."

Military Connection: http://www.militaryconnection.com—This comprehensive military directory provides information on job postings, job fairs, and listings.

Military Family Network: http://www.emilitary.org—The Military Family Network's mission is "to support military families and increase their readiness and well-being by connecting them with their communities and the organizations that provide the best service and value."

Military Homefront: http://www.homefrontamerica.org—This website provides reliable quality-of-life information designed to help troops, families, and service providers.

National Military Family Association (NMFA): http://www.militaryfamily.org—Serving the families of those who serve, the National Military Family Association—"the Voice for Military Families"—is dedicated to serving the families and survivors of the seven uniformed services through education, information, and advocacy. NMFA is the only national organization dedicated to identifying and resolving issues of concern to military families. Contact NMFA by phone at (800) 260-0218 or (703) 931-6632 or by fax at (703) 931-4600.

National Remember Our Troops Campaign: http://www.nrotc.org—The National Remember Our Troops Campaign works to recognize military service members and their families by providing them with an official US Blue or Gold Star Service Banner. Displaying the Star Service Banner in the window of a home is a tradition dating back to World War I.

Strategic Outreach to Families of All Reservists (SOFAR): http://www.sofarusa.org—Strategic Outreach to Families helps Reservist families reduce their stress and prepare for the possibility that their Reservist or Guard member may exhibit symptoms of trauma after serving in a combat zone. SOFAR aims to provide a flexible and diverse range of psychological services that foster stabilization, aid in formulating prevention plans to avoid crises, and help families to manage acute problems effectively.

Family Assistance

American Red Cross: http://www.redcross.org

Armed Forces Foundation: http://www.armedforcesfoundation.org

Army OneSource: http://www.myarmyonesource.com

Assistance with resume, job readiness training, and so forth: http://www.chooselifeinc.org

Cell Phones for Soldiers: http://www.cellphonesforsoldiers.com

Child Care Aware of America: http://www.naccrra.org

FOCUS Project: http://www.focusproject.org

Freedom Calls Foundation: http://www.freedomcalls.org

Freedom Hunters: http://www.freedomhunters.org

GrandCamps (for kids and grandparents): http://www.grandcamps.org

Homes for Our Troops: https://www.hfotusa.org

Military Family Network: http://www.emilitary.org

Military Impacted Schools Association (MISA): http://militaryimpactedschoolsassociation.org—MISA is a national organization of school superintendents whose mission is to serve school districts with a high concentration of military children.

Military OneSource: http://www.militaryonesource.com

Military Spouse Career Center: http://www.military.com/spouse

Military Spouse Resource Center (assistance with employment, education, scholarships): http://www.milspouse.org

Military.com (news with benefit information): http://www.military.com

National Military Family Association: http://www.nmfa.org

Operation Homefront: http://www.operationhomefront.org

Our Military: http://www.ourmilitary.com

Our Military Kids: http://www.ourmilitarykids.org

Project Sanctuary: http://www.projectsanctuary.us

Rebuilding Together: http://www.rebuildingtogether.org

Snowball Express: http://www.snowballexpress.org

Social Security Administration: http://www.ssa.gov

Soldiers Angels: http://www.soldiersangels.com

Swords to Plowshares (employment, training, health, and legal): http://www.swords-to-plowshares.org

Tragedy Assistance Program for Survivors: http://www.taps.org

United Services Organization: http://www.uso.org

USDA Women, Infants, and Children (WIC) Program: http://www.fns.usda.gov/wic

Veterans Holidays (discounted rates): http://www.veteransholidays.
com

Waves of Honor: http://wavesofhonor.com—Waves of Honor gives
any active-duty military, activated or drilling Reservist, or National Guardsman one complimentary admission per year to either
SeaWorld, Busch Gardens, Adventure Island, Water Country
USA, Sesame Place, or weekdays at Aquatica San Diego for military personnel and as many as three direct dependents. A valid
active military ID is necessary for the service member and his or
her direct dependents to participate.

EDUCATION

Air Force (CCAF) Transcript: http://www.au.af.mil/au/404.asp

Army/American Council on Education Registry Transcript System
(AARTS): http://aarts.army.mil

Coast Guard Institute Transcript: http://www.uscg.mil/hq/capemay/
Education/formsindex.asp

Defense Activity for Non-Traditional Education Support
(DANTES): http://www.dantes.doded.mil/dantes_web/
danteshome.asp

Department of Defense Voluntary Education Program: http://www.
defense.gov/specials/education/dod.html

Federal Student Aid: http://www.fafsa.ed.gov

GI Bill: http://www.gibill.va.gov

Navy and Marine Corps (SMART) Transcript: https://jst.doded.mil/
smart/welcome.do

Veterans Administration 22-1990 Application for Education Benefits: http://www.vba.va.gov/pubs/forms/VBA-22-1990-ARE.pdf

Veterans Administration Regional Office Finder: http://www1.va.
gov/directory/guide/home.asp

Veterans' Upward Bound: http://www2.ed.gov/programs/triovub/
index.html

Education Resources

AbilityInfo: http://www.abilityinfo.com

American Council on Education: http://www.acenet.edu

Association on Higher Education and Disability (AHEAD): http://www.ahead.org

National Center for Learning Disabilities: http://www.ncld.org

Office of Special Education and Rehabilitative Services (OSERS), National Institute on Disability & Rehabilitation Research (NIDRR): http://www2.ed.gov/about/offices/list/osers/nidrr

University Resources

Australian Disability Clearinghouse on Education and Training (ADCET): http://www.adcet.edu.au

Centennial College Centre for Students with Disabilities (CSD): http://www.cencol.on.ca/csd

Coalition of Rehab Engineering Research Orgs: http://www.crero.org

Curry School of Education: http://curry.virginia.edu

George Washington University Rehabilitation Counselor Education Programs: http://www.gwu.edu/graduate-programs/rehabilitation-counseling

International Center for Disability Information: http://www.icdi.wvu.edu

Johns Hopkins University Physical Medicine and Rehabilitation: http://www.hopkinsmedicine.org/rehab

National Clearing House of Rehabilitation Training Materials: https://ncrtm.org

Nebraska Assistive Technology Project: http://www.atp.ne.gov

Northwestern University Rehab Engineering, Prosthetics and Orthotics: http://www.nupoc.northwestern.edu

Ohio State University Disability Services: http://ods.osu.edu

Tarleton State University: http://www.tarleton.edu

Thomas Edison State College (distance learning): http://www.tesc.edu

University of California, Berkeley, School of Psychology: http://www-gse.berkeley.edu/program/SP/sp.html

University of California, Los Angeles, Disabilities and Computing Program (DCP): http://www.dcp.ucla.edu

University of Delaware, College of Engineering: http://www.ece.
udel.edu

University of Illinois, Urbana-Champaign: http://illinois.edu

University of Kansas Medical Center, School of Allied Health: http://
www2.ku.edu/~distinction/cgi-bin/2198

University of Minnesota, Disability Services: https://diversity.umn.
edu/disability

University of New Hampshire, Institute on Disability: http://iod.unh.
edu

University of Virginia, Special Education Web Site: http://curry.
virginia.edu/academics/areas-of-study/special-education

University of Washington, Department of Rehabilitation Medicine:
http://rehab.washington.edu

Wright State University Rehabilitation Engineering Info & Training:
http://www.wright.edu/~aja.ash/index.html

Education Scholarships

Air Force Aid Society (AFAS): http://www.afas.org—The Air Force
Aid Society provides need-based grants of up to $1,500 to se-
lected sons and daughters of current, former, and deceased air
force personnel. The AFAS website provides information on and
applications for the education grants offered by the society.
Phone: (800) 429-9475 or (703) 607-3072

Army Emergency Relief: http://www.aerhq.org—In addition to providing information on and applications for the scholarships it provides to spouses and children of deceased army personnel, the
Army Emergency Relief also maintains a listing of general financial aid links and scholarship search engines. Phone: (866) 878-
6378 or (703) 428-0000.

Hope for the Warriors: http://www.hopeforthewarriors.org—Hope
for the Warriors strives to enhance quality of life for US service
members and their families adversely affected by injuries or
death in the line of duty. It has developed a number of advocacy,
support, and educational programs.

PMB 48

1335 Suite E, Western Blvd.

Jacksonville, NC 28546

Phone: (910)-938-1817 or 877-2HOPE4W

info@hopeforthewarriors.org

Intrepid Fallen Heroes Fund: http://www.fallenheroesfund.org—
The Intrepid Fallen Heroes Fund serves US military personnel
wounded or injured in service to our nation, as well as their
families.

Marine Corps Scholarship Foundation: http://www.mcsf.org—The
Marine Corps Scholarship Foundation website provides information on and applications for scholarships offered by the foundation to the sons and daughters of current or former US marines
and to the children of current or former US Navy corpsmen who
have served with the US Marine Corps.

Phone: New Jersey Office: (800) 292-7777; Virginia Office: (703)
549-0060

Military.com: http://www.military.com—Military.com is a commercial, service-related organization that maintains a website offering
a scholarship search function for dependents of service members
as well as state-by-state education benefits listings.

Navy-Marine Corps Relief Society: http://www.nmcrs.org—The
Navy-Marine Corps Relief Society maintains a website for information on and applications for educational grants offered and
administered by the society. Phone: (703) 696-4960

Reserve Officers Association: http://www.roa.org—In addition to offering scholarship and loan programs to the families of its members, the Reserve Officers Association maintains a list of military-
dependent scholarships and scholarships for the children of deceased service members generally. Phone: (800) 809-9448

Scholarships for Military Children: http://www.militaryscholar.org—
Scholarships for Military Children is a scholarship program created by the Defense Commissary Agency. Its website provides information on and applications for scholarships funded through
the manufacturers and suppliers whose products are sold at military commissaries around the globe. Phone: (888) 294-8560

Society of Daughters of the United States Army (DUSA) Scholarship Program: https://bigfuture.collegeboard.org/scholarships/
societyof-daughtersof-united-states-army-scholarship-program—
The DUSA website provides information on applications for
DUSA scholarships, which are offered to daughters or grand-

daughters of chief warrant officers or officers of the US Army who died on active duty.

Children of Fallen Soldiers Relief Fund: http://www.cfsrf.org

Fish House Foundation: http://www.fishhouse.org

Freedom Alliance: http://www.freedomalliance.org

Scholarships for Military Children: http://www.militaryscholar.org/sfmc

Troops to Teachers: http://www.dantes.doded.mil/Programs/TTT.html

Service Specific

Air Forces Crossroads: http://www.afcrossroads.com

Marines: http://www.marines.mil/Pages/Default.aspx

Navy Personnel Command: http://www.public.navy.mil/bupers-npc/Pages/default.aspx

US Army Human Resource Command: http://www.hrc.army.mil

US Coast Guard: http://www.uscg.mil

RELOCATION

Chamber of Commerce Locator: http://www.uschamber.com/chambers/directory

Plan My Move: http://apps.militaryonesource.mil/MOS/f?p=PMM:ENTRY:0

Relocation Assistance Office Locator: http://www.militaryinstallations.dod.mil/smart/MHF-MI.

Military Personnel Portals

Air Force Portal: http://www.my.af.mil

Army Knowledge Online (AKO): http://www.army.mil/ako

"It's Your Move" Pamphlet: http://www.transcom.mil/dtr/part-iv/dtr_part_iv_app_k_1.pdf

Navy Knowledge Online (NKO): https://www.nko.navy.mil

Travel and Per Diem Information: http://perdiemhotels.com/per-diem-rates

INDEX

ABOUT THE AUTHORS

Cheryl Lawhorne is a clinical therapist with eighteen years' experience providing counseling services specializing in trauma care, posttraumatic stress, and traumatic brain injury treatment for wounded, ill, and injured service members and their families. As a senior consultant under the Office of the Secretary of Defense, she is part of a team that seeks innovative and proactive ways to enhance resources and services to military members and their families.

She recently participated in the corporate mission, vision, and implementation of projects for the Department of Defense to align current and future strategic plans and objectives. She possesses proven expertise in program management and clinical expertise in research, business development, and wounded care. She is proud spouse and teammate to Lieutenant Colonel Jeff Scott and mom to Evan and Quinn.

Jeff Scott is a twenty-six-year prior enlisted US Marine Corps lieutenant colonel who has held various leadership positions throughout his service, the most recent being as commanding officer of the world's first operational F-35 Lightning II Joint Strike Fighter squadron. In addition to being the first operational F-35 pilot and first operational F-35 commander, Lt. Col. Scott has received formal service training on sexual assault prevention and response as part of his leadership training and has mentored many marines. He has also served with senior leadership at the Pentagon and holds a BS in finance from San Jose State University and an MBA from Boston University.

Don Philpott is editor of *International Homeland Security Journal* and has been writing, reporting, and broadcasting about international events, trouble spots, and major news stories for almost forty years. For twenty years he was a senior correspondent with Press Association–Reuters, the wire service, and traveled the world on assignments, including to Northern Ireland, Lebanon, Israel, South Africa, and Asia.

He writes for magazines and newspapers in the United States and Europe and is a regular contributor to radio and television programs on security and other issues. He is author of more than 140 books on a wide range of subjects and has had more than five thousand articles printed in publications around the world. His recent books include the Military Life Series, *Terror: Is America Safe?*, *Workplace Violence Prevention*, and the *Education Facility Security Handbook*.

DATE DUE